Are Participants
Good Evaluators?

Are Participants Good Evaluators?

Jeffrey Smith
Alexander Whalley
Nathaniel Wilcox

2021

W.E. Upjohn Institute for Employment Research
Kalamazoo, Michigan

Library of Congress Cataloging-in-Publication Data

Names: Smith, Jeffrey A. (Jeffrey Andrew), 1962- author. | Whalley, Alexander, 1975- author. | Wilcox, Nathaniel Thomas, 1960- author.
Title: Are participants good evaluators? / Jeffrey Smith, Alexander Whalley, Nathaniel Wilcox.
Description: Kalamazoo, Michigan : W.E. Upjohn Institute for Employment Research, 2019. | Includes bibliographical references and index.
Identifiers: LCCN 2019003191| ISBN 9780880996587 (pbk. : alk. paper) | ISBN 0880996587 (pbk. : alk. paper) | ISBN 9780880996815 (cloth) | ISBN 0880996811 (cloth) | ISBN 9780880996594 (ebook) | ISBN 0880996595 (ebook)
Subjects: LCSH: Evaluation research (Social action programs) | Participant observation. | Social surveys—Evaluation.
Classification: LCC H62 .S5855 2019 | DDC 001.4—dc23 LC record available at https://lccn.loc.gov/2019003191

The facts presented in this study and the observations and viewpoints expressed are the sole responsibility of the authors. They do not necessarily represent positions of the W.E. Upjohn Institute for Employment Research.

Cover design by Carol A. S. Derks.
Index prepared by Diane Worden.
Printed in the United States of America.
Printed on recycled paper.

To Elsie Steele Smith

—Jeffrey Smith

To Oksana, Oliver, and Beatrix

—Alexander Whalley

To my spouse, Linda Jane Hayward

—Nathaniel Wilcox

Contents

Figures

Tables

Boxes

Acknowledgments

First and foremost, we thank the W.E. Upjohn Institute for Employment Research for funding this research, for their patience during the long process of completing it and writing it up in book form, and for their helpful substantive and editorial feedback.

We also thank MDRC for making available the data from its evaluation of the Connecticut Jobs First program. We thank MDRC, Mathematica Policy Research, and the Institute for Research on Poverty for creating the public use data from the National Supported Work Demonstration, and we thank the Inter-University Consortium for Political and Social Research for maintaining and distributing it.

For helpful comments, we are grateful to Iwan Barankay, Dan Black, Pam Giustinelli, Hilary Hoynes, Guy Michaels, Bob Schoeni, Gerard van den Berg, two anonymous readers, and audience members and discussants at Concordia University in Montreal, Quebec; Indiana University; the London School of Economics; Queens College, City University of New York; Queen's University in Kingston, Ontario; the universities of Mannheim; Warwick; California, Irvine; Chicago; and Michigan (the QMP, ISQM, and JPSM seminars); and University College London (especially Richard Blundell, Hidehiko Ichimura, and Costas Meghir).

Similarly, we are indebted to those who provided us with valuable feedback at the 2004 APPAM meetings in Atlanta; the 2004 SEA meetings in New Orleans; the 2006 SOLE meeting in Boston; the 2006 IZA/CEPR ESSLE in Ammersee, Germany; the 2006 IZA/IFAU Conference on Labor Market Policy Evaluation in Uppsala, Sweden; and the 2013 IZA/IFAU/IFS Conference on Labor Market Policy Evaluation in London. We appreciate Pam Jakiela and her coauthors' trying out our question wording ideas. Finally, for inspiration, we thank participants in a 2002 OECD conference in Vienna, Austria, on evaluating local economic development programs.

Despite our best efforts, any and all mistakes remain solely our own responsibility.

1
Are Participants Good Evaluators?

This book considers the value of survey questions that ask participants in social programs to evaluate those programs. We call measures constructed from such questions *participant evaluations*. The measures we study are widely used in evaluations of education and labor market interventions as well as in many other policy contexts. Evaluators sometimes offer them up as serious measures of causal effects. More deeply, the ability of individuals to learn from experience, and to express the knowledge thus gained in response to external queries, has implications in many areas of study.

Four important characteristics distinguish the measures we consider from other, more-or-less-related measures: First, they seek, however crudely, to capture causal impacts—i.e., effects on outcomes relative to a counterfactual world in which the respondent did not receive the treatment. Second, the participant evaluations we consider are constructed from survey responses to questions that are designed specifically for this purpose. Third, we study *participant* evaluations, rather than evaluations by observers of participants. Fourth, we limit ourselves to ex post evaluations—that is, evaluations that take place after the participant has experienced the program or policy being evaluated.

The first characteristic distinguishes the measures we study from typical customer satisfaction measures (which seek absolute judgments about quality rather than comparisons to an unrealized counterfactual) and from much of the contingent valuation literature. The second characteristic distinguishes our focus from studies of participant evaluations implicit in participants' behavior, as in the papers by Heckman and Smith (1998), Philipson and Hedges (1998), and Hoffmann and Oreopoulos (2009), which infer a negative evaluation from individual decisions to drop out of a program or course. The third characteristic separates us from impact estimates reported by persons other than the participant, as in Jacob and Lefgren's (2008) study of principals' evaluations of teachers. Finally, the fourth characteristic (and sometimes the third as well) distinguishes the measures we study from ex ante evalu-

1

ations by participants or program administrators, such as those considered in the context of job training programs (Bell and Orr 2002; Eyal 2010; Hirshleifer et al. 2014). In contrast, the class of measures we study does include survey-based evaluations of teacher value-added by students, as in Carrell and West (2010), and measures of pain relief in clinical trials, as in Branthwaite and Cooper (1981).

We frame our discussion in terms of evaluating labor market programs, and we draw our empirical case studies in that context. Our empirical focus on labor market programs arises not from any idea that they are particularly important in a policy sense (they are not, at least in the United States as measured in budgetary terms) or in an academic sense, but rather from the very practical fact that labor market programs are where the empirical "light" is (*light* in this context meaning experimental evaluations that feature large sample sizes and typical participant evaluation measures). We view this book as making a broad contribution based on evidence from a relatively narrow empirical context. We return to the question of the broader relevance of our theoretical and empirical contributions in our concluding chapter.

We have several motivations in pursuing this line of work. First, participant evaluation questions that provided even qualitative guidance on program impacts would have great value in improving policy. To quote Robert Schoeni, "There are thousands of programs that will never be able to afford a high-quality evaluation. But many of these programs can and do survey their program participants. If one could design a set of questions that did a decent job of capturing the causal effects, it would have huge benefits, particularly to state and local programs that just can't afford good evaluations."[1]

Participant evaluations constitute a potential alternative to the time, trouble, and expense of either the experimental or the nonexperimental (i.e., econometric) flavors of program evaluation. Econometric evaluations consume real resources, and, despite many advances in our understanding both of econometric methods and of the data requirements for their compelling application, evaluations based on such methods remain controversial. On the other hand, putting aside the limitations noted by Heckman and Smith (1995) and others, experimental methods remain politically problematic because a constituency almost always exists that does not really want compelling evidence on program impacts.[2] Given these issues with traditional evaluation approaches, and noting that surveys—even self-administered online surveys—also have their costs, if participant evaluations could be shown to capture real program impacts, they could substantially reduce the cost and increase the scope (and speed) of program evaluation, thereby allowing much more rapid growth in our stock of knowledge about what works and for whom.

Second, we observe the unhappy coincidence that both experimental and nonexperimental evaluations frequently collect participant evaluation responses and that participant evaluation measures sometimes (as in the U.S. Workforce Investment Act program) play a role in performance management, and yet there exists (to our knowledge, and we have been looking for over a decade) almost no serious theoretical or empirical literature on this topic that attempts to empirically evaluate participant evaluation measures. Of the three existing studies we know of, two of them, Kristensen (2014) and Brudevold-Newman et al. (2017), were inspired by presentations of our work. More broadly, the literature does not offer much in the way of evidence on the ability of either novices or experts to provide meaningful ex post program evaluations in the form of responses to survey questions.

The general lack of theoretical and empirical guidance in the literature leads to the uncritical use of participant evaluation questions in evaluation practice, as in U.S. Department of Education (2005) or Human Resources and Skills Development Canada (2009). We intend and expect that empirical findings from our case studies on the relationship between three typical participant evaluation measures and compelling estimates of program impacts, along with our theoretical critique of the existing question formats more generally, will lead readers to severely discount empirical analyses based on existing measures.

Third, from a broader academic perspective, our empirical inquiry into existing participant evaluation measures has been guided by a synthesis of theoretical and empirical knowledge from several disciplines. In turn, we believe that the guidance we provide, the theoretical frameworks we develop, and our new empirical results inform multiple scholarly literatures and also feed into our fourth aim, which is to lay out constructive suggestions for new participant evaluation measures that may improve on existing ones.

Given these motivating aims, the remainder of the book proceeds as follows: Chapter 2 lays out three theoretical frameworks drawn from the literatures in economics, survey research, and (most importantly) psychology—the "subjective rationality" view, the "lay scientist" view, and the "decision theory" view—the last of which we at times divide into two related but distinct bits. These frameworks guide the design of our three empirical case studies. In a limited sense, we can test the predictions from the theories; more generally, we use the theories to frame our interpretation of our findings and to guide qualitative judgments regarding the relative importance of the issues highlighted by the different frameworks in the empirical context of participant evaluations. In addition, we view our application of these theoretical frameworks to the context of participant evaluation as an independent contribution.

Chapter 3 develops an econometric framework in which to consider the relationship between participant evaluation responses and separate experimental and econometric estimates of program impact. In particular, we show how to use two different identification strategies to produce compelling impact estimates that vary at the individual (or subgroup) level; that variation allows us to relate them to the individual participant evaluations. We also describe the framework we use to examine the covariance between the participant evaluations and other variables, such as individual and program characteristics and simple empirical proxies for impacts, suggested by the theoretical frameworks in Chapter 2.

Chapters 4, 5, and 6 contain our three empirical case studies. In particular, Chapter 4 examines the U.S. National Job Training Partnership Act (JTPA) Study (NJS), Chapter 5 considers the data from the U.S. National Supported Work (NSW) Demonstration, and Chapter 6 addresses the Connecticut Jobs First program. The chapters share a common sequence of topics: we begin each chapter with a discussion of the program or policy and the population it serves. Following that, we describe the design and implementation of the experimental evaluation, with special attention paid to the participant evaluation measure. Next, we examine the correlation between the participant evaluation measure and the experimental and econometric estimates of program impacts obtained using the methods developed in Chapter 3. Finally, we examine the relationship between the participant evaluations and other factors, including respondent and program characteristics and poor but not unreasonable proxies for program impacts, such as the intensity of the services provided, labor market outcome levels in the post-random-assignment period, and before-and-after changes in labor market outcomes, motivated by the theoretical frameworks in Chapter 2.

In two of the three case studies, namely the JTPA and NSW experiments, we find essentially no relationship between the participant evaluations and predicted impacts. In the third, the Jobs First evaluation, we do find (modest) evidence of a positive relationship, particularly among older participants. We conjecture that the improved performance in the Jobs First context results from differences in the wording of the survey question underlying the participant evaluation measure. In contrast, we find strong evidence consistent with the "lay scientist" view in both its "lay theorist" and "lay empiricist" flavors, particularly from the JTPA data, which allow the most thorough investigation of the links between simple impact proxies and participant evaluations. We also find mixed evidence against the decision-theory frameworks we develop and, in a broad sense, evidence consistent with subjective rationality playing an empirically important role in the observed responses, especially in the JTPA data. Taken as a whole, our findings suggest little reason for confidence in analyses based on existing participant evaluation measures.

The findings from our case studies also strongly suggest the value of considering alternative participant evaluation questions and suggest some particular directions worthy of further investigation. To advance that aim, in Chapter 7 we first describe the (substantial) existing variation in the wording of questions from evaluations of labor market programs; this also serves the purpose of establishing that we did not, by any means, scrape the bottom of the participant-evaluation-measure barrel when choosing the evaluations to use in our case studies. We then critique the existing question formats in light of the existing literature; if the reader was not already convinced by the findings from our case studies, this critique should persuade the reader to dismiss analyses using extant question formats. Finally, we build on our critique and on the wider literature on survey design (and, more narrowly, on expectations measurement) to propose alternative participant-evaluation question formats that we think have some hope of capturing causal impacts of programs.

Chapter 8 concludes the book with a summary of our findings and some reflections on how those findings fit into the broader literatures in economics, psychology, and survey research.

Notes

1. Robert Schoeni, email message to author Jeffrey A. Smith, January 20, 2012.
2. For an amusing real-world example, see Bohm (1984), as described in Harrison (2013).

2
Three Viewpoints

This chapter outlines three viewpoints regarding how participants respond to survey questions that ask about how a treatment affected them. These viewpoints shape our empirical analysis and our interpretations of empirical results, and they motivate later suggestions for alternative participant-evaluation measures in Chapter 7. These are 1) a "subjective rationality" view, 2) a "decision theory" view, and 3) a "lay scientist" view. These three views draw upon several literatures that straddle psychology, economics, statistics, and survey design. We emphasize that the three views are not mutually exclusive; indeed, we expect that they all capture important aspects of the underlying reality. The empirical analyses in Chapters 4, 5, and 6 aim (in part) to sort out the relative importance of the issues highlighted by these three views in particular empirical contexts.

To fix ideas, and to introduce some notation, let $Y_i(D_i)$ be some outcome of interest to policymakers and econometricians, where i indexes individuals and $D_i = 1$ or 0 indicates whether respondent i was in the treatment or control condition, respectively. In the case of an active labor market program with a random assignment experiment, $Y_a(1)$ might be the earnings of a participant—let's call her "Anne" ($i = a$)—if she was randomly assigned to treatment ($D_a = 1$), while $Y_a(0)$ would be Anne's earnings if she was randomly assigned to the control condition ($D_a = 0$). Only one of these outcomes can occur for Anne. Therefore, any estimate of the expected value or sign of $\Delta_a = Y_a(1) - Y_a(0)$, the "program impact" on Anne, will require counterfactual reasoning, whether by Anne or an observing econometrician. Usually, treated respondents are the ones surveyed ($D_i = 1$ for all surveyed i) and are asked whether the program services were beneficial or helpful (in some sense specified by a question). Formally, this seems to request that a treated Anne estimate the sign of $\Delta_a = Y_a(1) - Y_a(0)$, knowing only $Y_a(1)$ for sure, for some kind of outcome.

The discussion here abstracts from complicating issues of compliance—i.e., from issues related to whether those randomly assigned to the treatment group actually receive the treatment and those randomly assigned to the control group do not. For the active labor market programs that we consider in the empirical applications in Chapters 4 and 5, not all treatment group members end up receiving program services, and, in Chapter 4, many control group members receive similar services from other sources. These issues do not arise for the budget-set treatment we consider in Chapter 6. We discuss the nature and extent of observed compliance in Chapters 4 and 5 and assume in both cases that the researcher cares about the effect of the offer of services through the program being evaluated, which all treatment group members receive and no control group members receive. See, e.g., Heckman et al. (2000) or Kline and Walters (2016) for additional discussion.

A BENCHMARK CASE

We can outline a set of conditions under which some form of participant evaluation could reveal more information than formal impact estimates. This optimistic benchmark case is characterized by *five assumptions*, each of which may or may not be true.

A1: Mutual outcome correspondence. Let $Y_i(D_i)$ be the outcomes of interest to researchers and policymakers, and let $\mathcal{Y}_i(D_i)$ be the outcomes respondent i answers questions about. Mutual outcome correspondence is true when $\mathcal{Y}_i(D_i) \equiv Y_i(D_i)$. When answering questions, respondents consider exactly the same outcomes the researcher analyzes for policymakers.

A2: Complete outcome resolution. At the time of questioning respondent i, all events on which the outcomes are conditioned have occurred. The outcomes $Y_i(D_i)$ are determined (or in the case of counterfactual outcomes, would now be fully determined): they are wholly things of the past.

A3. Event omniscience. Respondent i's information at the time of questioning is complete enough to compute both $Y_i(0)$ and $Y_i(1)$ with certainty. If $Y_i(0)$ and $Y_i(1)$ are conditioned on nonidentical sets of events, the respondent knows all events in the union of those sets.

A4. Conscious cognitive competence. Respondent i is cognitively able to compute the counterfactual outcome in consciousness and verbally report it.

A5. Motivational dominance. Respondent i is sufficiently motivated (by intrinsic or extrinsic rewards) to consciously compute the counterfactual outcome and report it. Any subjective costs of doing so are dominated by some positive motivation to do so.

To provide the intuition behind these assumptions, we can put them in the context of our example above. Suppose for instance that Anne was randomly assigned program services. She began them on January 1, 2008, and completed them six months later. She also may accumulate earnings at any time during the 2008 calendar year, including during the six months of the program. The earnings Anne accumulated from January 1, 2008, to December 31, 2008, is the outcome $Y_a(1)$ available to the econometrician. *Mutual outcome correspondence* (Assumption A1) says that if we ask Anne whether the services increased earnings, Anne fully understands that we are asking about exactly those earnings accumulated between January 1, 2008, and December 31, 2008. If the econometrician's data do not include unreported tips, Anne understands that and do not consider those tips either. *Complete outcome resolution* (Assumption A2) says that we interview Anne on or after January 1, 2009, so that the outcome (2008 earnings) is wholly a thing of the past: there is no remaining uncertainty about the outcome, and Anne understands that she should not include forecasts of future earnings when answering the question.

The other assumptions concern information, computation, and motivation. *Event omniscience* (Assumption A3) says that even though Anne received program services, she knows any and all past events needed to compute $Y_a(0)$—what she would have earned in 2008 if she had not received those services. *Conscious cognitive competence* (Assumption A4) says that Anne is cognitively equipped to consciously compute and verbally declare whether $\Delta_a = Y_a(1) - Y_a(0) > 0$ or not. Economic theory usually assumes that agents automatically know everything logically entailed by other things they know. That would imply that there is no distinction between Assumptions A3 and A4. The cognitive sciences do not assume this, so we make these two separate assumptions. To wrap things up, *motivational dominance* (Assumption A5) says that Anne is sufficiently well motivated to cooperate perfectly with the questioner. Note that A5 rules out both cognitive shirking and alternative motivations such as trying to please the interviewer by praising the program rather than by giving an accurate response.

Under these assumptions, Anne knows $Y_i(1)$ with certainty through experience, and she is willing, able, and sufficiently informed to compute $Y_i(0)$ without error or any remaining uncertainty. She compares the two outcomes, and her yes/no participant evaluation R_a is

$$(2.1) \quad R_a = 1[\Delta_a > 0] ,$$

where $1[expression]$ denotes the indicator function, equal to "1" when *expression* is true and "0" when it is not. In this benchmark case, these reports of respondents will reveal the direction of each respondent's impact perfectly. We could also imagine asking (treated) respondents to report $Y_i(0)$, their outcome in the absence of treatment, or Δ_i, the causal effect of treatment on their outcome, directly, though this is rarely done in practice (in Chapter 7 we return to alternative questions). Note that in this benchmark case, the information potential of participant evaluations actually exceeds that of an observing researcher. Even with a fully randomized experiment, a researcher only observes any participant in one "state"—the treated state or the control state. Event omniscience and conscious cognitive competence (Assumptions A3 and A4) essentially imply that the participant can observe her own counterfactual outcome and report it (or a function of it) to the researcher. Under this set of assumptions, then, participants will be better able to estimate their individual program impacts than an econometrician fully armed with a random assignment experiment.

Now we consider three ways in which the benchmark case can break down.

SUBJECTIVE RATIONALITY

Subjective rationality will matter if either *mutual outcome correspondence* (A1) or *complete outcome resolution* (A2), or both, fail to hold. The term *subjective rationality* comes from Simon (1956, p. 271): "[There is a] necessity for careful distinctions between *subjective* rationality (i.e., behavior that is rational, given the perceptual and evaluational premises of the subject), and *objective* rationality (behavior that is rational as viewed by the experimenter).... To predict how economic man will behave we need to know not only that he is rational, but also how he perceives the world—what alternatives he sees, and what consequences he attaches to them."

Put simply, a person's choice, estimate, or report depends on her choice set, what outcomes she values, and what she believes. Simon talks here about subjects and experimenters, but these could just as easily be survey respondents and econometricians. Simon's reference to "consequences" is like the outcomes $Y_i(D_i)$ of interest to the formal analyst and the outcomes $\mathcal{y}_i(D_i)$ considered by respondent i when answering questions.

Subjective rationality can break the link between program impacts reported by the participant and econometrician when $\mathcal{y}_i(D_i) \not\equiv Y_i(D_i)$. To illustrate this, consider a mainstream example of "rationality as viewed by the researcher." Schochet, Burghardt, and McConnell (2008) estimate the impact of Job Corps participation on specific outcomes $Y_i(D_i)$, such as earnings, GED receipt, and arrests. Presumably they chose these outcomes for several reasons (including data availability), but also because the program was designed to increase earnings and contained a significant GED training component, and because earlier evaluations had found effects on arrests during the residential component of the program.

"Rationality as viewed by the respondent" could be very different. One Job Corps survey question asks respondents (like our Anne) whether or not they would recommend the program to a friend. Would Anne naturally think of earnings, GED receipt, and arrests when answering this question? Perhaps she would, but nothing about this question demands or clearly suggests that she should. Suppose instead that Anne has a positive overall emotional remembrance of her Job Corps experience—today, what psychologists might call "positive affect" for the Job Corps experience. As it happens, Anne met a new friend at the Job Corps center, had a good time there, and found the instructors at the center well intentioned, sensitive, and knowledgeable; and her poor home situation made her stay at the Job Corps residential training center a welcome break. These kinds of outcomes loom large in the outcomes $\mathcal{Y}_i(D_i)$ that gave Anne her overall positive affect for Job Corps: those outcomes are the primary reasons she reports, "Yes (I would recommend Job Corps to a friend)." This report is neither frivolous nor a mistake. After all, Anne and her friends may value similar outcomes.

In this example, the outcomes $\mathcal{Y}_i(D_i)$ implicitly considered by Anne are clearly not the outcomes $Y_i(D_i)$ analyzed by Schochet, Burghardt, and McConnell (2008), nor are they the outcomes valued by policymakers. We have a failure of *mutual outcome correspondence* (A1) in this instance, the most pure form of a subjective rationality problem where one of two things happen: either 1) the respondent's interpretation of the question causes her to consider outcomes far different from the ones that interest researchers and policymakers, or 2) the respondent bases her answer on some overall evaluation of the program which mostly reflects outcomes that are not of interest to researchers or policymakers. In this case, Anne's participant evaluation is

$$(2.2) \quad R_a = 1[\mathcal{Y}_a(1) - \mathcal{Y}_a(0) > 0] ,$$

and whenever $\mathcal{Y}_i(D_i) \not\equiv Y_i(D_i)$, this is not identical to (2.1).

Anne might also focus on time periods different from those of the econometrician, who is constrained by the amount of follow-up data available on the quantitative outcomes. Anne could look ahead and consider the effects of having participated in Job Corps on future educational and employment outcomes. This is a failure of both A1 and A2, a less pure instance of a subjective rationality problem. In these cases, participant evaluation and econometric evaluation may diverge widely even if A3, A4, and A5 hold. However, the "decision theory" view discussed shortly also addresses failures of A2. The "subjective rationality" view assumes that both the participants who respond to the evaluation questions and the econometricians seeking to estimate program impacts make rational judgments about program success. If their conclusions differ, this happens merely because they consider different sets of valued consequences or outcomes. The subjective rationality view does not claim that respondents take cognitive shortcuts (the "lay scientist" view discussed below has some of that to it), but rather that respondents and econometricians have different definitions of desirable outcomes.

The "subjective rationality" view claims that respondents and econometricians interpret evaluation differently. Respondent interpretations are guided in part by the structure and wording of the survey questions that request the participant evaluation. In contrast, canonical econometric practice and ideal experimental data are aimed by design at precise outcomes of policy interest, measured in specific and well-defined ways over an exact time period in the past. For example, a formal experimental evaluation of an educational intervention may focus on specific test scores, administered on a particular day toward the end of the school year in which the intervention took place. In contrast, participant evaluations, particularly those based on vaguely worded survey items like the ones we analyze in Chapters 4, 5, and 6 and review in Chapter 7, instead measure program impacts on outcomes, over time periods, and relative to counterfactuals defined by respondents (at least in part) in their own ways.

As an analytical framework, the huge problem with the subjective rationality view is its predictive weakness. We left this out of Simon's previous quotation (1956, p. 271): "If we accept the proposition that organismic behavior may be subjectively rational . . . then the postulate of rationality loses much of its power for predicting behavior." All economists understand this (or should). Our own view is that the potential for subjective rationality problems should inspire researchers to write clear and closely defined evaluation questions that specifically ask about impacts relevant to policymakers. It also provides an attractive viewpoint for anyone who wishes to cling to the other four assumptions (no matter how strangely behaved participant evaluations may be), but we suspect it is a relatively weak framework for illuminating participant evaluations in active labor market program surveys.

DECISION THEORY I

The decision theory view becomes relevant if *complete outcome resolution* (A2) or *event omniscience* (A3) fails to hold. Manski (1990, p. 940) popularized this view, though he gives large credit to Juster (1964, 1966): "Divergences [between responses and outcomes] may simply reflect . . . events not yet realized at the time of the survey. Divergences will occur even if responses . . . to questions are the best predictions possible given the available information." Manski recognized that much of his analysis was more general than his particular subject matter (p. 935): "Although the substantive concern of this article is the use of intentions data, most of the analysis applies equally to a larger class of prediction questions asked in surveys."

There are two key features of the decision theory view. The first is uncertainty: the outcome in question depends either on future events (genuine uncertainty about the future, violating the assumption A2 of complete outcome resolution), or on past events that are simply unknown to the respondent (uncertainty about events relevant to the counterfactual outcome, violating the assumption A3 of event omniscience). Manski (1990) talks of "predictions" in both quotations above, since he addresses intentions data and how they can only bound future outcomes (unknown at the time that intentions are surveyed). However, respondent i could also be in a position of uncertainty when making participant evaluations. As mentioned earlier, Anne can consider the expected impact of Job Corps on future earnings (violating A2), while the researcher is necessarily constrained to outcomes resolved before the collection of his data.

Even assuming that A2 holds, we suspect that event omniscience (Assumption A3) must be viewed as particularly heroic. It may be absurd to assume that every outcome-relevant event along a path not taken is known. For example, Anne might be completely sure that if she had not participated in the program, she would have spent that time searching for an acceptable job. Moreover, she might know the objective probability distribution of wage offers she would have faced during that job-search time, and might also know the expected outcome of that search. Yet given program participation, that job search remains counterfactual, so she cannot know the actual outcome of it (as opposed to its expected outcome). Even in a mundane sense free of deep logical conundrums, some irreducible uncertainty about counterfactual outcomes seems almost necessary.

The second key feature is a discrete answer format—for instance, the binary yes/no response to questions such as "Did the program help?" Such questions are extremely common in the active labor-market program evaluation surveys we study here. With uncertainty and a binary decision, the respondent's situation resembles that of "the statistician" in modern statistical decision theory, and this is the perspective Manski (1990) develops. In this view, Anne does not know for sure whether $\Delta_a = Y_a(1) - Y_a(0) > 0$ or not. However, the decision theory view assumes that Anne knows the distribution $F(\cdot \mid Z_a)$ of Δ_a conditional on information Z_a available to her at the time of the survey, and that she can and does compute an objectively rational probabilistic forecast of the event $\Delta_a = Y_a(1) - Y_a(0) > 0$ given Z_a. We denote this probability as

(2.3) $P_a = 1 - F(0 \mid Z_a) = Prob[\Delta_a > 0 \mid Z_a]$.

When answering a binary-response participant evaluation question, Anne can make two kinds of errors (affirming that $\Delta_a > 0$ when it is false, and denying that $\Delta_a > 0$ when it is true). For many kinds of loss functions (associated with these two possible mistakes), we can characterize Anne's decision rule and participant evaluation in terms of a critical value c_a as follows:

(2.4) $R_a = 1[P_a > c_a]$.

The critical value c_a simply reflects the relative importance of the two kinds of mistakes (to Anne). Perhaps the most natural assumption is that Anne and most respondents view the two kinds of mistakes as equally costly. In that case, $c_a = 0.5$, and Anne's participant evaluation is "Yes, the program helped" if she believes it more likely that $\Delta_a > 0$ than not. We follow Manski in treating $c_i = c = 0.5 \, \forall i$ as a maintained hypothesis.

Manski (1990, p. 935) intended this view as an argument of poverty: "A primary lesson is that one should not expect too much of such data." Manski shows that binary response forecast data only provide very weak bounds on future binary outcomes under a decision-theoretic formulation like (2.4). Yet even these weak bounds allow for a test of the decision-theoretic view. Suppose we have a vector of observed characteristics X_i for each respondent i: following Manski, we assume these observed characteristics are a subset of the information Z_i, which each respondent knows when making their own evaluation. Let S be a "subgroup" of respondents i who share the same values of the vector X_i: formally, subgroup S is $\{i \mid X_i = X_s\}$. Let $R_s = E(R_i \mid X_i = X_s)$: this is just the expected participant evaluation (2.4) in subgroup S. Similarly, let P_s

$= Prob[\Delta_i > 0 \mid X_i = X_s]$: this is the expected proportion of participants in subgroup S who have a positive impact. Manski (p. 937, Equation [8]) shows that under the decision-theoretic view,

(2.5) $P_s \in [cR_s, c + (1 - c)R_s]$ for any subgroup S.

Expression (2.5) may be viewed as a predicted relationship between two different estimators—a consistent estimator of R_s and a consistent estimator of P_s—under the null hypothesis of the decision theory view. We can easily obtain a consistent estimate of R_s using the proportion of positive participant evaluations in subgroup S. Chapter 3 discusses a way to estimate P_s from experimental outcome data, and in Chapters 4, 5, and 6 we test for empirical evidence on (2.5). Under the maintained hypothesis that $c = 0.5$, the width of the interval in (2.5) is always 1/2—quite a weak bound for an expected proportion such as P_s.

DECISION THEORY II

Manski (1990) considered surveyed intentions (yes/no binary responses) concerning a future binary outcome, such as a future purchase or vote decision. In the previous section, we developed a decision theory view that stays very close to Manski's analysis. Generally, any decision theory view maintains that some uncertainty of outcomes lingers at the time of the survey. Because of that, respondents read questions such as "Did the program help?" or "Was the program helpful?" as meaning "Do you expect a helpful program impact, given the information you have right now?" In Manski's specific setting—where the future outcome in question is a discrete event such as a purchase or vote—there is little controversy about the underlying statistical entity a respondent would consult to answer the question "Do you expect (some discrete event)?" It is completely natural to assume she would inspect the probability of the discrete event.

In our program-evaluation setting, however, many interesting outcomes are not discrete: $Y_i(D_i)$ may be earnings or weeks of employment, and so forth. In such instances, it is far less clear that respondents ought to inspect the probability of some discrete event in order to answer participant evaluations. In the previous section, we implicitly assumed that respondents would in fact do so: Equations (2.3) and (2.4) say that respondent i inspects the *probability that Δ_i is positive*—discretizing an underlying continuous outcome into an event and its complement. This implicit assumption made our setting formally identical to the one considered by Manski (1990) and allowed us to borrow Manski's derivations to get Expression (2.5). But respondents might inspect other features of the underlying distribution $F(\Delta_i | Z_i)$, most notably its expectation.

For these reasons, we think there are several plausible "decision theory views" in our setting. An obvious second view is based on the respondent's expectation of Δ_i at the time of the survey. We maintain the two "decision theory assumptions," that 1) there is remaining uncertainty about Δ_i at survey time, and that 2) the survey response format is binary. As before, respondents have information and a conditional distribution $F(\Delta_i | Z_i)$ of Δ_i. Given conscious *cognitive competence* assumption (A4), respondents can then produce an expected impact $E(\Delta_i | Z_i)$ in consciousness, and we can imagine some critical value k_i such that the respondent is willing to declare that the expected program impact is positive, given the relative costs of judgment errors and the quality of her information Z_i. Under this "second decision theory view," the yes/no binary response is

(2.6) $R_i = 1[E(\Delta_i | Z_i) > k_i]$.

The researcher can also estimate program impacts for respondents i. Keeping within Manski's (1990) assumptions, we assume here that a researcher's information about respondents is some vector of individual characteristics X_i, and that this is a subset of the respondents' own information Z_i. Because $X_i \subseteq Z_i$, we can think of $E(\Delta_i | X_i)$ as the conditional expectation of $E(\Delta_i | Z_i)$, so that $E(\Delta_i | Z_i) = E(\Delta_i | X_i) + u_i$, where u_i is a mean zero error that is orthogonal to X_i. Therefore, across the sampled population of respondents i,

(2.7) $Cov[E(\Delta_i | Z_i), E(\Delta_i | X_i)] = Cov[E(\Delta_i | X_i) + u_i, E(\Delta_i | X_i)]$
$$= Var[E(\Delta_i | X_i)] \geq 0 .$$

Equation (2.7) says that *if* respondents reported consistent impact estimates (rather than the yes/no binary evaluations they are almost always asked to report), these would not be negatively correlated with a researcher's own consistent impact estimates.

Suppose now that we are willing to assume that $k_i = k \,\forall\, i$, just as we assumed that $c_i = c \,\forall\, i$ in the previous section. If R_i is given by (2.6), should it then be true that

(2.8) $Cov[R_i, E(\Delta_i | X_i)] \geq 0$?

Although Equation (2.8) looks quite plausible, it is not always true: a difficulty can occur when the fraction with $\Delta_i > 0$ negatively covaries with the expectations $E(\Delta_i | X_i)$ at the subgroup level. We discuss this further in Chapter 3, along with two different assumptions (associated with two different estimation strategies) that make Equation (2.8) a prediction of the second decision-theory view; and it is tested extensively in Chapters 4, 5, and 6. We emphasize that different kinds of questions could avoid the need for these extra assumptions. If respondents were asked to report impact estimates, Equation (2.7) could be tested directly regardless of the nature of the researcher's conditioning information X_i. We take this up again in Chapter 7, where we suggest new questions for future studies.

We should point out that Manski (1990) presented a decision-theoretic view of binary survey responses as a "best case" situation requiring objective rational expectations, and also requiring best predictions by respondents conditional on those expectations. He notes in passing, "I do not assert that this best-case hypothesis is necessarily realistic. My objective is to place an upper bound on the behavioral information contained in intentions data" (p. 934).

Why might Manski's best-case assumptions fail to hold when using conventional survey methods? So far we have said little about the *motivational dominance* assumption (A5)—the assumption that respondents are sufficiently motivated to do what the survey questioner wants them to do. If conscious counterfactual reasoning were simple, this might not be a problem, but experimental work suggests that real motivation starts to matter when choice and judgment involve relatively large stakes (Holt and Laury 2002) or relatively complex tasks (Wilcox 1993). Moreover, there is a large literature in psychology and experimental economics suggesting that elicited expectations and beliefs are generally biased when the elicitation scheme provides no real motivation (or trivial real motivation) for truthful revelation (Lichtenstein, Fischhoff, and Phillips 1982). When extrinsic motivation is used with a truthful revelation mechanism, both bias and measurement error variance tend to be reduced, though not eliminated (Ashton 1990; Grether 1980; Wright and Aboul-Ezz 1988; Wright and Anderson 1989).

Therefore, if we reject the bounds in Expression (2.5) or the covariance condition in Equation (2.8)—and we occasionally will—this is probably inconsequential to the theory of rational expectations, or to the assumption of best predictions made from rational expectations, as these are applied in most of economics (generally to highly motivated behavior). The survey data we use do not employ any sort of incentive-compatible, extrinsically motivated elicitation scheme. In the context of a methodological debate in experimental economics, Harrison (1992, p. 1441) famously asked, "Why attempt to verify or falsify models of motivated behavior with experiments that do not motivate subjects? . . . We arguably have no useful business fussing around in an attempt to make sense of unmotivated behavior." We need to remember that, from the perspective of respondents, there are no real consequences of insufficient thought when answering traditional survey questions about beliefs, expectations, or intentions. Therefore, it may be too much to expect the success of a rational expectations model of questionably motivated responses to survey questions about counterfactual states of the world.

LAY SCIENTISTS

In psychology, the term *lay scientist* goes back to Kelly (1955), but in contemporary cognitive psychology it is most widely associated with Nisbett and Ross (1980).[1] Nisbett and Ross discuss the idea that agents act as "lay scientists" when asked to produce verbal judgments about the causal structure of their social environment, their own behavior, or that of other agents. Like real scientists, lay scientists make these judgments using either empirical or theoretical reasoning, or some mixture of these, depending on how they interpret questions and, perhaps, which approach appears reasonable or appropriate to them. Yet lay scientists are not idealized professional scientists in two critical senses. First, when acting as "lay empiricists" at the behest of a survey questioner, they are not compelled to follow canons of formal inference on pain of professional embarrassment if they do not. The collection of "judgment heuristics" popularized by Kahneman, Slovic, and Tversky (1982) is, in the view of Nisbett and Ross, a large part of the lay empiricist's arsenal. Second, lay scientists may subscribe to a stock of implicit theories—we will call these "folk theories"—they share with others, and some of these folk theories may be poorly supported by formal evidence and analysis. These two possibilities, of course, can interact: following Ross (1989), if lay scientists use a poorly supported folk theory as an identifying restriction for empirical inference, their inferences will very likely be flawed.

Before delving more deeply into this "lay scientist" view, we need to underline a crucial distinction. The ability of a person's whole mind to store and use information, in order to make decisions and execute skilled performances (after a period of motivated adaptation to actual institutions and other persons), can be vast, without a corresponding ability to consciously know and verbally report on the stored information or the intermediate computations that undergird those vast capacities for choice and performance. As we use it here, the lay scientist view is only about the latter limits on conscious availability and verbalization. It is a violation of our Assumption A4, which we termed "*conscious* cognitive competence." For example, Anne may well need to know a conditional probability like $Prob[\Delta_a > 0 \mid Z_a]$ in the sense that her rational economic agency requires it for some motivated and recurring choice. If so, then somewhere in her brain, we might be roughly correct to say that this gets computed accurately on the way to making that motivated and recurring choice. But this does not imply that her mind can deliver $Prob[\Delta_a > 0 \mid Z_a]$ into her conscious awareness, or that natural language can easily express it, in any novel situation for no significant recurring purpose. Wilson (2004) argues that our adaptive unconscious (though vast and powerful) is largely hidden from introspection, so that we are in important ways "strangers to ourselves." The lay science view does not necessarily challenge the notion that people's minds can accurately track outcomes and their likelihoods for the purpose of making reasonable decisions. Instead, it challenges the notion that people can introspectively access such information, or accurately reconstruct it in consciousness.

Nisbett and Wilson (1977) document a widespread dissociation between experimentally verified causes of behavior and subjects' own verbal reports on those causes. Nisbett and Wilson review a large number of experiments showing that "there may be little or no direct introspective access to higher order cognitive processes. Subjects are sometimes (a) unaware of the existence of a stimulus that importantly influenced a response, (b) unaware of the existence of the response, and (c) unaware that the stimulus has affected the response" (p. 231).

Nisbett and Wilson (1977) point out that people have no trouble producing judgments about these things, and also point out that sometimes their judgments are correct. They suggest that people make these judgments not by introspection into their own thought processes, but rather on the basis of "a priori, implicit causal theories" (what we have called "folk theories"). Sometimes these theories are correct, and if so, the lay theorist makes correct judgments; but folk theories can be wrong, too.

In a survey of research on recall of personal history, Ross (1989, p. 351) endorses a similar view: "The research findings indicate the existence of two forms of systematic bias in personal memories. In some studies, people exaggerated their consistency over time. . . . In other studies, people overestimated the extent to which their present state differed from an earlier state. . . . Furthermore, there was evidence linking both biases to people's implicit theories of stability and change."

For one simple and pertinent example, suppose participants have a folk theory that outputs generally increase in input expense or resource intensity. They may then be more likely to say a program service had a positive impact on them if it seemed relatively expensive or resource intensive, all things being equal. We find evidence consistent with this sort of judgment process in Chapter 4. This particular lay theory is just one example of possible theories that participants might hold and which might influence their responses to participant evaluation questions; we single it out here because we have the means to look for its influence in some of our data.

Respondents may also act as lay empiricists. Lay empiricists may depend on the whole array of judgment heuristics laid out in Kahneman, Slovic, and Tversky (1982) and elsewhere, and these may produce predictable biases. Yet many potential mistakes of lay empiricism are quite humdrum—the kind of things we would teach new graduate students in a research methods class to avoid. For instance, Nisbett and Wilson (1977) point out that any potential cause that is not salient to people at the time of judgment, and hence ignored, can be a source of bias; this is simply omitted variable bias. Participants might wholly depend on relatively crude proxies, such as simple before-after comparisons, in order to make judgments, without accounting for the fact that other causes might have produced the change (or lack of it). In Chapter 4, the example of "Ashenfelter's dip" will appear as just such a confounding omitted variable (Heckman and Smith 1999). Interestingly, before-after comparisons and other crude impact proxies are commonly collected and used in administrative performance standards systems for employment and training programs, perhaps because they provide quick and inexpensive bureaucratic alternatives to the more difficult construction of consistent impact estimates.[2] Participants may rely on the very same proxies to construct their program evaluations. Indeed, we find evidence consistent with this, as these proxies often predict participants' own evaluations. This analysis has independent interest, since it suggests the extent to which participant evaluations might substitute for these measures in administrative performance systems.

SUMMARY: THE ROAD AHEAD

The next chapter discusses econometric strategies for estimating expected program impacts, probabilities of positive impact, the covariance between expected program impacts and participant evaluations, and other determinants of participant evaluations. We do not think the subjective rationality view is testable with the kind of data we have. However, its influence will reappear in Chapter 7 when we think about new questions for surveys. Moreover, Chapter 3 will occasionally use the subjective rationality distinction between $Y_i(D_i)$ and $\mathcal{Y}_i(D_i)$, the outcomes analyzed by the econometrician, and the outcomes considered by the respondent. This simply keeps track of things we don't know when we analyze participant evaluations.

We examine the first decision-theory view by checking whether the bounds of Expression (2.5) are violated. For the purpose of testing

Expression (2.5), we need an estimator of P_s, and the estimator we use depends on an auxiliary assumption commonly known as *rank preservation*, which we discuss in the next chapter. We examine the second decision theory view by testing the covariance proposition of Equation (2.8) in two different ways: one way depends on the rank preservation assumption, and the other depends on subgroup impact estimates and an additional assumption ruling out a pathological case.

We look on the lay scientist view as a way of thinking about apparent violations of the decision theory views. The available data from field experiments on active labor market programs are not really suited to a strong test of the lay scientist view. Our own opinion is that convincing tests of the lay scientist view require specific measurements (as part of a purposeful experimental design) that are not present in our data sets. Yet we think the idea has proved its mettle elsewhere, mainly in laboratory experiments but also in field experiments. In Chapters 4, 5, and 6, we put the lay science view to work as an interpretive lens to make sense of violations of the decision theory view, and to guide our empirical exploration of the correlates of participant evaluations. In Chapter 8, we will review a field experiment conducted by Conway and Ross (1984) that tests the notion of theory-driven participant evaluation in the context of a self-improvement class (a four-week "study skills" class).

Notes

1. The term *lay scientist* was most current during the 1980s. Although the currency of the term itself has diminished, the influence of the ideas is ongoing and widespread. Just since 2013, Google Scholar reports more than 2,500 citations of Nisbett and Wilson (1977), more than 4,000 citations of Nisbett and Ross (1980), and more than 250 citations of Ross (1989). We like the term because it creates a natural contrast to the researcher—the professional scientist—who estimates and interprets program impacts using formal canons of evidence.
2. See, e.g., Heckman, Heinrich, and Smith (2002), Barnow and Smith (2004), and Heckman et al. (2011) for reviews of the literature on administrative performance measures based on simple impact proxies.

3
Econometric Framework

This chapter presents the econometric methods we use for the empirical analyses in Chapters 4, 5, and 6. Each of those chapters uses a different data set, but all three data sets are "experimental data" in these two senses:

1) Participants i were randomly assigned to receive or not receive some treatment. In our applications, *treatment* means access to some program or service (Chapters 4 and 5) or a specific budget set (Chapter 6).

2) The data sets record one or more outcomes Y_i for those assigned to the treatment and control conditions. As in Chapter 2, we implicitly assume either full compliance with the experimental assignment or that we care about "intention to treat" effects. Additionally, for participants assigned to the treatment condition ($D_i = 1$), the data sets contain (or allow us to construct) a binary yes/no response, $R_i = 0$ or 1, to some participant evaluation question, coded so that $R_i = 1$ denotes a positive participant evaluation.

To begin, we lay out two identification strategies that we use to obtain compelling estimates of program impacts that vary among the individuals in our data. We require impact estimates that vary so that we can relate them to the participant evaluations. The first strategy relies only on the variation in treatment status induced by random assignment, but it produces estimates that do not vary among individuals with the same observed characteristics. The second strategy combines an additional assumption, called rank preservation, with the experimental data to produce impact estimates that do vary among individuals with the same observed characteristics. After explaining how we estimate program impacts, we describe and justify a regression that relates those estimated impacts and participant evaluations. We conclude the chapter with a description of the models we use to examine whether participant evaluations vary by background characteristics, along with proxies for impacts such as service intensity, outcome levels, or before-after out-come differences.

PREDICTED IMPACTS: SUBGROUPS

The first method we employ for generating impact estimates that vary among participants takes advantage of the experimental data and the fact that random assignment remains valid for subgroups defined on characteristics unaffected by the treatment, as discussed in (for example) Heckman (1997).

To create estimates of $E(\Delta_i \mid X_i = X_s)$, we estimate regressions of the form

$$(3.1) \quad Y_i(D_i) = \beta_0 + \beta_D D_i + \beta_X X_i + \beta_1 D_i X_i + \eta_i,$$

where $Y_i(D_i)$ is an outcome measure, D_i is an indicator equal to 1 for experimental treatment group members and 0 for experimental control group members, X_i denotes a vector of characteristics measured at or before random assignment, and $D_i X_i$ represents interactions between the characteristics and the treatment indicator. The interaction terms yield variation in predicted impacts among individuals at the subgroup level. For treated participants i in subgroup S, we want "predicted sub-group impacts" $\hat{\Delta}_s(X_s)$—that is, estimates of $E(\Delta_i \mid X_i = X_s)$. We base these on the estimated coefficients from Equation (3.1), and they are given by

$$(3.2) \quad \hat{\Delta}_s(X_s) = \hat{\beta}_D + \hat{\beta}_1 X_s = \hat{E}(\Delta_i \mid X_i = X_s).$$

Early in each empirical chapter, we begin by examining bivariate correlations between predicted subgroup impacts $\hat{\Delta}_s(X_s)$ and sample proportions $\bar{R}_s$ of positive participant evaluations. We do this for simple univariate definitions of subgroups S (e.g., X_s is a vector of age category indicators) and for a finer partition of participants into more subgroups based on multivariate differences in characteristics. In the first case, the vector X_i in Equation (3.1) consists of indicators for all but one of the subgroups; in the second, it consists of subgroup indicators for multiple underlying variables (e.g., age categories, years-of-schooling categories, and race/ethnicity categories). This is one way to test the covariance proposition in Equation (2.7) that is implied by the second decision theory view (when combined with assumptions discussed shortly). We can also think of predicted subgroup impacts as assigning a predicted impact to each respondent i, and we can examine the relationship between these estimates and the R_i by way of linear regression. We describe this regression-based approach shortly.

When we find evidence that $Cov[\hat{\Delta}_s(X_s), \bar{R}_s] < 0$, we intend to take this as evidence against the nonnegative covariance property in Equation (2.7) implied by the second decision theory view. However, $Cov[\hat{\Delta}_s(X_s), \bar{R}_s] < 0$ is really evidence against the nonnegative covariance shown in Equation (2.8). In Chapter 2, we noted that these two covariance properties are not identical, so we need an extra assumption to interpret such results as evidence against Equation (2.7). We illustrate the need for the assumption with an example from Heckman, Heinrich, and Smith (2011).

Suppose that respondents focus on earnings, that they behave according to the second decision theory view, and that $k_i = k = 0$ in Equation (2.6), so that respondents give a positive evaluation only if they expect a positive earnings impact. Now consider a population composed of just two groups. In Group One, 10 percent of the individuals expect a positive $1,000 impact, while the rest expect a zero impact: the mean Group One impact is $100, and the fraction giving positive participant evaluations is 0.1. In Group Two, 20 percent of the individuals expect a $400 impact, while the remainder expect a zero impact: the mean Group Two impact is $80, and the fraction giving positive evaluations is 0.2. This example shows that subgroup mean impacts could vary inversely with the fraction of respondents expecting a positive impact. When we interpret $Cov[\hat{\Delta}_s(X_s), \bar{R}_s] < 0$ as evidence against the second decision theory view (in Chapters 4, 5, and 6), we assume that this does not occur in our data.

The problem discussed above occurs for two reasons. First, the binary yes/no responses to typical participant evaluation questions are not a "representation of the underlying order" of expected impacts across respondents: most importantly, $R_h = R_i$ implies nothing about the ordering of $E(\Delta_h|Z_h)$ and $E(\Delta_h|Z_i)$. This is why subgroup means of the R_i and the $E(\Delta_h|Z_i)$ can move in different directions across groups. This point becomes quite important when we discuss new survey questions in Chapter 7: avoiding yes/no binary response formats will be recommended in most cases. Second, predicted subgroup impacts cannot vary across individuals in the same group: the counterexample of the previous paragraph depends on averaging within subgroups. If consistent impact estimates could be assigned at the individual level, this second reason would vanish (and with it the counterexample). The next section describes a different assumption (and estimation strategy) that allows us to derive individual-level impact estimates.

Though quite simple in a technical sense, the subgroup impact approach still raises some issues, to which we now turn. In the case of the finer multivariate partition into subgroups, the first issue is how to choose the specific variables used to define the partition. Any combination of the baseline variables in a given data set could be used to define subgroups. Put differently, how should we choose an indicator vector X_i for estimation of Equation (3.1)? In making this choice, we have two concerns. First, we want to avoid the "appearance of evil"—that is, the appearance of having chosen the variables to yield a particular conclusion. Second, we also want to avoid the inclusion of a lot of "junk" variables that yield highly imprecise estimates of subgroup impacts. To address the first concern, we choose subgroups using a method that does not look at the resulting covariance of the predicted subgroup impacts and participant evaluations. The second concern requires a method that yields a relatively modest set of subgroup variables. We describe our particular solutions in the individual chapters, as they vary somewhat across our three empirical studies. To keep things manageable, we limit ourselves to first-order interactions between the treatment indicator D and the indicator vectors X that define the subgroups.

A deeper and more fundamental issue concerns the amount of variation in impacts present in the data, and the extent to which subgroup variables capture that variation. Djebbari and Smith (2008) divide variation in impacts into two components: 1) systematic variation as a function of observed variables (what we here call subgroup variation), and 2) the idiosyncratic variation in impacts that remains after removing the systematic variation. Subgroup variation corresponds to the term $Var[E(\Delta_i|X_i)]$ in Equation (2.7); clearly, each definition of subgroups (choice of a particular vector X) yields a distinct division of the overall variation in impacts into systematic and idiosyncratic components.

Bitler, Gelbach, and Hoynes (2017) extend the conceptual discussion in Djebbari and Smith and provide a recent empirical example of such a decomposition.

Nothing guarantees, ex ante, any heterogeneity of impacts of either sort, though Heckman, Smith, and Clements (1997) show how to obtain upper and (more importantly) lower bounds on the total variation in impacts. We care more about the lower bound because it allows us to test the null of zero impact variation—i.e., the common effect model. Indeed, much of the prior literature on program evaluation explicitly or implicitly assumes a common impact for all participants. In such a world, $Var[E(\Delta_i|X_i)] = 0 \,\forall X_i$ and the population (i.e., the "true") value of the coefficient vector β_1 in Equation (3.1) equals zero regardless of our choice of X. Not surprisingly, our subgroup analyses will produce few insights in such a world. Alternately, we also cannot rule out, a priori, a world in which impacts vary substantially across participants but in which none of that variation depends on the possible X we can choose given our data or, more to the point, have chosen to use to define the subgroups for our analyses. In a world of only idiosyncratic variation in impacts, the population value of coefficient vector β_1 equals zero for our subgroup analysis (though not necessarily for the quantile analysis described in the next subsection), and our analysis will not provide any useful information about the performance of the participant evaluation variables. Strong evidence of subgroup variation in impacts (that is, strong evidence against the null $\beta_1 = 0$) casts serious doubt on the first of these worlds, while rejecting the null that the impact variance equals zero (or, put differently, finding that the lower bound on the impact variance statistically differs from zero) casts serious doubt on the second of these worlds (and provides hope to those looking for systematic variation in the first).

PREDICTED IMPACTS: QUANTILE DIFFERENCES

The second econometric method we use to derive individual-level treatment effect estimates continues to rely on the experimental data available in each of our three empirical applications, but it adds an additional assumption. The recent literature calls that assumption "rank preservation," while Heckman, Smith, and Clements (1997) call it the "perfect positive rank correlation" assumption. Invoking this assumption moves us from experimental estimates, as with the subgroup estimator, to nonexperimental estimates built on experimental data.

This approach builds on the literature on quantile treatment effects (QTEs); see, e.g., Abadie, Angrist, and Imbens (2002); Bitler, Gelbach, and Hoynes (2006); Djebbari and Smith (2008); Heckman, Smith, and Clements (1997); and Koenker and Bassett (1978). A quantile treatment effect is merely the effect of a treatment on a particular quantile (e.g., the median or the 30th percentile) of the outcome distribution. For example, if we have an experimental data set and a continuous outcome variable, we can obtain an estimate of the QTE for the median by taking the difference between the median value of the outcome in the experimental treatment group and the median of the outcome in the experimental control group. Repeating this exercise for other quantiles provides a much richer picture of how the treatment affects the entire distribution of outcomes than one obtains from mean impacts alone, a fact that inspired the title of Bitler, Gelbach, and Hoynes's (2006) paper, "What Mean Impacts Miss: Distributional Effects of Welfare Reform Experiments."

Without additional assumptions, QTEs do not provide any information about impacts for any particular individual, nor about the distribution of impacts across individuals. Instead, they represent impacts on quantiles of the distribution of outcomes. Put differently, without additional assumptions, the impact of treatment *on the median* outcome does not necessarily equal the impact of the treatment for the person *at the median* of the control group outcome distribution, because without additional assumptions, the QTEs make no presumption about the link between outcomes when treated and outcomes when not treated.

The rank preservation assumption provides the link between outcomes when treated and outcomes when not treated. In particular, it states that individuals occupy the same quantile of the outcome distribution in the world where they get assigned to the treated state as in the alternative world where they get assigned to the control state. Under this assumption, the median outcome in the control group estimates the counterfactual untreated outcome for the individual who experiences the median outcome in the treatment group. In more technical language, without additional assumptions, experimental data identify the marginal distributions of the treated (the treatment group) and untreated (the control group) outcomes, but not the joint distribution of outcomes. The rank preservation assumption represents one possible way of pinning down the joint distribution, and thereby of associating quantiles of the treated outcome distribution with quantiles of the untreated outcome distribution.

Under the assumption of rank preservation, quantile treatment effects represent treatment effects both *on quantiles* and *at quantiles*. Formally, we estimate the impact for the treated individual whose outcome falls at percentile j of the treatment group outcome distribution as

$$(3.3) \quad \hat{\Delta}_Q(j) = \hat{Y}^{(j)}(1) - \hat{Y}^{(j)}(0),$$

where the superscript (j) denotes the percentile. In other words, we estimate the QTE for a particular percentile of the outcome distribution as the difference in outcomes at that percentile of the treatment and control outcome distributions, and then interpret the QTE as the impact of treatment on an individual i who falls at percentile j of the treated distribution. Unlike the subgroup impact estimator defined in the preceding section, this estimator yields predicted impacts that may vary among individuals with the same observed characteristics; as a result, it may capture some of the underlying variation in impacts that the subgroups miss.

Does rank preservation make any substantive sense? One way to think about this assumption is to think about a world in which expected labor market outcomes depend on a single factor—call it "ability"—so that individuals who do well in the treatment state also do well in the control state. This represents a very different view of the world than, for example, the classic model of Roy (1951), which focuses on comparative advantage, as rank preservation embodies a very strong form of absolute advantage. We do not think rank preservation holds exactly, but it may provide a reasonable approximation, particularly in cases (such as the JTPA program examined in Chapter 4) that correspond to treatments of modest intensity which we would expect to yield only modest changes in individuals' relative labor market performances.

Bitler, Gelbach, and Hoynes (2005) show how to test an implication of rank preservation. The intuition is that if individuals at the corresponding quantiles of the treatment and control outcome distributions really represent one another's counterfactuals, then they should have the same baseline characteristics. For example, under rank preservation, the individuals with outcomes near the median of the treatment group distribution should "look like" the individuals near the median of the control outcome distribution. We follow Bitler, Gelbach, and Hoynes and operationalize this notion by testing the joint null hypothesis of equal means of selected baseline covariates in regions defined by percentiles of the outcome distribution. Rank preservation implies our null of equal means. Though the converse is not strictly true, for covariate balance conditional on quantile to hold without rank preservation requires very specific (and, in our view, implausible) departures from rank preservation in the joint distribution of outcomes.

Finally, rank preservation and QTEs give us a way to test the first decision theory view. We can compute QTEs at a large number of quantiles (say, the 91 centiles from $j = 0.05$ to $j = 0.95$ by 0.01) in a subgroup S. Under rank preservation, the proportion of these QTEs that are positive (call this $\hat{P}_{QS}$) gives us an estimator of $P_s = Prob[\Delta_i > 0 \mid X_i = X_s]$, one of the two quantities of interest in Expression (2.5) (implied by the first decision theory view). The other quantity in that expression, $R_s = E(R_i \mid X_i = X_s)$, is of course estimated by sample proportions $\bar{R}_s$ of positive participant evaluations in subgroup S. We compute the bounds implied by Expression (2.5) using $\bar{R}_s$ and $c = 0.5$, and we show how often $\hat{P}_{QS}$ falls within those bounds, as a simple test of the first decision theory view. This procedure follows Manski (1990) very closely.

PREDICTED IMPACTS AND PARTICIPANT EVALUATIONS: ESTIMATION

We can examine relationships between predicted impacts (based on either subgroup variation or rank preservation) and participant evaluations by simply regressing one on the other. In particular, we choose to estimate this equation:

$$(3.4) \quad \hat{\Delta}_i = \alpha_0 + \alpha_1 R_i + e_i,$$

in which the hat on the econometric impact on the left-hand side denotes an estimate and e_i includes all the unobserved factors that affect the predicted impact, including the estimation error in the predicted impact and any approximation error due to inappropriate linearization. When examining subgroup impact estimates, $\hat{\Delta}_i = \hat{\Delta}_s(X_{s(i)})$, where $S(i)$ is the subgroup of respondent i, as in Equation (3.2). When we examine quantile treatment effect estimates, $\hat{\Delta}_i = \hat{\Delta}_Q[j(i)]$, where $j(i)$ is the percentile of the treated outcome distribution in which respondent i falls, as in Equation (3.3). In both cases, we intend to take negative estimates of α_1 as evidence against the covariance property of the second decision theory view embodied in Equation (2.7), though of course estimates near zero also follow from a world with no (or no systemic) variation in impacts.

Despite its simplicity, three issues regarding Equation (3.4) warrant some discussion. First, we do not seek to measure the causal relationship between respondent evaluations and predicted impacts, but rather only their association. This follows immediately from the fact that we want to gather evidence about the covariance property in Equation (2.7); put simply, we want to know whether predicted impacts based on our two econometric approaches covary with the participant evaluations in the manner predicted by one of our viewpoints. Though obvious in some sense, this point bears repeating, given the current focus of most of the applied econometric literature on causal inference.

Second, we made the econometric impact estimate the dependent variable rather than the independent variable for a reason: we know that it embodies a lot of estimation error. In the linear regression model, putting a variable with measurement error on the right-hand side leads to biased and inconsistent estimates, while putting it on the left-hand side does not. Moreover, estimation error represents just one component of the measurement error in our dependent variable; depending on the particular variable in question, there may also be measurement error due to procedural errors in the original collection of data and its assembly into data sets. To be very clear, while it is the sign of α_1 that matters to us and not its precise value, because biased and inconsistent estimates also undermine hypothesis tests concerning the sign of the coefficient, we make the variable with the estimation error (and possibly other measurement error) the dependent variable.

One argument runs counter to our decision to make the econometric impact estimates the dependent variable in our analysis. It concerns the implicit assumption in the preceding paragraph that the participant evaluation as we measure it contains no measurement error. In fact, it may well contain substantial measurement error, but the literature provides no guidance, in the form of repeated measures taken a relatively short time apart, to inform us about the stability of the participant evaluation measure. A standard approach would imagine a latent "true" participant evaluation that gets measured with error each time an individual responds to the survey question. A measure with sufficient noise—that is, one that bounced around a lot from hour to hour or day to day despite no change in relevant circumstance—might well have enough measurement error to justify replacing the econometric impact estimates on the left-hand side.

Third, and finally, we include no additional covariates on the right-hand side. One of our two econometric impact estimates (namely the one based on subgroup variation in the experimental impact estimates) is already a linear combination of the covariates that we would otherwise include as regressors: it would of course be perfectly explained by such regressors, leaving nothing to be explained by R_i. We could include covariates when using the predicted quantile treatment effects as the dependent variable, but omit them to make the two analyses symmetrical.

As noted in Chapter 2, we do not believe that we can bring the subjective rationality view to any strong test. Yet a weak estimated relationship in Equation (3.4) might mean that impacts captured by the econometric estimates (whether subgroup impacts or quantile treatment effects) are based on outcomes that are of relatively small account to participants. Of course, we should not forget what lies in the error term. Among the items in the error term, we would expect impacts in the period after the period captured in our predicted short-term impacts to correlate positively with our predicted short-term impacts. In contrast, impacts on leisure likely correlate negatively with our predicted short-term impacts. A weak relationship in Equation (3.4) could thus also result from a combination of a positive direct correlation between the econometric impacts on labor market outcomes (such as employment or earnings) and a negative indirect correlation with the impact on leisure. Such a relationship would work through the correlation between the omitted impact on leisure and the included impact on employment or earnings. Put differently, omitted variable bias resulting from the correlation of the impact on labor market outcomes (the independent variable in Equation [3.4]) and impacts on leisure (which remain in the error term in Equation [3.4]) may lead to a small estimate of α_1.

Under the second decision theory view, only negative values of α_1 matter. Yet if we strongly reject the null hypothesis that $\beta_1 = 0$ in estimations of Equation (3.1), indicating the presence of subgroup variation in impacts, the explanatory significance of the second decision theory view would be called into question if estimates of α_1 rarely differ from zero. In other words, we might reject the second decision theory view only infrequently—rarely finding estimates of α_1 that are strongly negative—yet also rarely find strongly positive estimates of α_1. If we additionally know that there is substantively important variation in subgroup impacts (i.e., β_1 differs from zero both substantively and statistically), this would suggest that the second decision theory view is not a very useful view: it would have little hope of explaining observed variations in participant evaluations.

Under the lay scientist interpretation of our analysis, the absence of a relationship between the participant evaluations and our econometric estimates would have an additional possible meaning, namely that participants have used the less-than-formal inferential methods of lay science to construct flawed impact estimates. If the decision theory views appear to be empty in an explanatory sense, the lay science view gives us guidance for exploring the actual correlates of participant evaluations. It suggests variables that participants might use to create their estimates, such as outcomes or before/after outcome differences (in the case of lay empiricists) or measures of program inputs (in the case of lay theorists' depending on a theory of positive marginal products of training and education inputs). We discuss our econometric framework for examining those potential relationships in the next section.

Two reminders end this section. First, regardless of our interpretation, large estimated standard errors would suggest that our econometric impact estimates embody substantial estimation error. Second, in a common-effect world in which the program has the same impact on everyone, the true coefficient α_1 on the econometric estimate in Equation (3.4) equals zero.

DETERMINANTS OF A POSITIVE
PARTICIPANT EVALUATION

To explore the lay scientist view described in Chapter 2—that participants' evaluations depend on relatively crude proxies for impacts, such as program inputs, outcome levels, and before-after changes in outcomes—we need to examine relationships between participant evaluations and these potential proxies. As we examine only binary participant evaluation measures in our three applications, we use standard logit models to study these relationships. In formal notation, we estimate versions of

$$(3.5) \quad R_i = 1(\gamma_0 + \gamma_1 proxy[\mathcal{Y}_i(1) > \mathcal{Y}_i(0)] + \gamma_x X_i + v_i > 0),$$

where 1(*statement*) denotes the indicator function (which is equal to 1 when *statement* is true and equal to 0 otherwise). Here *proxy* $[\mathcal{Y}_i(1) > \mathcal{Y}_i(0)]$ indicates one observed proxy for impacts (or, in some cases, a vector of observed proxies), X_i denotes a vector of observed characteristics with corresponding coefficients γ_x, and we assume v_i has a logistic distribution. Following the notation in Chapter 2, the script $\mathcal{Y}$ in the notation for the impact proxies conveys that these particular proxies are for impacts on the *outcomes respondents consider* when answering participant evaluation questions. As the standard logit model identifies the coefficients only up to scale, we report mean derivatives rather than coefficient estimates.

Astute readers will have noticed that the participant evaluations (i.e., the R_i) have moved from the right-hand side of Equation (3.4) to the left-hand side of Equation (3.5). We do this because we think of both objects in Equation (3.5) as having been measured more or less without error, in which case the argument recounted above regarding relative variances points toward putting the variables with the larger variances—in this case the impact proxies—on the right-hand side. As discussed earlier in this chapter, one can reasonably worry about the actual extent of measurement error in the participant evaluations. The covariates X in Equation (3.5) soak up residual variance, yielding more precise estimates, and also help clarify the interpretation of the effects of the impact proxy.

We end with another reminder that we estimate the relationships in Equations (3.4) and (3.5) not to obtain casual effects. Rather, we seek "merely" to examine the relationships between variables, and we use the linear regression framework as a convenient and familiar (at least to economists) tool to accomplish that goal.

4

Evidence from the
National JTPA Study

This chapter lays out the results of our empirical analysis of the participant evaluation question from the National JTPA Study (NJS), an experimental evaluation of the Job Training Partnership Act (JTPA) program. It begins a sequence of three chapters analyzing participant evaluations from different experimental evaluations of programs targeted at disadvantaged populations. The NJS data have a number of attractive features for our purposes, including relatively large sample sizes, rich baseline and follow-up data, and high response rates. On the downside, we view the participant evaluation question as a relatively weak one, for reasons we discuss later in the chapter.

Our empirical analysis of the NJS data reveals very little in the way of relationships between predicted impacts and participant evaluations. We do find, however, substantial evidence to support both the "lay theorist" and "lay empiricist" interpretations of the participant evaluation responses described in Chapter 2.

This chapter shares a common format with the other two chapters that present our empirical findings. We begin by describing the program that participants are asked to evaluate in terms of the treatments offered and the populations served. The following section discusses the available data from the corresponding experimental evaluation and the construction of our analysis sample. We then consider the participant evaluation measure in some detail. With those preliminaries out of the way, we turn to our empirical analysis, starting with simple bivariate correlations between participant evaluations and impacts at the subgroup level, and continuing through the multivariate subgroup analysis, the quantile treatment effects, and the determinants of positive participant evaluations, as described in Chapter 3. The final section summarizes and provides some concluding remarks.

PROGRAM

The JTPA program was the primary federal program providing employment and training services to the disadvantaged from 1982, when it replaced the Comprehensive Employment and Training Act (CETA) program, to 1998, when it was replaced by the Workforce Investment Act (WIA) program, which was itself replaced by the Workforce Investment and Opportunity Act (WIOA) program in 2015. As described in Barnow and Smith (2016), all of these programs share more or less the same set of services (although JTPA, WIA, and WIOA omit the public-sector jobs that led to scandal under CETA) and serve the same basic groups. They differ primarily in their organizational details (e.g., do cities or counties play the primary role?) and in the emphasis on, and ordering of, the various services provided. Nonetheless, the commonalities dominate, with the implication being that our results for JTPA likely generalize to WIA and WIOA, as well as CETA.[1]

The JTPA eligibility rules included categorical eligibility for individuals receiving means-tested transfers such as Aid to Families with Dependent Children (AFDC) or its successor, Temporary Assistance for Needy Families (TANF), as well as food stamps. In addition, individuals were eligible if their family income in the preceding six months had fallen below a (relatively high) specific cutoff value. There were also special eligibility rules for several small groups and a 10 percent "audit" window that basically allowed local sites to enroll a limited number of individuals at their own discretion. These rules defined a broad eligible population, only a small (and highly selected) fraction of which participated in JTPA each year.[2] The populations served by the Supported Work program we study in Chapter 5—long-term AFDC recipients, youth high-school dropouts, ex-addicts and ex-convicts having trouble in the labor market—lie within the broader population of the JTPA eligible, as do the AFDC recipients served by the Connecticut Jobs First program we study in Chapter 6. But JTPA's eligible and participant populations also include many individuals not in these groups—for example, recently displaced workers who have completed high school, never had crime or drug problems, and never collected welfare.

The JTPA program provided five major services: 1) classroom training in occupational skills (CT-OS), 2) subsidized on-the-job training (OJT) at private firms, 3) job search assistance (JSA), 4) adult basic education (ABE), and 5) subsidized work experience (WE). Local sites had the flexibility to emphasize or deemphasize particular services in response to the needs of the local population and the availability of local service providers. In general, CT-OS was the most expensive service, followed by OJT, ABE, and WE. JSA cost a lot less.[3]

JTPA caseworkers assigned services to individual participants, taking into account the participant's abilities and desires as well as the mix of locally available service types and the site budget. This process leads to clear patterns in terms of the observed characteristics of participants assigned to each service in our data.The most job-ready individuals are typically assigned to JSA or OJT, while less job-ready individuals are typically assigned to CT-OS, ABE, or WE. CT-OS is often followed by JSA for participants who do not find employment during their course. Kemple, Doolittle, and Wallace (1993) analyze the service assignment process in detail. This strongly nonrandom assignment process has implications for our analyses below, in which we examine the relationship between participant evaluations and the types of services received.

In comparing JTPA to the other two programs whose data we analyze in later chapters, Supported Work and Jobs First, several notable differences emerge. JTPA was an ongoing national program at the time our data were collected. In contrast, Supported Work was a demonstration project operating in a small number of locations, and Jobs First represented a new and challenging design for welfare in a single state. In terms of the treatments, JTPA provided a wide variety of low-to-medium-intensity services, while Supported Work provided a single very intense (and very expensive) service, namely supported employment. The Jobs First treatment mainly involved changing the budget set, but it also included low-intensity job-search activities. For our purposes, this variation in programs and treatments across our three data sets provides useful but, in some sense, excessive variation. In statistical terms, we have only three data points but (many) more than three aspects of our programs and treatments that vary in possibly important ways. This fact necessarily complicates interpretation.

DATA AND SAMPLE

The National JTPA Study (NJS) evaluated the JTPA program using a random assignment design. It was the first major social experiment to evaluate an ongoing program rather than a demonstration program brought into existence solely for the purposes of the experiment. Random assignment in the NJS took place at a nonrandom sample of 16 of the more than 600 JTPA service delivery areas (SDAs). Each SDA had a local geographic monopoly on the provision of employment and training services funded under the JTPA. The exact period of random assignment varied among the sites, but in most cases random assignment ran from late 1987 or early 1988 until sometime in the spring or summer of 1989. A total of 20,601 individuals were randomly assigned, usually but not always with the probability of assignment to the treatment group set at 0.67.[4] Kemple, Doolittle, and Wallace (1993) present descriptive statistics on the experimental sample in the NJS.

As discussed in detail in Heckman et al. (2000), many NJS treatment group members did not ever enroll in the JTPA program (though some of the nonenrollees did receive low-intensity services), and many control group members received the same or similar services from other sources or, in the case of community-college training courses, simply by paying for them out-of-pocket. Given the empirical importance of these issues, we focus on the "intent-to-treat parameter"—that is, we think of the treatment as adding the option of JTPA participation to the other employment and training services present in the community.

The experimental evaluation provides separate estimates for four demographic groups: 1) adult women ages 22 and above, 2) adult men ages 22 and above, 3) female out-of-school youth ages 16–21, and 4) male out-of-school youth ages 16–21. The JTPA programs for in-school youth and for displaced workers were not included in the experiment. The demographic subgroups analyzed in the NJS spring from institutional features of the JTPA program, which included separate funding streams for youth and adults as well as separate performance measures and some different regulations. The preexisting evaluation literature, which frequently found differing impacts for these groups, provided additional motivation. We follow the evaluation by performing our own analyses separately for these groups.

The NJS data come from multiple sources. First, respondents completed a Background Information Form (BIF) at the time of random assignment. The BIF collected basic demographic information along with information on past schooling and training and on labor market outcomes at the time of random assignment and earlier. Second, all experimental sample members were asked to complete the first follow-up survey around 18 months after random assignment. This survey collected information on employment and training services (and any formal schooling) received in the period since random assignment, as well as monthly information on employment, hours, and wages, from which a monthly earnings measure was constructed. Third, a random subset (for budgetary reasons) of the experimental sample members was asked to complete a second follow-up survey around 32 months after random assignment. This survey collected similar information for the period since the completion of the first follow-up survey or, in the case of individuals who did not complete the first follow-up survey, over the period since random assignment. (In such instances, we treat this survey as the individual's first follow-up survey.) Response rates to both follow-up surveys were around 80 percent. Because of these high response rates, we do not use any weights in our analysis to correct for differences in response probabilities as a function of observed characteristics. Finally, administrative data on quarterly earnings and unemployment from state unemployment insurance (UI) records in the states corresponding to the 16 NJS sites were collected.[5] Our analysis relies on data from the BIF and the first follow-up survey, along with the UI earnings data. Table 4A.1 in the appendix documents the number of observations lost on each step from the raw data to our analysis samples. Box 4A.1 defines the variables we construct and use in greater detail.

Three features of our data merit mention here. First, the self-reported earnings data available for our "SR sample" is a subset of that used in Bloom et al. (1993), the official 18-month impact report. These data include the recoded values for outliers (which were examined individually and by hand by staff at Abt Associates, one of the two main contractors on the evaluation).[6] Second, the administrative earnings data from state UI records available for our "UI sample" consist of earnings in each calendar quarter. As a result, for some sample members, the 18 months corresponding to the six calendar quarters after the calendar quarter of random assignment (the period used in some of our earnings variables constructed from the UI data) differ somewhat from the 18 months immediately after the month of random assignment over which we define our earnings measures based on the self-reported data. Third, to include individuals in our study, we require that the first follow-up survey occur at least 18 whole months (548 days) after random assignment, a somewhat stronger selection than the 18 calendar months used by others. We do this for two reasons. First, because it results in a better match between the observed characteristics of individuals in our SR Sample and those in our UI Sample (see Table 4.1). Second, we want our "complete outcome resolution" condition from Chapter 2 to hold for the 18-month self-reported earnings measure.

Reporting results using earnings outcomes constructed from both the UI administrative records and the self-reported information from the surveys might seem like unnecessary extravagance in a time of austerity, but in fact the two measures differ substantially in ways that make each one a useful check on the other. First of all, the survey measure will catch informal jobs and off-the-books earnings (likely relatively important in the population served by JTPA) missed by the UI data, as well as formal jobs in sectors, like the government, not necessarily covered by the UI program. Second, the self-reported data will capture jobs in other states, something potentially important at a few of the NJS sites. On the other side of the ledger, the UI data come directly from firm reports of wages paid. Thus, they avoid measurement error due to failures of participant recall and also due to underlying survey measures that do not allow month-to-month variation in hours on a job within the period covered by a particular survey. Given these differences, we feel it makes sense to look at both types of data in our application.

PARTICIPANT EVALUATION MEASURE

Box 4.1 presents the two survey questions that, taken together, define the participant evaluation measure from the NJS. The questions appear on both the first and second follow-up surveys, but respondents were asked these questions in the second follow-up survey only if they did not complete the first follow-up survey.

Box 4.1 JTPA Participant Evaluation Survey Questions

(D7)

According to (LOCAL JTPA PROGAM NAME) records, you applied
to enter (LOCAL JTPA PROGRAM NAME) in (MONTH/YEAR OF
RANDOM ASSIGNMENT). Did you participate in the program after
you applied?

YES (SKIP TO D9)
NO (GO TO D8)

(D9)

Do you think that the training or other assistance that you got from the
program helped you get a job or perform better on the job?

YES
NO

NOTE: Question (D8) elicits reasons for nonparticipation in JTPA. Respondents who
are diverted to (D8) skip (D9).
SOURCE: National JTPA Study, First Follow-Up Survey instrument.

The first question asks whether the respondent participated in JTPA.
The question assumes application to JTPA because it is implied by the
respondent having been randomly assigned. The JTPA program had
different names in the various sites participating in the evaluation; the
interviewer included the appropriate local name in each site, as indicated in the question. In the second question, respondents who self-
report having participated in the program get asked whether the program helped them get a job or perform better on the job.

For treatment-group members only, we code the usable responses to
both of these questions as indicator variables, and the participant evaluation measure employed in our empirical work consists of the product
of these two indicators. Put differently, our participant evaluation measure equals one if the respondent replies "Yes" to Question (D7) and
"Yes" to Question (D9). Otherwise, it equals zero.

Table 4.1 Sample Members' Characteristics at Random Assignment, by Demographic Group and Treatment Status —NJS Experimental Sample Members with Valid Self-Reported Earnings or Valid Quarterly State UI Earnings

Demographic group	Adult males				Adult females				Male youth				Female youth			
Treatment status	Control		Treat		Control		Treat		Control		Treat		Control		Treat	
Sample	SR	UI	SR	UI	SR	UI	SR	UI	SR	UI	SR	UI	SR	UI	SR	UI
Race																
White	62	61	60	59	56	56	56	55	53	53	54	54	47	48	50	48
Black	26	27	26	27	30	29	30	30	30	31	30	29	34	34	32	32
Hispanic	9	8	9	9	12	12	11	12	15	15	14	14	17	17	16	18
Other	3	3	4	4	3	3	3	3	2	1	2	2	1	1	2	2
Age	33	33	33	33	33	33	33	34	19	19	19	19	19	19	19	19
	(10)	(10)	(10)	(10)	(10)	(10)	(10)	(10)	(1)	(1)	(1)	(1)	(1)	(1)	(1)	(1)
Education																
< 10 years	16	17	18	18	19	19	17	17	29	27	29	31	26	27	25	25
10–11 years	24	23	22	22	23	23	22	22	34	35	33	33	27	28	29	29
12 years	39	39	39	39	40	40	42	42	31	32	33	31	39	38	40	40
13–15 years	14	14	15	14	13	13	14	14	5	5	5	5	6	6	5	5
16+ years	5	5	5	5	3	3	3	3	0	0	0	0	0	0	0	0
Marital status																
Single	39	39	37	37	30	30	29	29	86	86	86	86	77	77	76	76
Married	33	33	37	36	20	20	21	21	10	10	10	10	12	12	10	11
Div/wid/sep	24	24	21	22	41	41	42	42	1	1	1	2	8	8	9	9
English not 1st language	3	3	4	4	4	4	4	4	3	3	2	2	2	2	2	2

Receiving AFDC	6	6	7	6	34	35	34	33	4	5	6	6	28	28	27	27
Never worked for pay	7	7	9	9	15	15	14	14	13	12	17	16	24	24	22	22
Have children under age 6	19	19	21	21	35	35	34	34	8	8	9	9	43	43	43	43
Observations	1,375	1,429	2,829	3,018	1,783	1,845	3,732	3,875	530	577	1,142	1,256	693	737	1,531	1,667

NOTE: The SR Sample consists of 13,615 NJS experimental sample members with valid self-reported earnings who were interviewed at least 18 whole months—548 days—after random assignment. The UI Sample consists of the 14,404 NJS experimental sample members with valid quarterly state UI earnings records who, if interviewed, were interviewed at least 18 whole months—548 days—after random assignment. For each demographic and treatment group, and each sample, table entries are the observed percentage of observations having the characteristics listed in the row headings. For the age variable, we give the mean and (in parentheses) the standard deviation of age in years. Observed percentages do not sum to 100 for some categorical variables (e.g., "Education" and "Marital status") because of missing values.

SOURCE: Authors' calculations using the SR Sample and the UI Sample from the NJS data.

We have several concerns with this participant evaluation measure. We mention a couple of them here and defer a more thorough discussion to Chapter 7. First, it does not either explicitly or implicitly mention a counterfactual. Thus, a respondent who got a job as a result of an on-the-job training opportunity provided by the program might reasonably offer a positive response even if she believes she would have found employment just as quickly had she not participated in JTPA. Second, the term *help* leaves the reader with a wide variety of possible interpretations. Does a training course provide help or cause delay in getting a job? That depends on how broadly the respondent interprets *help*, as a narrow definition might include only direct measures such as job search assistance or an on-the-job training slot but ignore human capital investment. At the same time, the question's concentration on labor market outcomes should increase the strength of the relationship between the participant evaluations and the econometric estimates of labor market impacts, relative to a broader question that asked about generic program benefits. Whatever the pluses and minuses, the JTPA evaluation includes only this one participant evaluation measure, and so we proceed to analyze it.

Tables 4.2 and 4.3 tabulate, for each of the four demographic groups and each of the analysis samples, the full set of responses to both underlying questions in Panels A and B and, for the treatment group only, the cleaned and recoded participant evaluation measure we actually analyze in Panel C. Overall, our participant evaluation measure turns out positive less than half the time, and thus it is much less positive than the measures we examine in Chapters 5 and 6. Negative responses to the first of the two questions (i.e., to D7 rather than D9) account for much of this pattern: many treatment group members, even many who formally enrolled in the program, do not recall participating in it.

EMPIRICAL RESULTS

Descriptive Statistics

Table 4.1 offers basic descriptive statistics. Within each demographic group, we present four columns of statistics. From left to

Table 4.2 Participation and Evaluation Responses and Derived Participant Evaluation Measure, by Demographic Group and Treatment Status—NJS Experimental Sample Members with Valid Self-Reported Earnings

Demographic group	Adult males		Adult females		Male youth		Female youth		All participants		
Treatment status	Control	Treat	Control	Treat	Control	Treat	Control	Treat	Control	Treat	Total
Panel A. Self-reported participation question (D7):											
Yes (1)	13.09	62.21	12.23	68.76	15.47	63.05	12.99	66.36	13.01	65.65	48.71
No (2)	85.16	36.48	86.60	30.09	81.70	35.03	85.28	31.81	85.35	32.94	49.81
Refused (7)	0.00	0.25	0.22	0.21	0.19	0.00	0.14	0.26	0.14	0.21	0.18
Don't know (8)	0.80	0.60	0.17	0.59	1.13	1.14	0.72	0.91	0.57	0.71	0.67
Missing (9)	0.95	0.46	0.79	0.35	1.51	0.79	0.87	0.65	0.94	0.49	0.63
Total observations	1,375	2,829	1,783	3,732	530	1,142	693	1,531	4,381	9,234	13,615
Panel B. Participant evaluation question (D9):											
Yes (1)	46.60	61.21	53.78	63.83	49.44	67.26	61.46	70.89	52.08	64.67	63.54
No (2)	45.55	36.10	37.33	33.36	39.33	30.83	29.17	25.92	38.94	32.60	33.17
Refused (7)	0.00	0.39	1.78	0.31	1.12	0.00	1.04	0.39	1.00	0.31	0.37
Don't know (8)	2.09	0.95	2.22	0.96	3.37	0.68	5.21	1.35	2.83	0.99	1.16
Missing (9)	5.76	1.35	4.89	1.54	6.74	1.23	3.13	1.45	5.16	1.43	1.76
Total observations	191	1,784	225	2,596	89	733	96	1,034	601	6,147	6,748
Panel C. Participant evaluation measure:											
Positive (1)		38.60		44.29		42.64		47.81		42.93	
Negative (0)		59.07		53.14		54.55		49.31		54.49	
Missing		2.33		2.57		2.80		2.87		2.58	
Total observations		2,829		3,732		1,142		1,531		9,234	

NOTE: The SR Sample consists of the 13,615 NJS experimental sample members with valid self-reported earnings who were interviewed at least 18 whole months—548 days—after random assignment. Total observations are shown in the final row of each panel, and the figures above them are percentages of the total. (Percentages may not sum to 100.0 because of rounding.) The top panel, A, details responses to Question (D7) in either follow-up interview. The middle panel, B, details responses to Question (D9). Only the 6,748 respondents in the response categories "Yes," "Refused," or "Don't know" for Question (D7) were asked Question (D9). The bottom panel, C, shows our derived participant evaluation measure for respondents in the treatment condition with valid responses to both Questions (D7) and (D9). Numbers in parentheses are the numerical codes for the survey responses. For example, a "Yes" on (D7) is coded as "1" in the data.

SOURCE: Authors' calculations using the SR Sample.

Table 4.3 Participation and Evaluation Responses and Derived Participant Evaluation Measure, by Demographic Group and Treatment Status—NJS Experimental Sample Members with Valid Quarterly State UI Earnings

Demographic group	Adult males		Adult females		Male youth		Female youth		All participants		
Treatment status	Control	Treat	Control	Treat	Control	Treat	Control	Treat	Control	Treat	Total
Panel A. Self-reported participation question (D7):											
Yes (1)	13.37	61.43	12.63	68.39	15.94	62.18	13.30	65.15	13.38	64.90	48.49
No (2)	84.67	37.24	85.91	30.40	81.11	35.83	84.94	32.99	84.76	33.64	49.92
Refused (7)	0.07	0.23	0.22	0.21	0.17	0.00	0.14	0.24	0.15	0.19	0.18
Don't know (8)	0.91	0.63	0.27	0.59	1.39	1.19	0.81	0.96	0.70	0.74	0.73
Missing (9)	0.98	0.46	0.98	0.41	1.39	0.80	0.81	0.66	1.00	0.52	0.67
Total observations	1,429	3,018	1,845	3,875	577	1,256	737	1,667	4,588	9,816	14,404
Panel B. Participant evaluation question (D9):											
Yes (1)	46.34	61.49	54.13	63.86	50.50	65.45	58.10	69.62	51.76	64.35	63.20
No (2)	44.39	35.85	36.36	33.35	36.63	32.41	30.48	27.31	37.98	32.93	33.39
Refused (7)	0.49	0.37	1.65	0.30	0.99	0.00	0.95	0.36	1.07	0.29	0.37
Don't know (8)	1.95	1.01	2.48	0.93	3.96	0.88	5.71	1.36	3.06	1.02	1.21
Missing (9)	6.83	1.28	5.37	1.57	7.92	1.26	4.76	1.36	6.13	1.41	1.84
Total observations	205	1,880	242	2,681	101	796	105	1,106	653	6,463	7,116
Panel C. Participant evaluation measure:											
Positive (1)		38.30		44.08		41.00		46.13		42.26	
Negative (0)		59.38		53.32		56.13		51.05		55.15	
Missing		2.32		2.61		2.87		2.82		2.59	
Total observations		3,018		3,875		1,256		1,667		9,816	

NOTE: The UI Sample consists of 14,404 NJS experimental sample members with valid quarterly state UI earnings records who were interviewed at least 18 whole months—548 days—after random assignment. Figures are percentages of the total observations shown in the final row of each panel. (Percentages may not sum to 100.0 because of rounding.) The top panel, A, details responses to Question (D7) in either follow-up interview. The middle panel, B, details responses to Question (D9). Only the 7,116 respondents in the response categories "Yes," "Refused," or "Don't Know" for Question (D7) were asked Question (D9). The bottom panel, C, shows our derived participant evaluation measure for respondents in the treatment condition with valid responses to both Questions (D7) and (D9). Numbers in parentheses are the numerical codes for the survey responses. For example, a "Yes" on (D7) is coded as "1" in the data.
SOURCE: Authors' calculations using the UI Sample.

right in the table, they are control-group SR sample, control-group UI sample, treatment-group SR sample, and treatment-group UI sample. Overall, the tables present few surprises, given the nature of the program and its eligibility rules. Demographically, our samples are mostly white, combined with a sizable minority of African Americans and smaller groups of Hispanics and others (i.e., Asians, Pacific Islanders, and Native Americans). This characteristic varies the most across sites (by far) because of geographic differences in the representation of these groups. High school completers with no further education make up the modal education group, with high school dropouts (i.e., persons with 10–11 years of schooling) the second largest, and nontrivial numbers in the "some college" and "early dropout" groups. Some of the other characteristics differ in predictable ways among the demographic groups. For example, youth are less likely to be presently or formerly married than adults, and more likely never to have worked. Women are much more likely than men to have a child under six in the home, and female youth are more likely to have a child under six than adult women.

Table 4.4 details our outcome variables, which appear in its first column. The first two outcomes (Earnings One and Employ One) are self-reported earnings and any self-reported employment in the first 18 months after random assignment, which corresponds roughly to the whole period prior to the survey response for most sample members. The second two outcomes (Earnings Two and Employ Two) instead focus on the respondent's status right around the time of the survey question: these are self-reported earnings and any employment in month 18 after random assignment. The remaining four outcomes (Earnings Three, Employ Three, Earnings Four, and Employ Four) repeat the first four but use the quarterly data from the matched UI earnings records instead of respondents' self-reported outcome data. Throughout our discussion of results, we refer to these collectively as the "eight outcomes." The earnings outcomes represent nominal dollars (i.e., not adjusted for inflation). See the appendix for slightly more detailed definitions of the outcome variables.

The table reveals that our sample members have low but not trivial levels of mean earnings and relatively high employment rates in the post-random-assignment period, given the barriers to employment they face. As expected, we find higher average earnings for adult men than for adult women, and for male youth than for female youth. The dif-

Table 4.4 Employment and Earnings Outcomes of Analysis Sample Members—NJS Experimental Sample Members with Valid Self-Reported Earnings or Valid Quarterly State UI Earnings

Demographic group	Adult males		Adult females		Male youth		Female youth	
Treatment status	Control	Treat	Control	Treat	Control	Treat	Control	Treat
Earnings One ($)	12,619	13,157	7,439	8,257	10,790	10,052	6,149	6,151
(Total self-reported earnings over 18 months)	(11,666)	(11,546)	(7,733)	(8,229)	(9,444)	(8,776)	(6,657)	(6,510)
Employ One (%)	85	87	77	80	89	91	77	81
(Any self-reported employment over 18 months)	(36)	(34)	(42)	(40)	(31)	(29)	(42)	(39)
Earnings Two ($)	768	795	475	536	690	632	396	393
(Total self-reported earnings in 18th month)	(823)	(801)	(562)	(603)	(706)	(626)	(530)	(500)
Employ Two (%)	66	68	56	60	69	67	51	52
(Any self-reported employment in 18th month)	(47)	(47)	(50)	(49)	(46)	(47)	(50)	(50)
Observations	1,375	2,829	1,783	3,732	530	1,142	693	1,531
Earnings Three ($)	8,728	8,645	5,694	6,313	6,039	5,723	4,437	4,234
(Total state UI earnings over 6 quarters)	(9,086)	(9,115)	(6,785)	(6,861)	(6,651)	(6,503)	(5,371)	(5,087)
Employ Three (%)	86	85	77	81	89	89	82	83
(Any state UI employment over 6 quarters)	(35)	(36)	(42)	(39)	(31)	(31)	(39)	(38)
Earnings Four ($)	1,628	1,580	1,094	1,231	1,170	1,058	833	825
(Total state UI earnings in 6th quarter)	(2,034)	(2,036)	(1,475)	(1,589)	(1,484)	(1,460)	(1,177)	(1,152)
Employ Four (%)	61	58	53	57	62	61	52	53
(Any state UI employment in 6th quarter)	(49)	(49)	(50)	(50)	(49)	(49)	(50)	(50)
Observations	1,429	3,018	1,845	3,875	577	1,256	737	1,667

NOTE: For employment, table entries are the observed percentage of participants employed; for earnings, table entries are mean earnings. Standard deviations of each outcome appear in parentheses. Times in the row headings are after random assignment.

SOURCE: Authors' calculations using the SR Sample and the UI Sample from the NJS data.

ference in employment rates (those not employed enter mean earnings with a zero) accounts for much of the difference in mean earnings.

Outcomes and Experimental Impacts

In brief, the experiment found substantively and statistically significant earnings impacts on adult women. These impacts persisted for several years after random assignment in the long-term follow-up study summarized in USGAO (1996). Heckman, LaLonde, and Smith (1999) find that these estimates suffice to pass cost-benefit tests under some reasonable assumptions about discount rates, the marginal social cost of public funds, and the persistence of the impacts beyond the data. In stark contrast, the NJS yielded disappointing impacts for both male and female youth, with the point estimates close to zero (for the females) and negative (for the males) and rarely statistically different from zero. The estimates for adult men lie in between.[7]

Impact Variance

Before we launch into our discussion of subgroup effects and their correlations with participant evaluations, we take a brief but informative detour to consider the strength of the evidence on the question of whether or not the data contain any variation in impacts at all. Estimating the lower bound on the standard deviation of the impacts on self-reported earnings in the 18 months after random assignment using the methods described in detail in Heckman, Smith, and Clements (1997) and briefly in Chapter 3, we find lower bounds of $458, $587, $960, and $278 for adult males, adult females, male youth, and female youth, respectively. These represent substantively meaningful lower bounds, particularly for the groups other than female youth.

Of course, these estimates embody sampling variation. We cannot simply do the usual test that compares the estimated lower bounds to their estimated standard errors because the null we care about, namely that they equal zero in the population, lies at the boundary of the parameter space—i.e., of the set of possible values for a standard deviation. Instead, we undertake the test described in Appendix E of Heckman, Smith, and Clements (1997). We find that our estimated lower bounds lie below the 90th or 95th percentiles of the distributions of such estimates under the null; put differently, the data do not allow us to strongly reject the null at even the 10 percent level for any of the four demographic groups. Taken together, and combining it with our prior that impacts likely vary in a context like the JTPA program, in which the treatment itself exhibits substantial heterogeneity, we view the data as providing modest but not zero evidence of impact variation large enough to matter.

Bivariate Correlations

We begin our analysis of the data from the NJS with simple bivariate relationships between mean experimental impacts and fractions of treated participants giving a positive evaluation of JTPA. This analysis, presented in Table 4.5, extends that presented in Table 8.11 of Heckman and Smith (1998). The four rows in Table 4.5 correspond to the four demographic groups already defined. The first columns of Panels A and B present the fraction of treated individuals in each group that give JTPA a positive evaluation in the NJS survey, and thus they repeat information from the bottom panels of Tables 4.2 and 4.3.

The remaining eight columns of Panels A and B report experimental impact estimates (for each group) for the eight outcomes. The final two rows of Table 4.5 display the correlation between the fraction with a positive evaluation and the impact estimates across subgroups, along with p-values from tests of the null of a zero correlation. Be clear that this correlation relies on just four observations, so we do not expect a great deal of precision; at the same time, it summarizes eight numbers in a convenient and comparable way.

Table 4.5 reveals that adult women have both large mean earnings impacts and a higher fraction of positive participant evaluations than adult men; the parallel pattern holds for male and female youth. On the other hand, female youth have lower earnings impacts than adult women, but a higher fraction of positive participant evaluations; the parallel pattern by age holds for males. Consistent with this mixed picture, the last row reports five positive correlations and four negative ones, none (not surprisingly) statistically different from zero at conventional levels. At this crude level, then, we find no *consistent* evidence of a positive association between participant evaluations and experimental impact estimates.

Table 4.5 Bivariate Relationships between Experimental Impacts and Positive Participant Evaluation, by Demographic Group

	Experimental impacts, based on valid self-reported earnings					Experimental impacts, based on valid state UI earnings records				
	Positive participant evaluation (%)	Earnings One ($)	Employ One (%)	Earnings Two ($)	Employ Two (%)	Positive participant evaluation (%)	Earnings Three ($)	Employ Three (%)	Earnings Four ($)	Employ Four (%)
Adult males	39.52	538	2.05	28	1.88	39.21	-83	-0.36	-48	-3.05
	(0.93)	(382)	(1.16)	(27)	(1.55)	(0.90)	(292)	(1.13)	(65)	(1.58)
Adult females	45.46	819	3.03	62	4.00	45.26	619	3.90	137	3.86
	(0.83)	(227)	(1.20)	(17)	(1.42)	(0.81)	(193)	(1.16)	(43)	(1.41)
Male youth	43.87	-738	1.57	-58	-1.99	42.21	-316	-0.49	-112	-1.12
	(1.49)	(486)	(1.61)	(36)	(2.44)	(1.41)	(332)	(1.56)	(74)	(2.45)
Female youth	49.23	2	4.26	-4	0.43	47.47	-203	1.24	-8	0.83
	(1.30)	(303)	(1.88)	(24)	(2.29)	(1.24)	(234)	(1.70)	(52)	(2.21)
Correlation with positive participant evaluation	—	-0.17	0.81	-0.10	-0.08	—	0.23	0.62	0.49	0.77
		[0.83]	[0.19]	[0.90]	[0.92]		[0.77]	[0.38]	[0.51]	[0.23]

NOTE: "Positive participant evaluation" is the percentage of nonmissing participant evaluations that are positive. Entries in the "Experimental impact" columns are experimental impacts on these outcomes for each demographic group in the row headings. (See Table 4.4 and its notes for definitions of the outcome variables heading each column.) Employment impacts are expressed as a difference of percentages. The values in parentheses are heteroskedasticity-robust standard errors, and the values in square brackets are p-values. Blank cells = not applicable.

SOURCE: Authors' calculations using the subsamples of the SR Sample and the UI Sample (from the NJS data) with nonmissing participant evaluation.

Given that the survey-question wording focuses more on employment than earnings, one might expect a more consistent picture in employment outcomes alone. Yet no uniform pattern of correlation signs across the four alternative employment impact measures (three are positive and one is negative) emerges from the table. More broadly, if the rank preservation assumption described in Chapter 3 holds true even approximately, the quantile treatment effects show that the program improved the employment situation of at most a few percent of the respondents, yet around 40 percent gave positive participant evaluations in all four groups.

Tables 4.6 to 4.9 (one for each of the four basic demographic groups) show summaries of similar analyses for subgroups defined using a variety of baseline variables. As in Table 4.5, the columns correspond to the eight outcomes. Row labels indicate the variable used to create finer subgroups, and each row contains correlation coefficients (and p-values from tests of the null of a zero correlation) between positive participant evaluation fractions and estimated experimental impacts across those finer subgroups (similar to the final row of Table 4.5). We use race/ ethnicity, years of schooling categories, marital status, time since last employment categories, site, and age categories to define the subgroups (we omit the age subgroups for the youth because of lack of variation).

The bottom of each table presents the number of positive and negative correlations in the table and, for each sign, the number of statistically significant coefficients at the 5 and 10 percent levels. Though the statistics literature offers more sophisticated ways to summarize this information, for our purposes, and given the clear message from the data, these "vote counts" provide a useful summary of the 48 (or 40 for the youth) entries in each table. For adults, for instance, random variation would lead to an expected four or five statistically significant estimates at the 0.10 level, and two or three at the 0.05 level. Of course, this simple summary measure ignores the lack of independence among the estimates used to create each table and does not attempt to weight or value the different estimates based on their precision. The results in Tables 4.6 to 4.9 reinforce the impression made by Table 4.5: no clear or consistent patterns emerge in terms of the signs of the correlations, and the number of statistically significant correlations roughly resembles what one would expect if the population coefficients all equal zero. We do observe some quite large correlations, both positive and negative;

Table 4.6 Correlations between Experimental Impacts and Positive Participant Evaluations for Eight Outcomes, Adult Males

Category variable	Earnings One	Employ One	Earnings Two	Employ Two	Earnings Three	Employ Three	Earnings Four	Employ Four
Race	-0.66	-0.11	-0.91	-0.19	-0.86	-0.77	-0.86	-0.67
	[0.34]	[0.89]	[0.09]	[0.81]	[0.14]	[0.23]	[0.14]	[0.33]
Age	-0.90	0.92	-0.78	-0.05	0.77	0.73	-0.23	0.69
	[0.29]	[0.25]	[0.43]	[0.97]	[0.44]	[0.48]	[0.85]	[0.52]
Education	-0.43	-0.43	-0.86	-0.93	0.47	0.15	-0.82	-0.51
	[0.39]	[0.40]	[0.03]	[0.01]	[0.35]	[0.77]	[0.05]	[0.30]
Marital status	0.21	0.19	-0.24	0.36	0.70	0.95	0.99	0.63
	[0.79]	[0.81]	[0.76]	[0.64]	[0.30]	[0.05]	[0.01]	[0.37]
Employment status	0.18	0.47	0.07	0.49	0.15	-0.19	-0.66	0.07
	[0.82]	[0.53]	[0.93]	[0.51]	[0.85]	[0.81]	[0.34]	[0.93]
Site	0.42	0.34	0.03	0.06	0.29	0.11	0.15	0.25
	[0.11]	[0.19]	[0.92]	[0.84]	[0.28]	[0.67]	[0.59]	[0.36]

Positive Correlations: 27 of 48 (56.25%); 2 of 48 (4.17%) significant at 0.10; 2 of 48 (4.17%) significant at 0.05.
Negative Correlations: 21 of 48 (43.75%); 4 of 48 (8.33%) significant at 0.10; 3 of 48 (6.25%) significant at 0.05.

NOTE: Table entries are unweighted Pearson correlations between the percentage of positive nonmissing participant evaluations and experimental impacts, across the subgroups defined by distinct levels of each categorical variable in the row headings (p-values appear below each correlation in square brackets). The subgroups of each categorical variable are as follows. Race: White, Black, Hispanic, and Other. Age: 22–25 years, 26–34 years, and 35+ years. Education: missing, less than 10 years, 10–11 years, 12 years, 13–15 years, and 16+ years. Marital status: missing, single, married, and divorced/widowed/separated. Employment status: missing, out of the labor force, unemployed, and employed. Site: 16 sites. See the row headings of Table 4.4 for definitions of the outcome variables heading each column.
SOURCE: Authors' calculations using the subsamples of the SR Sample and the UI Sample (from the NJS data) with nonmissing participant evaluations.

Table 4.7 Correlations between Experimental Impacts and Positive Participant Evaluations for Eight Outcomes, Adult Females

Category variable	Earnings One	Employ One	Earnings Two	Employ Two	Earnings Three	Employ Three	Earnings Four	Employ Four
Race	-0.17	-0.19	0.06	-0.32	-0.40	-0.46	-0.28	-0.33
	[0.83]	[0.81]	[0.94]	[0.68]	[0.60]	[0.54]	[0.72]	[0.67]
Age	0.17	-0.75	-1.00	-0.98	-0.36	-0.09	-0.87	-0.97
	[0.89]	[0.46]	[0.04]	[0.12]	[0.76]	[0.94]	[0.33]	[0.15]
Education	0.11	-0.80	-0.85	-0.20	-0.82	-0.92	-0.85	-0.90
	[0.83]	[0.05]	[0.03]	[0.70]	[0.05]	[0.01]	[0.03]	[0.01]
Marital status	-0.57	-0.81	-0.75	-0.79	0.01	-0.64	0.72	-0.52
	[0.43]	[0.19]	[0.25]	[0.21]	[0.99]	[0.36]	[0.28]	[0.48]
Employment status	0.50	0.67	-0.08	0.15	0.46	0.70	-0.33	-0.54
	[0.50]	[0.33]	[0.92]	[0.85]	[0.54]	[0.30]	[0.67]	[0.46]
Site	-0.41	-0.37	0.07	0.02	-0.30	-0.15	0.13	0.18
	[0.12]	[0.15]	[0.81]	[0.94]	[0.27]	[0.57]	[0.63]	[0.51]

Positive correlations: 14 of 48 (29.17%); 0 of 48 (0.00%) significant at 0.10; 0 of 48 (0.00%) significant at 0.05.
Negative correlations: 34 of 48 (70.83%); 7 of 48 (14.58%) significant at 0.10; 7 of 48 (14.58%) significant at 0.05.

NOTE: Table entries are unweighted Pearson correlations between the percentage of positive nonmissing participant evaluations and experimental impacts, across the subgroups defined by distinct levels of each categorical variable in the row headings (*p*-values appear below each correlation in square brackets). The subgroups of each categorical variable are as follows. Race: White, Black, Hispanic, and Other. Age: 22–25 years, 26–34 years, and 35+ years. Education: missing, under 10 years, 10–11 years, 12 years, 13–15 years, and 16+ years. Marital status: missing, single, married, and divorced/widowed/separated. Employment status: missing, out of the labor force, unemployed, and employed. Site: 16 sites. See the row headings of Table 4.4 for definitions of the outcome variables heading each column.
SOURCE: Authors' calculations using the subsamples of the SR Sample and the UI Sample (from the NJS data) with nonmissing participant evaluations.

Table 4.8 Correlations between Experimental Impacts and Positive Participant Evaluations for Eight Outcomes, Male Youth

Category variable	Earnings One	Employ One	Earnings Two	Employ Two	Earnings Three	Employ Three	Earnings Four	Employ Four
Race	−0.80	−0.76	−0.86	−0.74	−0.79	−0.81	−0.64	−0.90
	[0.20]	[0.24]	[0.14]	[0.26]	[0.21]	[0.19]	[0.36]	[0.10]
Education	0.96	−0.83	−0.97	−0.95	0.91	−0.88	−0.86	−0.94
	[0.01]	[0.08]	[0.01]	[0.01]	[0.03]	[0.05]	[0.06]	[0.02]
Marital status	0.43	0.56	−0.20	0.89	−0.83	−0.89	−0.71	−0.76
	[0.57]	[0.44]	[0.80]	[0.11]	[0.17]	[0.11]	[0.29]	[0.24]
Employment status	0.17	0.92	0.69	0.48	0.43	0.97	0.77	0.96
	[0.83]	[0.08]	[0.31]	[0.52]	[0.57]	[0.03]	[0.23]	[0.04]
Site	0.07	−0.09	−0.06	−0.09	−0.01	−0.16	−0.17	−0.10
	[0.81]	[0.75]	[0.83]	[0.76]	[0.98]	[0.57]	[0.53]	[0.72]

Positive correlations: 14 of 40 (35.00%) significant at 0.10; 5 of 40 (12.50%) significant at 0.05.
Negative correlations: 26 of 40 (65.00%) significant at 0.10; 8 of 40 (20.00%) significant at 0.10; 5 of 40 (12.50%) significant at 0.05.

NOTE: Table entries are unweighted Pearson correlations between the percentage of positive nonmissing participant evaluations and experimental impacts, across the subgroups defined by distinct levels of each categorical variable in the row headings (p-values appear below each correlation in square brackets). The subgroups of each categorical variable are as follows. Race: White, Black, Hispanic, and Other. Age: less than 19 years and 19–21 years. Education: missing, under 10 years, 10–11 years, 12 years, and 13+ years. Marital status: missing, single, married, and divorced/widowed/separated. Employment status: missing, out of the labor force, unemployed, and employed. Site: 16 sites. See the row headings of Table 4.3 for definitions of the outcome variables heading each column.
SOURCE: Authors' calculations using the subsamples of the SR Sample and the UI Sample (from the NJS data) with nonmissing participant evaluations.

Table 4.9 Correlations between Experimental Impacts and Positive Participant Evaluations for Eight Outcomes, Female Youth

Category variable	Earnings One	Employ One	Earnings Two	Employ Two	Earnings Three	Employ Three	Earnings Four	Employ Four
Race	-0.22	-0.63	-0.54	-0.66	0.52	0.22	0.70	-0.10
	[0.78]	[0.37]	[0.46]	[0.34]	[0.48]	[0.78]	[0.30]	[0.90]
Education	-0.93	-0.90	-0.94	-0.88	-0.34	-0.84	-0.81	-0.91
	[0.02]	[0.04]	[0.02]	[0.05]	[0.58]	[0.08]	[0.1]	[0.03]
Marital status	0.26	0.24	0.47	0.20	0.64	0.88	0.83	0.55
	[0.74]	[0.76]	[0.53]	[0.80]	[0.36]	[0.12]	[0.17]	[0.45]
Employment status	-0.34	0.97	-0.04	-0.19	0.03	0.52	0.04	0.18
	[0.66]	[0.03]	[0.96]	[0.81]	[0.97]	[0.48]	[0.96]	[0.82]
Site	0.06	-0.05	0.19	0.03	0.04	0.05	0.00	0.03
	[0.84]	[0.85]	[0.51]	[0.93]	[0.89]	[0.85]	[0.99]	[0.92]

Positive correlations: 23 of 40 (57.50%); 1 of 40 (7.50%) significant at 0.10; 1 of 40 (5.00%) significant at 0.05.
Negative correlations: 17 of 40 (42.50%); 7 of 40 (17.50%) significant at 0.10; 5 of 40 (12.50%) significant at 0.05.

NOTE: Table entries are unweighted Pearson correlations between the percentage of positive nonmissing participant evaluations and experimental impacts, across the subgroups defined by distinct levels of each categorical variable in the row headings (*p*-values appear below each correlation in square brackets). The subgroups of each categorical variable are as follows. Race: White, Black, Hispanic and Other. Age: less than 19 years and 19–21 years. Education: missing, under 10 years, 10–11 years, 12 years, and 13+ years. Marital status: missing, single, married, and divorced/widowed/separated. Employment status: missing, out of the labor force, unemployed, and employed. Site: 16 sites. See the row headings of Table 4.4 for definitions of the outcome variables heading each column.
SOURCE: Authors' calculations using the subsamples of the SR Sample and the UI Sample (from the NJS data) with nonmissing participant evaluations.

these follow from the small number of categories associated with most of the variables.

Subgroup Impacts

We now turn to our multivariate subgroup analysis. As described in Chapter 3, we obtain predicted impacts for each individual in our treatment group sample by estimating an experimental impact regression in which we interact the treatment group indicator with a variety of baseline covariates. We then regress the predicted impacts on the participant evaluation measure.

Though quite straightforward conceptually, our experimental subgroup impact estimates do raise two important issues, which we now discuss. The first issue concerns the choice of variables to interact with the treatment indicator. We address this issue by presenting two sets of estimates based on vectors of characteristics selected in very different ways. One set of estimates simply borrows the vector of characteristics employed by Heckman, Heinrich, and Smith (2002, 2011) in their analyses of the JTPA data. The note to Table 4.10 lists these variables. The second set of estimates utilizes a set of characteristics selected using the somewhat undesirable method of stepwise regression. While economists typically shun stepwise procedures as atheoretic, for our purposes here that characteristic represents a feature rather than a bug, as it makes the variable selection procedure completely mechanical and thus immune from charges that we "cooked the books" by selecting variables that provide a particular conclusion. In both cases, we restrict our attention to main effects in order to keep the problem manageable.

We implement the stepwise procedure using essentially all of the variables from the background information form, including variables measuring participant demographics, site, receipt of means-tested monetary and in-kind transfers, labor force status, and work history. We include a missing indicator for each variable (to avoid losing a large fraction of the sample from listwise deleting observations with item nonresponse on one or more variables), and we interact both the variables and the missing indicators with the treatment group indicator. The stepwise procedure has to keep or drop each variable along with the missing indicator and interactions with the treatment indicator as a group. The stepwise procedure, which we perform separately for each

Table 4.10 Regression Results for the Relationship between Predicted Impacts and Positive Participant Evaluation for Eight Outcomes, by Demographic Group

	Adult males		Adult females		Male youth		Female youth		All participants		
	(1)	(2)	(1)	(2)	(1)	(2)	(1)	(2)	(3)	(4)	(5)
Earnings One	118.43	157.27**	10.09	−92.96**	−72.15	81.45	−6.41	18.09	30.06	6.70	−43.62
	(112.61)	(70.74)	(54.45)	(39.91)	(200.92)	(190.96)	(75.82)	(90.45)	(50.24)	(40.21)	(32.11)
	{1.70}	{0.63}	{1.40}	{0.73}	{1.60}	{1.17}	{1.35}	{0.93}	{1.56}	{0.82}	{1.41}
	[0.0045]	[0.9702]	[0.0354]	[0.8977]	[0.0200]	[0.2213]	[0.1158]	[0.5916]	[0.0000]	[0.9598]	[0.0160]
Employ One	0.05	0.54**	−0.39	−0.11	0.36	−0.27	0.91	1.15*	7.59	0.29	−0.28**
	(0.30)	(0.27)	(0.28)	(0.23)	(0.39)	(0.64)	(0.62)	(0.62)	(18.50)	(0.18)	(0.13)
	{1.35}	{0.91}	{1.31}	{0.87}	{1.86}	{1.12}	{1.94}	{1.19}	{1.53}	{0.95}	{1.35}
	[0.0753]	[0.6428]	[0.0849]	[0.7163]	[0.0469]	[0.2820]	[0.0035]	[0.1979]	[0.0002]	[0.6731]	[0.0350]
Earnings Two	7.44	0.79	0.01	−3.24	5.83	8.07	−0.46	2.15	3.00	−0.15	−2.86
	(7.31)	(5.64)	(3.32)	(2.65)	(22.16)	(15.76)	(5.80)	(8.71)	(3.97)	(3.26)	(2.14)
	{1.47}	{0.83}	{0.97}	{0.57}	{2.31}	{1.56}	{1.46}	{1.34}	{1.59}	{1.03}	{1.36}
	[0.0394]	[0.7730]	[0.5191]	[0.9880]	[0.0003]	[0.0151]	[0.0994]	[0.0763]	[0.0001]	[0.3809]	[0.0381]
Employ Two	−0.30	0.39	0.32	−0.09	0.38	−0.23	−0.48	0.17	−4.41	0.02	−0.31**
	(0.32)	(0.29)	(0.25)	(0.22)	(0.66)	(0.95)	(0.68)	(0.89)	(20.26)	(0.23)	(0.15)
	{0.96}	{0.67}	{1.00}	{0.57}	{1.46}	{1.13}	{2.23}	{1.59}	{1.30}	{0.99}	{1.31}
	[0.5378]	[0.9515]	[0.4605]	[0.9883]	[0.1045]	[0.2645]	[0.0026]	[0.0122]	[0.0245]	[0.5108]	[0.0597]
Earnings Three	123.86*	110.26*	−41.54	−51.74	−25.91	79.40	121.36*	72.15	48.43	49.10	−67.63***
	(66.53)	(66.74)	(43.14)	(34.48)	(117.27)	(125.66)	(63.46)	(65.71)	(32.73)	(31.92)	(25.26)
	{1.33}	{0.99}	{1.06}	{0.77}	{2.07}	{1.22}	{1.50}	{0.97}	{1.30}	{0.93}	{1.19}
	[0.0938]	[0.4864]	[0.3669]	[0.8562]	[0.0031]	[0.1623]	[0.0544]	[0.5241]	[0.0113]	[0.7331]	[0.1122]

	(1)	(2)	(3)	(4)	(5)	(6)	(7)	(8)	(9)	(10)	(11)
Employ Three	0.26 (0.27) {1.10} [0.3118]	0.95*** (0.27) {0.94} [0.5785]	-0.50* (0.26) {1.67} [0.0094]	-0.30 (0.27) {1.31} [0.0881]	0.74** (0.35) {2.61} [0.0112]	0.47 (0.56) {0.91} [0.6272]	0.53 (0.53) {1.94} [0.0041]	0.34 (0.46) {0.81} [0.7938]	19.86 (16.82) {1.62} [0.0001]	0.43** (0.17) {1.00} [0.4957]	-0.15 (0.12) {1.30} [0.0627]
Earnings Four	14.25 (17.65) {1.46} [0.0516]	37.04*** (14.08) {0.85} [0.7395]	4.83 (7.00) {0.69} [0.9224]	-12.94*** (6.53) {0.55} [0.9927]	-16.69 (24.08) {2.20} [0.0050]	22.17 (29.25) {1.29} [0.1123]	20.39 (15.27) {2.51} [0.0011]	-9.02 (13.22) {0.73} [0.8914]	14.98*** (7.38) {1.40} [0.0053]	14.03*** (6.85) {0.81} [0.9601]	5.03 (4.88) {1.22} [0.1324]
Employ Four	0.19 (0.31) {0.83} [0.7355]	0.77** (0.36) {0.83} [0.7759]	-0.71** (0.30) {1.29} [0.1121]	-0.65*** (0.27) {0.88} [0.6944]	0.47 (0.46) {1.04} [0.4110]	0.22 (0.85) {0.91} [0.6270]	-0.15 (0.56) {2.03} [0.0152]	-0.75 (0.73) {1.19} [0.1909]	0.05 (0.19) {1.04} [0.3687]	0.11 (0.23) {0.98} [0.5419]	0.05 (0.12) {0.97} [0.5205]

NOTE: Each cell in the table reports four numbers. The top number is a coefficient estimate from a univariate linear regression in which the dependent variable is the estimated treatment impact for an individual's subgroup (taken from a supporting model), and the independent variable is that individual's participant evaluation. The second number (in parentheses) is the heteroskedasticity-consistent standard error of the coefficient estimate. Significance of the coefficient estimate at the 0.10, 0.05, and 0.01 levels is indicated by symbols *, **, and ***, respectively. The data for these regressions are the subsamples of the SR Sample and UI Sample that are treated and have nonmissing participant evaluations. The last two numbers concern the supporting model itself, which estimates impacts using a linear regression in which the dependent variable is the outcome variable in the row headings and the independent variables are subgroup characteristics X, a treatment indicator D, and their interactions DX. The third number {in braces} is an F-statistic against the null hypothesis that there is no heterogeneity of treatment impacts across subjects (that is, that the coefficients on the interactions DX are jointly zero), and the final number [in brackets] is the p-value against that null hypothesis. Several specifications are used for the supporting model. Specifications (1), (3), and (5) select the X used to estimate impacts for each individual by a stepwise procedure. Specifications (2) and (4) use the X set of Heckman, Heinrich, and Smith (2002) to estimate impacts for each individual: that X set is race, age, education, marital status, employment status, AFDC receipt, receipt of food stamps, and site. The specifications (3), (4), and (5) introduce demographic group indicators G. Specifications (3) and (4) allow all coefficients on the X, D, and XD to vary with G, while specification (5) allows this only for D and for the intercept in X. See the row headings of Table 4.4 for definitions of the outcome variables in the row headings for this table. The data for these supporting models are the entire SR Sample or the entire UI Sample. The boxes within the table indicate the three cases that have both an estimate of α_1 that differs statistically from zero and subgroup effects that jointly differ statistically from zero.

SOURCE: Authors' calculations using the NJS data.

of the four demographic groups, iteratively drops variables with coefficients not statistically different from zero in a regression with self-reported earnings in the 18 months after random assignment as the dependent variable.[8]

The second issue concerns the amount of subgroup variation in impacts in the NJS data within the four demographic groups for which both we and the official reports conduct separate analyses. Although the NJS impact estimates differ substantially between youth and adults (and between male and female youth when considering the full samples), the experimental evaluation reports—see Exhibits 4.15, 5.14, 6.6, and 6.5 in Bloom et al. (1993) for the 18-month impacts and Exhibits 5.8, 5.9, 5.19, and 5.20 in Orr et al. (1996) for the 30-month impacts—do not reveal a huge amount of statistically significant variation in impacts among subgroups defined by the variables available on the background information form. If the impact does in fact vary a lot among individuals, but not in a way that is correlated with the characteristics we use in our model, then we may reach the wrong conclusions about participants' ability to construct consistent estimates of earnings impacts.

Table 4.10 presents our evidence based on regressions of experimental subgroup impact estimates for the eight outcomes on participant evaluations. Entries in Table 4.10 correspond to the combination of the dependent variable given by the row label and the demographic group and covariate set given by the column headings. The columns headed by (1), (3), and (5) contain the estimates using the covariate set chosen by the stepwise procedure described earlier, while the columns headed by (2) and (4) contain the estimates based on the covariates from Heckman, Heinrich, and Smith (2002). The three right-hand columns pool the four demographic groups so as to incorporate their variation in treatment effects into the regression framework.

Each entry in Table 4.10 contains four values: The top two values represent estimates of α_1 from Equation (3.4) in Chapter 3 and the associated estimated standard error. The second two values consist of the F-statistic and p-value from a test of zero coefficients on all of the interaction terms in the corresponding version of Equation (3.1) from Chapter 3 (i.e., a test of the null of no subgroup variation in treatment effects). As such, the last two numbers in each entry give a sense of the amount of precisely estimated subgroup variation in impacts.

The regression evidence in Table 4.10 suggests little, if any, consistent relationship between the experimental impact estimates based on subgroup variation and the participant evaluations, echoing the results of Table 4.5 and Tables 4.6 through 4.9. While the estimates of α_1 lean positive in the aggregate, only a handful of the estimates reach conventional levels of statistical significance (and not all of those fall on the positive side of the ledger). The boxes in Table 4.10 highlight the 3 cases, out of 64, with both an estimate of α_1 that differs statistically from zero (positive in two cases and negative in the other) and subgroup effects that jointly differ statistically from zero. While we wish we had more precise estimates of the subgroup impacts, given the information available, we conclude that either the participants do not weigh labor market impacts very heavily in their response, or else their impact estimates (or ours, or both) do not do a very good job of capturing the actual impacts.

Quantile Treatment Effects

This section presents evidence on the relationship between participant evaluations and impact estimates constructed under the rank preservation assumption defined in Chapter 3, which holds that the counterfactual outcome associated with a particular percentile of the treated outcome distribution equals the corresponding percentile of the untreated outcome distribution. Like the literature, we refer to these estimates as quantile treatment effects (QTEs). We focus on one particular outcome in this analysis: self-reported earnings over the whole 18 months since random assignment (quantiles of employment provide little in the way of insight, for obvious reasons). The predicted impacts from this approach still rely on the experimental data, but they build on a different identifying assumption than the subgroup impacts just considered.

Figure 4.1, Panels A through D (one for each demographic group) present our results in graphical form. The horizontal axis in each figure corresponds to percentiles of the untreated outcome distribution. The solid line in each figure represents impact estimates at every fifth percentile (5, 10, 15, ... , 95), constructed as in Equation (3.3). The broken line in each graph represents an estimate of the fraction with a positive

Figure 4.1 Quantile Treatment Effects (self-reported earnings over 18 months) and Positive Participant Evaluation (%)

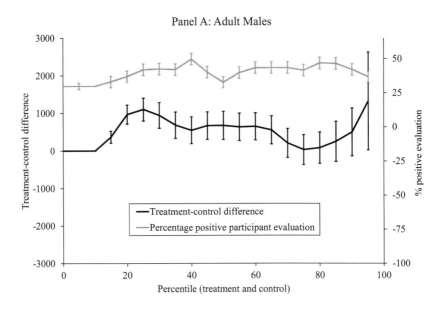

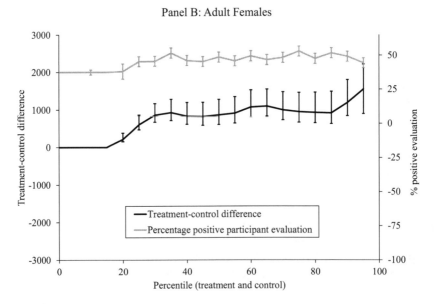

Figure 4.1 (continued)

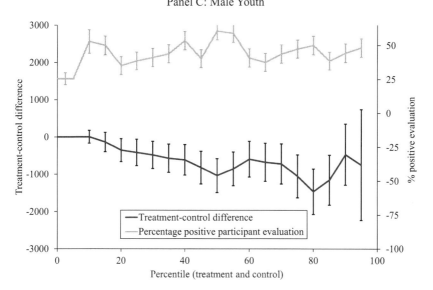

Panel C: Male Youth

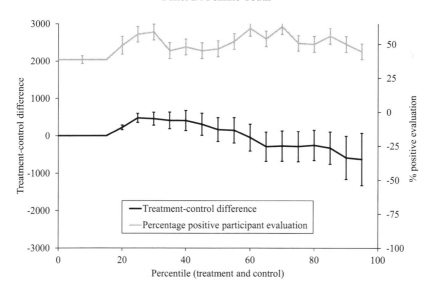

Panel D: Female Youth

SOURCE: Authors' calculations using the SR sample.

participant evaluation at every fifth percentile. For percentile j, this estimate consists of the fraction of the treatment-group sample members in the interval between percentile $j - 2.5$ and percentile $j + 2.5$ with a positive participant evaluation. If the rank preservation assumption holds, if participants care enough about labor market outcomes in answering the survey question, and if participants consistently estimate their own impacts, then the two lines should move together in the figures.

Two features of the figures merit notice. First, in the lower percentiles in each figure, the econometric impact estimate equals zero. This results from the fact that the lowest percentiles in both the treated and untreated outcome distributions have zero earnings in the 18 months after random assignment; the difference between the two then equals zero as well. Surprisingly, a substantial fraction of treatment group members at these percentiles provide positive participant evaluations, even though they have zero earnings in the 18 months after random assignment. This could mean that respondents view the question as asking about longer-term labor market impacts beyond the 18-month window of the measured outcomes (i.e., "employability," in the jargon of the active labor market policy literature), but it also could mean that respondents are acting as lay theorists (more on this shortly).

Second, the fraction with a positive participant evaluation has remarkably little variation across percentiles of the outcome distribution. For all four demographic groups, it remains within a band of width 0.3 centered on the unconditional proportion. For all four groups, the fraction is lowest for those with zero earnings in the 18 months after random assignment. Above that earnings level, the data fail to reveal a clear pattern.

Table 4.11 presents some of the estimates underlying the figures. In particular, the first five rows present the values for the 5th, 25th, 50th, 75th, and 95th percentiles. The last two rows of the table give the correlation between the quantile treatment effects and the fraction with a positive participant evaluation for each group (and the corresponding p-value from a test of the null that the correlation equals zero), along with the estimated coefficient from a regression of the quantile treatment effects on the fraction with a positive participant evaluation (and the corresponding standard error). The correlation and regression estimates quantify and confirm what the figures indicate: a strong, positive relationship for adult women, a weak and statistically insignificant

Table 4.11 Relationship between Quantile Treatment Effects for 18-Month Earnings and the Percentage with Positive Participant Evaluation, by Demographic Group

	Adult males		Adult females		Male youth		Female youth	
	Quantile treatment effects	Positive participant evaluation (%)	Quantile treatment effects	Positive participant evaluation (%)	Quantile treatment effects	Positive participant evaluation (%)	Quantile treatment effects	Positive participant evaluation (%)
5th	0	29.83	0	37.56	0	25.49	0	38.63
	—	(2.41)	—	(1.70)	—	(4.34)	—	(2.93)
25th	1099	41.91	607	45.50	−417	38.60	479	57.33
	(307)	(4.25)	(132)	(3.74)	(355)	(6.51)	(121)	(5.75)
50th	670	32.61	863	48.65	−1036	60.71	169	46.58
	(372)	(4.01)	(256)	(3.68)	(455)	(6.59)	(319)	(5.88)
75th	27	41.43	945	52.97	−1054	47.37	−284	50.67
	(398)	(4.18)	(280)	(3.68)	(575)	(6.67)	(404)	(5.81)
95th	1323	36.69	1547	44.32	−748	48.21	625	44.59
	(1303)	(4.10)	(653)	(3.66)	(1483)	(6.74)	(696)	(5.82)
Pearson correlation	0.08		0.78		−0.34		−0.02	
	[0.7360]		[0.0000]		[0.1556]		[0.9202]	
Regression coefficient	5.68		67.82		−15.18		−1.15	
	(19.59)		(12.96)		(11.16)		(9.57)	

NOTE: The upper part of the table has a pair of columns for each demographic group: the left-hand column shows five quantile treatment effect estimates, while the right-hand column shows the percentage of positive nonmissing participant evaluations in each quantile of the outcome distribution for those in the treatment group. Standard errors appear in parentheses. The first row of the lower part of the table contains Pearson correlations between quantile treatment effect estimates and the percentage of positive participant evaluations by quantile (in which one observation is one of the 19 quantiles), and the p-value for the correlation appears in square brackets. The second row of the lower part of the table contains the estimated coefficient from a univariate linear regression in which the dependent variable is the quantile treatment effect estimate, and the independent variable is the percentage of positive nonmissing participant evaluations (for which one observation is one of the 19 quantiles). Heteroskedasticity-consistent standard errors for these estimates appear in parentheses. — = data not available.

SOURCE: Authors' calculations using the SR Sample from the NJS data.

positive relationship for adult men, a moderately strong and negative relationship for male youth, and a similar but not statistically significant relationship for female youth.

Skeptical readers may wonder, rightly, whether the lack of strong associations in Table 4.11 says more about the large standard errors of our estimated quantile treatment effects than about the goodness of the NJS participant evaluation measure. To address this concern, we examined whether participants in the top or bottom 5 percent of the distribution of estimated QTEs are more likely to report that the program did (or did not, in the case of the lower group) benefit them. We find that individuals who experience these particularly large positive or negative QTEs do not differ from the remainder of the sample in their probability of a positive participant evaluation.

Appendix Table 4A.2 presents results from undertaking the test of covariate balance within quantile intervals from Bitler, Gelbach, and Hoynes (2005), described in Chapter 3. As noted there, rank preservation implies covariate balance (in samples of reasonable size), but covariate balance does not imply rank preservation. The tests yield little evidence of strong departures from covariate balance, rejecting the null at the 5 percent level only for the bottom half of the distribution for male youth. These findings provide support for interpreting the quantile differences as causal effects, as we have done here.

To summarize, we find only weak evidence of a positive relationship between participant evaluations and quantile treatment effects, where we interpret the quantile treatment effects as individual impact estimates by invoking a rank preservation assumption. At the same time, a substantial minority of treatment group members provide positive participant evaluations. This basic pattern appears, with remarkably little variation in levels, for all four demographic groups and across the distribution of untreated outcomes. Even many individuals with zero earnings over the 18 months following randomized assignment say that the program helped them get a job. With these disappointing and somewhat puzzling findings in hand, we turn in the next section to an examination of just what variables do predict a positive participant evaluation response.

Testing the Decision Theory Viewpoint

In this subsection, we consider the (weak) test of the first decision theory viewpoint advanced in Chapter 2. In particular, we use estimates of R_s and P_s from the NJS data to test whether the relationship in Equation (2.5) holds, under the assumption that $c = 0.5$. Estimates of R_s, the proportion with a positive participant evaluation, for the four demographic groups and the SR sample appear in the first column of Table 4.4. Based on these estimates, the bounds on the right-hand side of (2.5) equal [0.1976, 0.6976] for adult males, [0.2273, 0.7273] for adult females, [0.2194, 0.7194] for male youth, and [0.2461, 0.7461] for female youth.

The subgroup estimates based on the moderators from Heckman, Heinrich, and Smith (2002, 2011) (and self-reported earnings in the 18 months after random assignment) yield fractions positive 0.61, 0.74, 0.39, and 0.44 for adult males, adult females, male youth, and female youth, respectively. The corresponding values from the moderators chosen via stepwise regression equal 0.60, 0.67, 0.35, and 0.47. Seven of these eight values lie within the intervals implied by the first decision theory viewpoint with $c = 0.5$. In contrast, using the estimates of the fraction positive based on the QTE analysis (i.e., those shown in Figure 4.1), we have fractions positive of 0.80, 0.80, 0.05, and 0.40 for the four demographic groups, in the usual order. Only for the female youth does R_s lie in the interval consistent with the first decision theory view.

Thus, in the data from the NJS, a conclusion about the consistency of the data with the first decision theory viewpoint depends on the particular identification strategy for the subgroup effects. We call this mixed evidence in its favor.

Determinants of Positive Participant Evaluations: Motivation and Caveats

The general lack of an empirical relationship between participant evaluations and predicted impacts, whether based on subgroup variation or rank preservation, could simply reflect very imprecise impact estimates, little actual variation in impacts across subgroups or, in the case of the quantile treatment effects, complete failure of the rank preservation assumption. Absent one or more of these factors at work, our results so far broadly comport with our subjective rationality interpretation: participants may care mostly about effects of JTPA not captured by our particular quantitative labor market outcomes measured over the specific periods in which we measure them.

Yet the results also strongly suggest lay scientists at work. For instance, consider the finding that participant evaluations vary remarkably little across the four demographic groups, across subgroups within those four groups, and across quantiles of outcome distributions within those groups. This suggests that participants' evaluations may be largely theory-driven inferences based on shared folk theories. For example, one such folk theory might hold that impacts increase monotonically in inputs (the expense or resource-intensiveness of program services received). We examine the evidence for this particular folk theory in the next subsection by estimating relationships between participant evaluations and services received by participants and looking to see if having received relatively resource-intensive services increases the probability of a positive participant evaluation.

An obvious interpretive caveat is that different program services may themselves have different subjective or direct costs and benefits not captured by the labor market outcomes we consider. For example, classroom training may be more fun (or more tedious) than, say, job search assistance. Alternatively, classroom training at a distant community college imposes higher direct costs than job search assistance provided at a local neighborhood location. Thus, the subjective rationality interpretation also allows for relationships between participant evaluations and service types—though it makes no obvious prediction about the direction of those relationships.

Our results so far also suggest that some participants may act as lay empiricists, making judgments based on proxy variables that correlate only weakly with true impacts, and perhaps with insufficient notice of potential confounding factors. If so, their evaluations can be both inconsistent and full of nuisance variance, undermining any relationship between them and consistent impact estimates. The proxies we examine are actual labor market outcomes (employment and earnings) and simple before-after differences in those outcomes. If respondents really do know the impacts, then such proxies should have little explanatory power except to the extent that they correlate with actual impacts, which, as Heckman and Smith (1999) and Heckman, Heinrich, and Smith (2002) show, they largely do not.

Determinants of Positive Participant Evaluation: Service Types

Table 4.12 presents estimates of Equation (3.5) that include administrative measures of the service type received by JTPA treatment group members. For this analysis, we employ five service types: 1) classroom training in occupational skills (CT-OS), 2) on-the-job training or work experience (OJT/WE) (which is almost all OJT), 3) job search assistance (JSA), 4) adult basic education (ABE), and 5) "other." CT-OS means what it says, while OJT, despite the name, is a wage subsidy to private firms with some expectation that the firm will provide some training (though it need not, and often does not, exceed that provided to unsubsidized workers) and retain satisfactory workers when the subsidy runs out. WE subsidizes nonprofit or government enterprises to hire participants and does not entail an expectation that the worker will stay on after the subsidy runs out. JSA can include instruction in job search techniques and self-presentation as well as group activities such as "job clubs." ABE aims to have the participant finish high school or obtain a general education diploma (GED). We code an indicator variable for each service type indicating whether or not the respondent received it; many individuals receive more than one service type. To the extent that respondents employ the lay theory that impacts increase with resources expended, we expect relatively more positive participant evaluations among those receiving the expensive service types, namely CT-OS and OJT/WE.

The logit models presented in Table 4.12 also include a variety of background variables. These variables play two roles. First, we expect them to pick up parts of the overall impact of participation unrelated to the labor market outcomes we examine. The variable "never worked for pay" relates to the opportunity cost of participation, as does the variable for having a young child. The variable for AFDC receipt at random assignment captures variation in the cost of classroom training due to the availability of an income source not tied to employment. Taking account of these other sources of consistent variation in the participant evaluation variable clarifies our interpretation of the effects of the service-type variables by removing potential confounds. Second,

Table 4.12 Logistic Regression Estimates of the Determinants of Positive Participant Evaluation, by Demographic Group

	Adult males	Adult females	Male youth	Female youth
Race				
Black	6.76	−1.76	11.04	2.79
	(2.54)	(2.00)	(4.33)	(3.24)
	[0.0078]	[0.3778]	[0.0109]	[0.3894]
Hispanic	2.36	2.95	14.33	9.30
	(3.16)	(2.62)	(4.64)	(3.67)
	[0.4549]	[0.2614]	[0.0020]	[0.0114]
Other	5.02	−2.63	4.52	5.99
	(4.64)	(4.31)	(9.37)	(9.64)
	[0.2795]	[0.5412]	[0.6295]	[0.5343]
Age				
19–21 years			−0.69	−0.86
			(3.53)	(2.64)
			[0.8443]	[0.7453]
26–34 years	−1.14	0.36		
	(2.19)	(1.82)		
	[0.6021]	[0.8421]		
35+ years	−2.91	−7.83		
	(2.25)	(1.81)		
	[0.1951]	[0.0000]		
Education				
10–11 years	2.68	−1.07	2.71	0.72
	(2.46)	(2.10)	(3.85)	(3.13)
	[0.2756]	[0.6102]	[0.4812]	[0.8180]
12 years	3.82	−2.74	3.24	4.52
	(2.19)	(1.76)	(3.88)	(3.04)
	[0.0802]	[0.1180]	[0.4039]	[0.1368]
13–15 years	1.96	−1.40	0.42	−1.26
(For youth, 13+ years)	(2.72)	(2.45)	(6.51)	(5.29)
	[0.4707]	[0.5673]	[0.9482]	[0.8120]
16+ years	5.95	5.18		
	(4.31)	(4.31)		
	[0.1675]	[0.2289]		
Marital status				
Married	−2.18	4.52	−6.22	0.73
	(2.18)	(2.18)	(4.83)	(4.09)
	[0.3175]	[0.0378]	[0.1980]	[0.8575]

Table 4.12 (continued)

	Adult males	Adult females	Male youth	Female youth
Marital status				
Div/wid/sep	−3.34	3.17	−10.34	−4.42
	(2.44)	(1.87)	(10.52)	(4.30)
	[0.1705]	[0.0910]	[0.3261]	[0.3032]
English not primary	9.74	4.21	7.14	−6.44
language	(4.61)	(3.83)	(9.78)	(10.09)
	[0.0346]	[0.2708]	[0.4652]	[0.5232]
AFDC receipt	−1.44	−0.61	0.06	−0.13
	(3.66)	(1.88)	(6.60)	(3.24)
	[0.6949]	[0.7474]	[0.9924]	[0.9690]
Never worked for pay	−3.90	−0.70	−0.35	−0.36
	(3.24)	(2.42)	(4.44)	(3.27)
	[0.2291]	[0.7727]	[0.9367]	[0.9127]
Child less than six	−0.93	0.05	−1.59	0.49
	(2.45)	(1.80)	(5.25)	(2.85)
	[0.7051]	[0.9771]	[0.7626]	[0.8636]
Service				
CT-OS	30.90	33.62	23.46	28.52
	(2.88)	(2.34)	(4.66)	(3.77)
	[0.0000]	[0.0000]	[0.0000]	[0.0000]
OJT/WE	25.47	27.19	14.78	17.73
	(2.78)	(2.63)	(4.41)	(4.11)
	[0.0000]	[0.0000]	[0.0008]	[0.0000]
JSA	13.20	7.35	5.84	5.32
	(2.50)	(2.16)	(4.02)	(3.50)
	[0.0000]	[0.0007]	[0.1466]	[0.1284]
ABE	25.06	8.53	8.14	7.42
	(4.22)	(2.94)	(4.22)	(3.51)
	[0.0000]	[0.0038]	[0.0541]	[0.0347]
Other	8.85	15.63	4.14	18.90
	(2.73)	(2.68)	(4.43)	(4.17)
	[0.0012]	[0.0000]	[0.3502]	[0.0000]

NOTE: The four columns of the table report the results from a logistic regression in which the binary positive participant evaluation variable is the dependent variable and the categorical variables listed in the row headings are the independent variables. The values in the table are mean numerical derivatives, with standard errors in parentheses. Indicator variables for missing values for the independent variables are also included in the regression. The omitted age category for adults is aged 22–25 years; for youths, it is less than 19. The omitted marital status is single, the omitted education category is less than 10 years, the omitted racial group is white, and the omitted training type is no report of training for all demographic groups. Blank cells = not applicable.

SOURCE: Authors' calculations using the subsample of the NJS data with follow-up interviews at least 18 whole months—548 days—after random assignment and nonmissing participant evaluations.

and more prosaically, we expect the additional covariates to make the estimates of the effects of the service-type variables more precise by soaking up residual variance.

The columns in Table 4.12 give results for the four demographic groups. The table presents mean derivatives, estimated standard errors for the mean derivatives in parentheses, and p-values from tests of the null hypothesis that the mean derivative equals zero in square brackets. Table 4.13 summarizes the results in Table 4.12 by presenting test statistics and p-values from tests of the joint null that the mean derivatives for groups of related covariates (e.g., all of the service-type variables) equal zero.

Consider the variables other than the service-type variables first. Although they do not appear in the table, the site indicators have a substantively strong effect on the probability of a positive participant evaluation. Moreover, Table 4.13 shows that these variables are strongly statistically significant as a group. Respondents may take account of nonpecuniary aspects of their JTPA experience, such as staff friendliness and efficiency, or the attractiveness and ease of access of the JTPA office and the local service providers. Variation in local environmental conditions across sites, such as hiring opportunities, also might affect respondents' evaluations through an influence on outcomes. Site differences in impacts could in principle matter as well, though we would have expected to find evidence of this in Tables 4.6–4.9, which we did not.

Looking at the remainder of Table 4.13, we see that with the exception of age for adult women, race for adult males and male youth, and "other individual characteristics" for adult women, we cannot reject the nulls of zero coefficients on the background variables. Substantively, too, they typically add little to the explanatory power of the covariate set. For adult women, age has a substantively large effect toward negative participant evaluations. For adult males, some nonwhite groups have substantively and statistically higher probabilities of positive participant evaluations. We do not have good stories for either of these patterns. The limited role played by the background characteristics in the analysis surprised us.

In contrast to these background characteristics, service type plays a major role in determining individual participant evaluations. The magnitudes of the average derivative estimates for service types in Table

Table 4.13 Test Statistics from Logistic Regressions of Determinants of Positive Participant Evaluation, by Demographic Group

Category variable	Adult males	Adult females	Male youth	Female youth
Race	7.23	2.41	11.27	3.87
	[0.0649]	[0.4920]	[0.0103]	[0.2759]
	$R^{*2} = 0.21$	$R^{*2} = 0.05$	$R^{*2} = 0.80$	$R^{*2} = 0.19$
Age	1.48	21.03	0.05	0.10
	[0.4764]	[0.0000]	[0.8233]	[0.7506]
	$R^{*2} = 0.05$	$R^{*2} = 0.48$	$R^{*2} = 0.00$	$R^{*2} = 0.00$
Education	7.66	6.69	1.46	3.54
	[0.1762]	[0.2445]	[0.8333]	[0.4726]
	$R^{*2} = 0.21$	$R^{*2} = 0.15$	$R^{*2} = 0.11$	$R^{*2} = 0.18$
Marital status	2.19	5.23	2.53	1.32
	[0.5339]	[0.1555]	[0.4695]	[0.7239]
	$R^{*2} = 0.06$	$R^{*2} = 0.13$	$R^{*2} = 0.19$	$R^{*2} = 0.07$
English not primary language	3.93	0.89	0.76	0.80
	[0.1401]	[0.6415]	[0.6847]	[0.6695]
	$R^{*2} = 0.11$	$R^{*2} = 0.02$	$R^{*2} = 0.05$	$R^{*2} = 0.05$
Other individual characteristics	3.21	9.63	0.65	0.64
	[0.6681]	[0.0863]	[0.9855]	[0.9859]
	$R^{*2} = 0.10$	$R^{*2} = 0.21$	$R^{*2} = 0.05$	$R^{*2} = 0.04$
Service type	272.82	429.31	59.75	125.38
	[0.0000]	[0.0000]	[0.0000]	[0.0000]
	$R^{*2} = 9.88$	$R^{*2} = 11.83$	$R^{*2} = 4.71$	$R^{*2} = 7.53$
Site	70.83	46.64	47.48	66.19
	[0.0000]	[0.0000]	[0.0000]	[0.0000]
	$R^{*2} = 2.10$	$R^{*2} = 1.08$	$R^{*2} = 3.59$	$R^{*2} = 3.75$

NOTE: The four columns of the table report the results from a logit model in which the binary positive participant evaluation variable is the dependent variable and the categorical variables summarized in the row headings are the independent variables. The values in the table are χ^2-statistics for joint tests that all of the coefficients equal zero for a given group of variables, with the p-values in square brackets. The value for R^{*2} are the partial r-squared times 100 for the group of covariates in the row in the corresponding linear probability model. The variables in "Other individual characteristics" are indicators of current AFDC receipt, the presence of children younger than age six, and having ever worked for pay. Indicator variables for missing values for the independent variables are also included in the regressions.

SOURCE: Authors' calculations using the subsample of the NJS data with follow-up interviews at least 18 whole months—548 days—after random assignment and nonmissing participant evaluations.

4.12 reveal that both CT-OS and OJT/WE have large positive effects on the probability of a positive participant evaluation (relative to no service receipt) in all four demographic groups. Recall that CT-OS and OJT/WE generally represent the largest resource investment in the JTPA participant. In contrast, JSA is the cheapest of the services and, as expected, elicits less of a positive effect, though one statistically distinguishable from zero for adults and almost so for youth. The ABE and "other" service types matter pretty consistently in the statistical sense; the average derivative estimates almost always lie between those for CT-OS and OJT/WE and those for JSA, which corresponds to their relative costs.

Overall, these findings comport with the patterns expected under our specific lay theorist interpretation, as relatively more expensive services correlate with positive participant evaluations. At the same time, these patterns also comport with the subjective rationality interpretation, if respondents take the nonpecuniary aspects of the service type into account in their response and if those nonpecuniary aspects line up with relative costs.

Determinants of Positive Participant Evaluations: Labor Market Outcomes

Table 4.14 reports estimates of Equation (3.5) that include the same background variables as the models of Table 4.12 but adds various versions of Y_1, the labor market outcome in the treated state, in place of the service-type indicators. Acting as lay empiricists, respondents may be relatively more likely to infer a positive program impact if they have done well in the labor market over the period between random assignment and the survey, or if they are doing well around the time of the survey.

Panel A of Table 4.14 shows results from two specifications that include an indicator variable for any employment (defined as nonzero earnings) in the 18 months after random assignment, the first based on the self-reported earnings data and the second on the UI data. Similarly, Panel B of Table 4.14 displays results from two specifications in which we divide earnings in the 18 months after random assignment into five categories—zero and four quartiles of the distribution of positive earnings—and then include indicator variables for four of these five catego-

Table 4.14 Logistic Regression Estimates of the Relationship between Outcomes and Positive Participant Evaluation: Four Outcomes, by Demographic Group

	Adult males	Adult females	Male youth	Female youth
Panel A. Employment: change in % positive participant evaluation				
Employ One	8.69	9.52	18.32	13.97
	(3.89)	(3.45)	(5.97)	(4.33)
	[0.0256]	[0.0058]	[0.0022]	[0.0013]
Employ Three	7.61	2.22	2.08	5.67
	(3.54)	(3.36)	(4.94)	(3.96)
	[0.0315]	[0.5094]	[0.6738]	[0.1526]
Panel B. Earnings: change in % positive participant evaluation				
Earnings One (SR): Bottom quartile	7.37	7.30	13.67	13.15
	(3.03)	(2.98)	(4.07)	(4.05)
	[0.0150]	[0.0143]	[0.0008]	[0.0012]
Earnings One (SR): Lower middle quartile	8.62	9.37	22.20	10.47
	(3.02)	(3.01)	(4.23)	(4.10)
	[0.0043]	[0.0018]	[0.0000]	[0.0107]
Earnings One (SR): Upper middle quartile	9.66	12.21	16.53	19.46
	(3.02)	(3.05)	(4.22)	(4.19)
	[0.0014]	[0.0001]	[0.0001]	[0.0000]
Earnings One (SR): Top quartile	9.56	9.69	21.61	13.75
	(3.06)	(3.10)	(4.52)	(4.32)
	[0.0018	[0.0017]	[0.0000]	[0.0014]
Earnings Three (UI): Bottom quartile	3.97	0.08	1.26	5.56
	(2.92)	(3.33)	(4.95)	(4.17)
	[0.1746]	[0.9815]	[0.7999]	[0.1823]
Earnings Three (UI): Lower middle quartile	9.39	1.57	0.21	3.03
	(2.99)	(3.36)	(4.69)	(4.18)
	[0.0017]	[0.6400]	[0.9646]	[0.4679]
Earnings Three (UI): Upper middle quartile	6.85	4.58	1.17	4.47
	(2.89)	(3.37)	(4.80)	(4.17)
	[0.0177]	[0.1742]	[0.8078]	[0.2836]
Earnings Three (UI): Top quartile	10.80	3.25	7.35	10.93
	(2.97)	(3.42)	(5.23)	(4.43)
	[0.0003]	[0.3420]	[0.1599]	[0.0135]

NOTE: The four columns of this table report the results from logistic regressions in which the binary participant evaluation variable is the dependent variable, the categorical variables listed in the row headings of Table 4.1 are independent variables, and, additionally, an outcome variable is included in each regression. The values in the table are mean numerical derivatives, with the standard errors in parentheses and p-values in square brackets. For earnings outcomes, the

(continued)

Table 4.14 (continued)

continuous variables are entered as four categorical variables: 1) zero earnings, an indicator for being in the lowest quartile of the nonzero earnings distribution; 2) lower middle quartile of the nonzero earnings distribution; 3) upper middle quartile of the nonzero earnings distribution; and 4) highest quartile of the nonzero earnings distribution. The omitted category is for zero earnings. For the employment outcomes, a binary variable is included indicating whether the respondent was employed. Each set of cells in the table is the result for a different specification in which the outcome to be included as an independent variable is different. The sets of cells are defined as two groups of four and two groups of two, depending on how the outcome enters the regression. Indicator variables for missing values for the independent variables are also included in the regression. Employment measures are expressed in percentage terms.

SOURCE: Authors' calculations using the subsamples of the SR Sample and the UI Sample (from the NJS data) that were treated and have nonmissing participant evaluations.

ries, with zero earnings as the excluded category. The first specification does this with self-reported 18-month earnings, while the second uses UI administrative earnings (in the six calendar quarters after random assignment) instead of self-reported earnings.

The broad picture from Table 4.14 is that labor market outcomes predict positive participant evaluations. We obtain uniformly statistically and substantively significant estimates for the self-reported outcomes but smaller estimates—often not statistically distinguishable from zero—for the outcomes constructed from the UI data. Differences in coefficients, rather than differences in standard errors, generate the contrast in findings between the two sets of outcome measures. We expect that the difference in coefficients, in turn, springs from the measurement differences between the two data sources discussed earlier.

For the estimates using the categories based on self-reported earnings, we usually find the smallest estimates for the lowest nonzero earnings category but no consistent pattern above that, which makes some sense, given the focus of the participant evaluation measure on employment rather than on earnings. For instance, for adult females, we estimate that self-reported earnings over the 18 months after random assignment in the lowest quartile increase the probability of a positive participant evaluation by about 7.3 percentage points, while the estimates for the remaining quartiles range from 9.4 to 12.2 percentage points.

Table 4.15 summarizes the evidence in Table 4.14, as well as evidence from alternative specifications not fully reported here for reasons of space. As in Table 4.13, the summary takes the form of chi-square statistics, and their p-values, for tests of the null hypothesis that a coefficient (or all coefficients) on a specific labor market outcome measure

Table 4.15 Test Statistics from Logistic Regressions of the Relationship between Positive Participant Evaluation and Outcomes, by Demographic Group

	Adult males	Adult females	Male youth	Female youth
Panel A. Employment				
Employ One	9.36	19.73	11.80	16.39
	[0.0022]	[0.0000]	[0.0006]	[0.0000]
	$R^{*2} = 0.32$	$R^{*2} = 0.52$	$R^{*2} = 1.02$	$R^{*2} = 1.05$
Employ Two	5.48	8.86	6.01	2.22
	[0.0193]	[0.0029]	[0.0142]	[0.1364]
	$R^{*2} = 0.19$	$R^{*2} = 0.24$	$R^{*2} = 0.51$	$R^{*2} = 0.14$
Employ Three	8.79	1.09	0.21	2.95
	[0.0030]	[0.2959]	[0.6447]	[0.0859]
	$R^{*2} = 0.28$	$R^{*2} = 0.03$	$R^{*2} = 0.02$	$R^{*2} = 0.17$
Employ Four	4.83	2.15	0.93	0.40
	[0.0279]	[0.1422]	[0.3337]	[0.5260]
	$R^{*2} = 0.16$	$R^{*2} = 0.06$	$R^{*2} = 0.07$	$R^{*2} = 0.02$
Panel B. Earnings				
Earnings One	10.18	23.29	16.91	21.61
	[0.0374]	[0.0001]	[0.0020]	[0.0002]
	$R^{*2} = 0.35$	$R^{*2} = 0.62$	$R^{*2} = 1.46$	$R^{*2} = 1.38$
Earnings Two	7.87	16.18	7.12	6.17
	[0.0963]	[0.0028]	[0.1295]	[0.1868]
	$R^{*2} = 0.27$	$R^{*2} = 0.43$	$R^{*2} = 0.60$	$R^{*2} = 0.39$
Earnings Three	15.89	4.60	3.48	7.74
	[0.0032]	[0.3309]	[0.4809]	[0.1015]
	$R^{*2} = 0.52$	$R^{*2} = 0.12$	$R^{*2} = 0.26$	$R^{*2} = 0.45$
Earnings Four	9.00	11.57	12.48	5.92
	[0.0611]	[0.0208]	[0.0141]	[0.2056]
	$R^{*2} = 0.29$	$R^{*2} = 0.30$	$R^{*2} = 0.98$	$R^{*2} = 0.34$

NOTE: The four columns of this table report the results from logistic regressions in which the binary participant evaluation variable is the dependent variable, the categorical variables listed in the row headings of Table 4.1 are independent variables, and, additionally, an outcome variable is included in each regression. Each cell in the table is the result for a different specification in which the outcome to be included as an independent variable is different. The values in the table are χ^2-statistics for joint tests of the null in which all of the coefficients equal zero for a given outcome, with the p-values in square brackets. The value for R^{*2} is the partial r-squared times 100 for the group of covariates in the row in the corresponding linear probability model. For earnings outcomes, the continuous variables are entered as four categorical variables: 1) an indicator for being in the lowest quartile of the nonzero earnings distribution, 2) lower middle quartile of the nonzero earnings distribution, 3) upper middle quartile of the nonzero earnings distribution, and 4) upper quartile of the nonzero earnings distribution. The omitted category is for those with zero earnings. For the employment outcomes, a binary variable is included indicating whether the respondent was employed. Indicator variables for missing values for the independent variables are also included in the regression. Employment measures are expressed in percentage terms.
SOURCE: Authors' calculations using the subsamples of the SR Sample and the UI Sample (from the NJS data) that were treated and have nonmissing participant evaluations.

(or vector of outcome measures) equals zero. These results show that relationships tend to be statistically stronger for adults than for youth. Also, earnings measures tend to yield more statistically significant relationships than employment measures, especially for outcomes at or just around the time of the survey.

Overall, we find strong evidence consistent with the notion that participants use outcomes as proxies for impacts. This finding is consistent with lay science, but with real science too, as outcomes may be correlated with actual impacts. Indeed, some fraction of the treated group would have zero counterfactual (untreated) earnings outcomes in the period after random assignment; in such cases, their observed outcome levels coincide with their otherwise unobserved impacts. Our concerns about the potential for large amounts of error in our predicted impacts mean that we cannot rule out a broader correlation between outcomes and impacts.

Determinants of Positive Participant Evaluations: Before-After Comparisons

In this section, we explore the relationship between participant evaluations and before-after comparisons of employment and earnings. The cognitive appeal and simplicity of before-after comparisons as an estimator of impacts is undeniable. Moreover, despite their simplicity, before-after comparisons are consistent impact estimates in the absence of confounds—that is, if there is no change in any outcome-relevant factor other than the treatment over the period between the two measurements. (Initial outcomes will then consistently estimate the final outcome that would have occurred in the absence of treatment.) Unfortunately, there is a dramatic confound over the NJS experiment period. Heckman and Smith (1999) show that, because of "Ashenfelter's dip" in earnings in the preprogram period, before-after impact estimates tend to have a strong upward bias. Remembering that lay empiricists may fail to correct for nonsalient confounds, participants making judgments on the basis of before-after comparisons may well fail to appreciate a confounding factor like Ashenfelter's dip and, as a result, will produce upward-biased impact estimates.

The background information form survey includes responses to the question "How much did you earn last year?" We will call this "earnings before (random assignment)" and, when it is positive, we will call it "employed before (random assignment)." This response is missing for an appreciable number of individuals, so we regard "employed before" as a trinary categorical variable (with levels *yes*, *no*, and *missing*). For a comparable one-year period after random assignment, we choose to use the sum of self-reported earnings across the seventh through eighteenth months after random assignment. We call this "earnings after (random assignment)" and, when this is positive, we call it "employed after (random assignment)." Finally, for the difference between earnings after and earnings before, we will use the term "(self-reported) before-after earnings difference."

Given that the second of the two survey questions that compose our self-reported evaluation measure asks directly about finding a job, in Table 4.16 we first consider its relationship to before-after employment changes. We coded an employment status difference variable based on the two self-reported employment status variables just described. This coding yields six patterns: 1) (missing, no), 2) (missing, yes), 3) (no, no), 4) (no, yes), 5) (yes, no), and 6) (yes, yes). We include indicators for five of these, with "not employed both before and after" as the omitted category. The first column of Panel A of Table 4.16 assigns names to the coefficients on these indicators (e.g., μ_{yy}), which makes it easier to define the joint null hypotheses tested in Panel B of Table 4.16.

Three patterns emerge from the findings: First, respondents employed in the "after" period, as we define it here, have a higher probability of providing a positive participant evaluation. Second, the extent of the first pattern does not depend on employment status in the before period. For example, for adult men, the (yes, yes) coefficient equals 10.42, the (missing, yes) coefficient equals 12.08, and the (no, yes) coefficient, which a story that emphasizes use of before-after comparisons would predict to have the largest value, equals 8.64. The joint tests in the second panel of the table comport with this interpretation, as we find essentially zero evidence against the null that the "employed after" difference does not depend on the "employed before" status. Thus, this aspect of the findings provides additional support to the preceding analysis that focused on outcome levels. Third, we observe larger coefficient estimates for men than for women, but we have no good theoretical story as to why.

84

Table 4.16 Logistic Regression Estimates of Effects of Employment Status before and after Random Assignment on Positive Participant Evaluation, by Demographic Group

Panel A. Change in % positive participant evaluation

Parameter name	Employed before status	Employed after status	Adult males	Adult females	Male youth	Female youth
μ_{yy}	yes	yes	10.42	3.23	18.17	15.81
			(2.99)	(3.22)	(4.41)	(4.20)
			[0.0005]	[0.3152]	[0.0000]	[0.0002]
μ_{yn}	yes	no	4.62	−1.07	11.79	4.04
			(3.72)	(4.06)	(6.05)	(5.17)
			[0.2149]	[0.7918]	[0.0513]	[0.4346]
μ_{my}	missing	yes	12.08	2.25	19.56	11.94
			(3.27)	(3.41)	(4.89)	(4.35)
			[0.0002]	[0.5108]	[0.0001]	[0.0061]
μ_{mn}	missing	no	4.93	−2.30	4.95	5.75
			(5.55)	(4.61)	(12.83)	(6.57)
			[0.3741]	[0.6175]	[0.6996]	[0.3811]
μ_{ny}	no	yes	8.64	8.33	16.12	10.81
			(3.30)	(3.45)	(4.46)	(4.05)
			[0.0089]	[0.0158]	[0.0003]	[0.0076]

Panel B. Tests of restrictions

All five parameters are zero.	8.65	12.06	6.46	12.86
	[0.1239]	[0.0339]	[0.2641]	[0.0247]
	$R^{*2}=0.30$	$R^{*2}=0.32$	$R^{*2}=0.55$	$R^{*2}=0.81$

No effects of employed before status $\mu_{yn} = \mu_{mn} = 0, \mu_{ny} = \mu_{yy} = \mu_{my}$	1.33 [0.8558] $R^{*2} = 0.04$	4.26 [0.3723] $R^{*2} = 0.11$	1.42 [0.8406] $R^{*2} = 0.11$	1.73 [0.7856] $R^{*2} = 0.11$
No effects of employed after status $\mu_{ny} = 0, \mu_{yy} = \mu_{yn}, \mu_{my} = \mu_{mn}$	7.23 [0.0649] $R^{*2} = 0.24$	9.66 [0.0216] $R^{*2} = 0.26$	6.19 [0.1026] $R^{*2} = 0.53$	11.51 [0.0093] $R^{*2} = 0.73$
Employed after difference does not depend on employed before status. $\mu_{ny} = \mu_{yy} - \mu_{yn} = \mu_{my} - \mu_{mn}$	0.27 [0.8717] $R^{*2} = 0.01$	0.90 [0.6372] $R^{*2} = 0.02$	1.20 [0.5501] $R^{*2} = 0.09$	0.47 [0.7912] $R^{*2} = 0.03$

NOTE: "Employed before" status is derived from self-reported earnings over the year prior to random assignment (positive is "yes," zero is "no," and missing is "missing"). "Employed after" status is derived from self-reported earnings over the year from the seventh to the eighteenth month after random assignment (positive is "yes" and zero is "no"). The 3×2 classification induced by these two status variables implies six patterns: we omit the "no, no" pattern and estimate a parameter on an indicator for each of the other five included patterns, as shown in the row heading and first two columns of Panel A. Each estimation includes all five of these indicators as well as all the variables in the row headings of Table 4.1. Entries in Panel A are mean numerical derivatives with respect to each indicator, with standard errors in parentheses and p-values in square brackets. In Panel B, entries are χ^2 statistics against the restrictions on the included parameters that are listed in the first column, along with p-values in square brackets, and the R^{*2} (the partial r-squared times 100 for the tested effects) associated with relaxing each restriction in the corresponding linear probability model.

SOURCE: Authors' calculations using observations from the SR Sample in the NJS data that were treated and have nonmissing participant evaluations.

Table 4.17 presents logit models with participant evaluations as the dependent variable, but now with the self-reported before-after earnings differences joining the set of independent variables. We code a categorical before-after earnings differences variable with five categories: 1) After = 0, Before Missing; 2) After > 0, Before Missing; 3) After − Before < 0; 4) After − Before = 0; and 5) After − Before > 0—and use the first category as the omitted category. With the exception of a single individual, when "After − Before = 0," "earnings before" and "earnings after" both equal zero. We again also include all of the variables in column 1 of Table 4.1 as independent variables in the models.

We find clear evidence in Panel A that before-after differences in labor market outcomes predict participant evaluations for all four demographic groups. In particular, we obtain substantively large and statistically significant estimates for the "After − Before > 0" indicator for all four groups, and similar point estimates, statistically significant only for males, for the "After > 0, Before Missing" indicator. The remaining estimates turn out relatively small and not statistically distinguishable from zero. Overall, the strong findings for before-after earnings changes provide clear support to the view that respondents implicitly or explicitly use natural and cognitively simple (but nonetheless quite biased in this substantive context) before-after comparisons in constructing their participant evaluations.

Determinants of Positive Participant Evaluations: Impact Proxies and Program Impacts

There are two potential reasons that some impact proxies correlate more strongly with positive participant evaluations than others. First, individuals may focus particular attention on, say, employment status changes when attempting to construct counterfactuals as lay scientists. Employment status changes then correlate with participant evaluations for this reason. Alternatively, some of the proxies may be less poor than others. Which of the proxies that individuals use to form their participant evaluation responses are better at predicting true program impacts has important implications for our lay scientist interpretation. In particular, if individuals rely most heavily on the proxies that best predict impacts, then we might think of our results partly in terms of respondents using effective but cognitively cheap alternatives to constructing

Table 4.17 Logistic Regression Estimates of the Relationship between Before-After Self-Reported Earnings Changes and Positive Participant Evaluation, by Demographic Group

	Adult males	Adult females	Male youth	Female youth
Panel A. Change in % positive participant evaluation				
After > 0, before missing	7.11	4.69	14.54	6.07
	(3.51)	(3.29)	(5.11)	(4.57)
	[0.0431]	[0.1535]	[0.0044]	[0.1845]
After − before < 0	2.11	−0.15	7.08	2.11
	(3.29)	(3.33)	(5.10)	(4.75)
	[0.5223]	[0.9648]	[0.1645]	[0.6573]
After − before = 0	−4.28	1.27	−3.2	−2.05
	(4.63)	(3.47)	(7.18)	(4.74)
	[0.3552]	[0.7153]	[0.6564]	[0.6658]
After − before > 0	5.42	8.26	13.67	9.51
	(3.27)	(3.18)	(4.74)	(4.10)
	[0.0980]	[0.0095]	[0.0040]	[0.0204]
Panel B. Joint test of significance				
	5.75	16.28	6.37	8.92
	[0.0563]	[0.0003]	[0.0414]	[0.0115]
	$R^{*2} = 0.26$	$R^{*2} = 0.48$	$R^{*2} = 0.63$	$R^{*2} = 0.63$

NOTE: "Before-after self-reported earnings changes" are the difference between the total self-reported earnings over the year from the seventh to the eighteenth month after random assignment and total self-reported earnings over the year prior to random assignment. The estimates are from logistic regressions in which the binary participant evaluation is the dependent variable. A vector of four indicators for categories of the before-after difference is included: 1) an indicator for "After > 0, before missing"; 2) an indicator for "After − before < 0"; 3) an indicator for "After − before = 0"; and 4) an indicator for "After − before > 0." The omitted category is "After > 0, before = 0." The categorical variables listed in the row headings of Table 4.1 are also included as independent variables, along with indicators for missing values. The values in Panel A are mean numerical derivatives, with standard errors in parentheses and p-values in square brackets. The values in Panel B are χ^2-statistics for joint tests of the null hypothesis that all of the coefficients equal zero for a given outcome, with the p-values in square brackets; and R^{*2} is the partial r-squared times 100 for the four quartile indicators from the corresponding linear probability model.

SOURCE: Authors' calculations using those observations from the SR Sample in the NJS data that were treated and have nonmissing participant evaluations.

a counterfactual. This view of our evidence would complement (but not necessarily replace) the view that sees it as showing that respondents make mistakes due to acting as lay theorists, lay empiricists, or both.

To examine whether individuals use the best of the proxies to form their counterfactuals, we proceed in two steps. We first test which of the proxies has the strongest correlation with positive participant evaluations when we include *all* of the proxies in the specification. We report the results from this exercise under the heading "Positive participant evaluations" (left panel) in Table 4.18. We then examine which of the proxies correlate most strongly with the predicted subgroup impacts from specification (1) in Table 4.10 under the heading "Positive predicted subgroup impacts" (right panel) of Table 4.18.

The left panel of Table 4.18—i.e., Panel A—shows that the service-type variables overwhelmingly have the strongest statistical relationship with participant evaluations for all four demographic groups. Self-reported employment over the 18 months after random assignment also always attains statistical significance, while self-reported earnings and self-reported employment changes do so for adult females but not for the other three groups.

We now turn to the second step and correlate the impact proxies with our predicted subgroup impacts. Given the highly nonrandom service assignment process in JTPA, we do not view these as estimates of the impacts of particular services. The experiment did not randomly assign services, merely access to JTPA.[9] We have no reason to think that our set of conditioning variables satisfies the conditional independence assumption required for our analysis to produce causal effects of different service types. Indeed, we have good reason not to, as we know that caseworkers observe, and use in their service assignments, a variety of information that we lack, including test scores and the participant's attitude and self-presentation. Moreover, our service-type indicators simply code whether an individual received any of a particular service—not how much that individual received. Thus, from an evaluation standpoint, our service type indicators measure the treatment with error. Finally, we remark once again on the relatively imprecise predicted impacts that emerge from our subgroup regression.

With that whole paragraph of caveats firmly in mind, we proceed to the right panel of Table 4.18—Panel B—which presents evidence on the strength of the statistical association between the impact proxies

Table 4.18 Positive Participant Evaluations versus Positive Predicted Subgroup Impacts on Self-Reported Employment over the 18 Months after Random Assignment: Statistical Tests on Impact Proxies, by Demographic Group

	Panel A. Positive participant evaluations				Panel B. Positive predicted subgroup impacts			
	Adult males	Adult females	Male youth	Female youth	Adult males	Adult females	Male youth	Female youth
Training type	267.74 [0.0000]	404.89 [0.0000]	58.07 [0.0000]	109.17 [0.0000]	8.45 [0.1331]	52.58 [0.0000]	20.15 [0.0012]	75.46 [0.0000]
Any SR employment during 18 months	3.70 [0.0544]	13.37 [0.0003]	6.12 [0.0133]	3.97 [0.0464]	0.49 [0.4827]	2.05 [0.1522]	1.01 [0.3140]	0.01 [0.9111]
Any SR employment in the 18th month	0.34 [0.5580]	0.01 [0.9430]	1.92 [0.1664]	0.85 [0.3570]	2.77 [0.0962]	1.95 [0.1626]	2.96 [0.0854]	0.02 [0.8747]
SR earnings over 18 months	0.60 [0.8957]	7.74 [0.0518]	4.37 [0.2240]	5.61 [0.1325]	1.87 [0.6001]	17.81 [0.0005]	16.1 [0.0011]	1.45 [0.6943]
Before-after SR employment changes	0.80 [0.9390]	12.5 [0.0140]	5.06 [0.2813]	0.55 [0.9682]	37.69 [0.0000]	19.73 [0.0006]	6.26 [0.1803]	23.79 [0.0000]
Before-after SR earnings changes	0.61 [0.7363]	3.35 [0.1870]	0.59 [0.7432]	0.52 [0.7708]	18.71 [0.0000]	1.64 [0.4407]	8.41 [0.0149]	11.92 [0.0026]

NOTE: Panels A and B report χ^2 statistics (and their p-values in square brackets), testing hypotheses that each row's displayed outcome (in column 1) has no explanatory value for positive participant evaluations (the dependent variable of linear regressions underlying Panel A) and positive predicted subgroup impacts on self-reported employment over the 18 months after random assignment (the dependent variable of linear regressions underlying Panel B). The latter is a binary indicator derived from the predicted subgroup impacts from the specification (1) supporting models underlying the "Employ One" row of Table 4.10. All six outcomes in the row headings are included as independent variables in every estimation (each row of the table simply focuses on results concerning one of the six outcomes), and all the categorical variables in the row headings of Table 4.1 are additional independent variables in the Panel A estimations. A single binary indicator is included for the employment outcomes in the second and third rows. The continuous earnings outcome enters as four categorical variables indicating membership in the four quartiles of the nonzero earnings distribution, as in Table 4.14, with zero earnings as the omitted category. The before-after employment changes are entered as indicators for five of six categories, as in Table 4.16. Similarly, the before-after earnings changes are entered as indicators for four of five categories as in Table 4.17. Indicator variables for missing values of any independent variable are also included wherever relevant.
SOURCE: Authors' calculations using those observations from the SR Sample in the NJS data that were treated and have nonmissing participant evaluations.

and our predicted impacts based on subgroup variation, with impacts on self-reported earnings over the 18 months after random assignment as the dependent variable. Overall, two sets of proxies have statistically strong relationships with predicted impacts for at least three of the four demographic groups: the service-type variables measured using the administrative data and the before-after employment status changes. Some other proxies matter statistically for one or two demographic groups, such as self-reported employment in the eighteenth month after random assignment for males.

In analyses not reported in detail here, we examined the sensitivity of the findings in Panel B of Table 4.18 to replacing the predicted impacts from subgroup specification (1) with predicted impacts from subgroup specification (2) and with the quantile treatment effects. The service-type variables remain statistically important in every case, while the before-after employment changes remain important with the alternative subgroup impacts but not the quantile treatment effects. Perhaps oddly, replacing the administrative measure of service receipt with the self-reported measure yields weaker and less consistent relationships with predicted impacts. In sum, the estimates in Table 4.18 provide support for our view that the correlation between participant evaluations and before-after employment changes largely represents respondents acting as misguided lay theorists. In contrast, the correlation between participant evaluations and service type may spring in part from a clever strategy by respondents to economize on cognitive effort by relying on a good proxy for impacts. However, we wonder why this same pattern does not appear more strongly using the self-reported service types.

SUMMARY AND CONCLUSIONS

Broadly speaking, we have two main findings. First, the participant evaluations by treatment group members from the JTPA experimental evaluation have, in general, little if any relationship either to experimental impact estimates at the subgroup level or to what we regard as relatively plausible econometric impact estimates based on percentile differences. Second, the participant evaluation measures do have consistent relationships with crude proxies for impacts, such as measures of service type (a proxy for resources expended on the participant), labor market outcome levels (which measure impacts only if the counterfactual state consists of no employment or earnings, which it does not for the vast majority of our sample), and before-after earnings differences.

Taken together, these two findings provide strong support for the view that respondents avoid the cognitive burden associated with trying to construct (implicitly or explicitly) the counterfactual outcome they would have experienced had they been in the control group and thus excluded from JTPA. Instead, they appear to act as lay scientists, using readily available proxies and simple heuristics to conclude, for example, that if they are employed at the time of the survey or if their earnings have risen relative to the period prior to random assignment, the program probably helped them find a job or get a better job. At the same time, our evidence does not rule out the view that respondents consider factors in their answers not captured in our experimental and econometric impact estimates, such as expected impacts in later periods or subjective and direct costs and benefits associated with the services they received. The proxy variables still leave much variation in the participant evaluation measure to be explained by other factors.

Notes

1. One possible caveat is that potential participants may have better information to guide them in making participation decisions about a relatively old program, as JTPA was at the time of the experiment, than about a relatively new program. This reasoning suggests greater selection on impacts over time as a program matures.
2. See Devine and Heckman (1996) for more details on the JTPA eligibility rules and Heckman and Smith (1999, 2004) for thorough analyses of the determinants of participation in JTPA conditional on eligibility.
3. See Heinrich, Marschke, and Zhang (1998) for a detailed study of costs in JTPA, and see Wood (1995) for information on costs at the NJS study sites.
4. Making the treatment group two-thirds of the data, rather than one-half, reduced the recruiting burden on the evaluation sites, which were asked to serve the same number of participants during the experiment as they usually did, while at the same time filling the control group. Assuming homogeneous treatment effects, and thus equal residual variances in the treatment and control groups, the statistically preferred division is one-half of the sample members in each group.
5. These data were collected twice: once for 12 of the 16 sites by Abt Associates, one of the prime contractors on the original experiment, and then for all 16 sites later on by Westat under a separate contract. We use the latter data set in our analysis.

6. Note that we do not use the imputed values based on the matched UI earnings records employed in the final evaluation report and related publications—e.g., Bloom et al. (1993). The benefit to using those imputed values is that they allow the avoidance of issues related to survey nonresponse. The cost is that the UI data differ from the survey responses in important and interesting ways; see, e.g., Smith (1997) and Kornfeld and Bloom (1999). Despite the differences documented in the literature, impact estimates tend to coincide for both adult groups and for female youth. Thus we do not think that the choice makes a difference to our qualitative findings.

7. See Doolittle and Traeger (1990) on the design of the NJS, Orr et al. (1996) and Bloom et al. (1993) for the official impact reports, and Heckman and Smith (2000) and Heckman et al. (2000) for further interpretation.

8. We employ the "step up" stepwise procedure, as it has more power than the "step down" and "single step" procedures. See Dunnett and Tamhane (1992) and Liu (1997) for details. We set the p-value for choosing variables in the final specification at 0.05.

9. The researchers did categorize individuals into three "treatment streams" (CT-OS, OJT/JSA, and "other") based on the service recommendations they received prior to random assignment, but only for the CT-OS stream do the services that were received correlate very well with the treatment stream designation. See Exhibit 5.1 in Orr et al. (1996). Heckman et al. (2000) provide more compelling nonexperimental estimates of the effect of CT-OS using the NJS data in the context of their exploration of the implications of service receipt in the control group.

Appendix 4A

SOURCE: National JTPA Study Background Information Form; authors' compilation.

Box 4A.2 Outcome Variables

Predicted impact: This consists of the experimentally estimated impact of the program for an individual based on subgroup variation in average treatment effects or the nonexperimentally estimated impact based on quantile treatment effects interpreted under an assumption of rank preservation.

Percent positive participant evaluation: This is the mean of a binary indicator for a positive participant evaluation. It is defined only for individuals in the treatment group.

Earnings One: This is total earnings (in nominal dollars) over the 18 months after random assignment based on the self-reported earnings data.

Employ One: This is a binary variable indicating any employment over the 18 months after random assignment using self-reported earnings data. The variable equals one if self-reported earnings over the 18 months after random assignment are positive and zero otherwise.

Earnings Two: This is total earnings (in nominal dollars) in the 18th month after random assignment based on the self-reported earnings data.

Employ Two: This is a binary variable indicating employment in month 18 after random assignment based on the self-reported earnings data. The variable equals one if self-reported earnings in the 18th month after random assignment are positive and zero otherwise.

Earnings Three: This is total earnings (in nominal dollars) in the six calendar quarters after the calendar quarter of random assignment based on the matched UI administrative earnings data.

Employ Three: This is a binary variable indicating any employment over the six calendar quarters after the calendar quarter of random assignment based on the matched UI administrative earnings data. This variable equals one if UI earnings over the six calendar quarters after the calendar quarter of random assignment are positive and zero otherwise.

Earnings Four: This is total earnings (in nominal dollars) in the sixth calendar quarter after random assignment based on the matched UI administrative earnings data.

Employ Four: This is a binary variable indicating any employment in the sixth calendar quarter after random assignment based on the matched UI administrative earnings data. This variable equals one if UI earnings in the sixth calendar quarter after random assignment are positive and zero otherwise.

SOURCE: National JTPA Study Background Information Form; authors' compilation.

Table 4A.1 Sample Selection

	Total observations (% of total experimental sample)		
	Control group	Treatment group	Total
Total NJS experimental sample	6,629	13,972	20,601
1) Excluding observations with no follow-up interview	5,620 (84.78)	12,069 (86.38)	17,689 (85.86)
2) 1, and excluding observations with follow-up interviews less than 18 whole months after random assignment	4,732 (71.38)	10,104 (72.32)	14,836 (72.02)
3) 2, and excluding missing participant evaluations		9,842 (70.44)	
4) 2, and excluding invalid self-reported earnings	4,381 (66.09)	9,234 (66.09)	13,615 (66.09)
5) 4, and excluding missing participant evaluations		8,996 (64.39)	
6) 2, and excluding invalid state UI earnings	4,588 (69.21)	9,816 (70.25)	14,404 (69.92)
7) 6, and excluding missing participant evaluations		9562 (68.44)	

NOTE: We examine relationships between demographic and training type variables, and positive participant evaluations, using the treatment group sample in row 3. We estimate experimental impacts on self-reported earnings using the total sample in row 4, and we examine their relationship to participant evaluations using the treatment group subsample in row 5. We estimate experimental impacts on State UI earnings using the total sample in row 6, and we examine their relationship to participant evaluations using the treatment group subsample in row 7. Blank cells = not applicable.
SOURCE: Authors' calculations using the NJS data.

Table 4A.2 Rank Preservation Tests, by Demographic Group

Panel A. Adult males

	$q \leq 50$			$50 < q \leq 75$			$75 < q$		
	Mean diff.	90% C.I.	p-value	Mean diff.	90% C.I.	p-value	Mean diff.	90% C.I.	p-value
White	−0.009	[−0.040,0.040]	0.7310	−0.063	[−0.048,0.054]	0.0430	0.016	[−0.051,0.053]	0.6430
Black	−0.009	[−0.037,0.035]	0.7143	0.039	[−0.047,0.043]	0.1588	−0.006	[−0.046,0.044]	0.8432
26 to 34 years old	−0.004	[−0.034,0.037]	0.8731	0.019	[−0.054,0.054]	0.5784	−0.025	[−0.055,0.056]	0.4326
> 34 years old	0.008	[−0.037,0.035]	0.7343	−0.012	[−0.052,0.053]	0.7123	−0.003	[−0.052,0.052]	0.9191
< 10 years school	0.026	[−0.031,0.028]	0.1449	0.001	[−0.041,0.041]	0.9540	0.018	[−0.037,0.036]	0.4306
10 to 11 years school	−0.020	[−0.033,0.035]	0.3237	0.008	[−0.043,0.044]	0.7772	−0.037	[−0.041,0.041]	0.1399
12 years school	−0.014	[−0.038,0.035]	0.5105	−0.007	[−0.056,0.055]	0.8162	0.038	[−0.052,0.054]	0.2298
13 to 15 years school	0.020	[−0.026,0.026]	0.2098	−0.005	[−0.036,0.040]	0.8082	0.008	[−0.040,0.043]	0.7473
Never married	−0.010	[−0.039,0.041]	0.6364	0.005	[−0.054,0.053]	0.8631	−0.065	[−0.049,0.049]	0.0250
Married	0.050	[−0.036,0.036]	0.0300	0.038	[−0.052,0.052]	0.2318	0.041	[−0.055,0.054]	0.2098
Div/wid/sep	−0.038	[−0.031,0.032]	0.0589	−0.053	[−0.047,0.046]	0.0659	0.027	[−0.045,0.043]	0.3067
Out of labor force	0.054	[−0.032,0.031]	0.0030	−0.033	[−0.037,0.035]	0.1379	0.011	[−0.035,0.034]	0.6024
Unemployed	−0.023	[−0.035,0.036]	0.2977	−0.028	[−0.051,0.055]	0.3616	−0.025	[−0.057,0.057]	0.4655
Employed	−0.029	[−0.028,0.025]	0.0749	0.035	[−0.046,0.045]	0.1978	0.025	[−0.046,0.049]	0.3856
Household receives AFDC	0.023	[−0.022,0.018]	0.0699	−0.044	[−0.026,0.024]	0.0030	0.029	[−0.024,0.022]	0.0480
Receives food stamps	0.035	[−0.037,0.035]	0.1169	−0.039	[−0.049,0.047]	0.1838	0.017	[−0.047,0.043]	0.5534
Joint F-test:									
Statistic	1.3877			1.2834			1.1749		
p-value	0.0989			0.1878			0.2867		

Panel B. Adult females

	q ≤ 50			50 < q ≤ 75			75 < q		
	Mean diff.	90% C.I.	p-value	Mean diff.	90% C.I.	p-value	Mean diff.	90% C.I.	p-value
White	0.006	[-0.035,0.035]	0.7742	-0.038	[-0.049,0.049]	0.1968	0.016	[-0.047,0.046]	0.5714
Black	0.006	[-0.032,0.031]	0.7692	0.007	[-0.043,0.044]	0.7882	0.005	[-0.039,0.042]	0.8192
26 to 34 years old	-0.014	[-0.034,0.033]	0.5075	0.004	[-0.052,0.050]	0.9081	-0.015	[-0.049,0.045]	0.6234
> 34 years old	0.012	[-0.032,0.034]	0.5664	-0.001	[-0.049,0.046]	0.9670	0.014	[-0.046,0.050]	0.6114
< 10 years school	-0.023	[-0.026,0.026]	0.1439	-0.016	[-0.035,0.034]	0.4396	-0.027	[-0.030,0.031]	0.1419
10 to 11 years school	-0.019	[-0.030,0.027]	0.2767	0.021	[-0.039,0.041]	0.3896	0.010	[-0.036,0.037]	0.6743
12 years school	0.031	[-0.033,0.033]	0.1209	0.019	[-0.047,0.047]	0.5005	0.015	[-0.044,0.045]	0.5914
13 to 15 years school	0.006	[-0.020,0.022]	0.6733	-0.001	[-0.035,0.031]	0.9610	0.004	[-0.037,0.038]	0.8981
Never married	-0.040	[-0.033,0.030]	0.0360	0.005	[-0.040,0.044]	0.8641	0.016	[-0.043,0.039]	0.5285
Married	0.017	[-0.027,0.027]	0.3107	-0.019	[-0.040,0.038]	0.4436	0.027	[-0.038,0.038]	0.2348
Div/wid/sep	0.023	[-0.030,0.035]	0.2607	0.016	[-0.050,0.045]	0.5574	-0.015	[-0.043,0.050]	0.6044
Out of labor force	-0.026	[-0.034,0.032]	0.1818	0.022	[-0.039,0.042]	0.3526	0.003	[-0.034,0.039]	0.8901
Unemployed	0.027	[-0.028,0.031]	0.1399	0.001	[-0.048,0.045]	0.9700	0.006	[-0.050,0.046]	0.8442
Employed	-0.001	[-0.023,0.023]	0.9431	-0.036	[-0.042,0.043]	0.1558	0.011	[-0.044,0.044]	0.6893
Household receives AFDC	-0.018	[-0.034,0.034]	0.3457	0.052	[-0.043,0.041]	0.0430	-0.006	[-0.039,0.037]	0.7782
Receives food stamps	-0.032	[-0.032,0.033]	0.0999	0.046	[-0.048,0.046]	0.1069	-0.061	[-0.045,0.048]	0.0280
Joint F-test:									
Statistic	1.1040			0.7669			0.8415		
p-value	0.3277			0.8132			0.7083		

(continued)

Table 4A.2 (continued)

Panel C. Male youth

	q ≤ 50			50 < q ≤ 75			75 < q		
	Mean diff.	90% C.I.	p-value	Mean diff.	90% C.I.	p-value	Mean diff.	90% C.I.	p-value
White	0.041	[−0.061,0.059]	0.2747	−0.009	[−0.086,0.091]	0.8671	0.008	[−0.083,0.082]	0.8641
Black	−0.042	[−0.060,0.056]	0.2268	0.020	[−0.080,0.075]	0.6573	0.020	[−0.072,0.068]	0.6434
19 to 21 years old	−0.088	[−0.065,0.067]	0.0220	0.020	[−0.090,0.090]	0.7003	−0.002	[−0.076,0.075]	0.9670
<10 years school	0.080	[−0.053,0.065]	0.0240	−0.073	[−0.077,0.077]	0.1209	−0.087	[−0.069,0.068]	0.0370
10 to 11 years school	−0.006	[−0.059,0.053]	0.8751	−0.034	[−0.084,0.081]	0.5055	0.009	[−0.079,0.085]	0.8631
12 years school	−0.049	[−0.056,0.053]	0.1369	0.095	[−0.086,0.090]	0.0749	0.074	[−0.090,0.084]	0.1518
Never married	0.006	[−0.035,0.040]	0.7952	−0.017	[−0.066,0.061]	0.6663	−0.008	[−0.069,0.073]	0.8511
Married	−0.010	[−0.031,0.028]	0.5994	0.006	[−0.058,0.054]	0.8462	0.027	[−0.071,0.067]	0.4845
Out of labor force	0.070	[−0.059,0.061]	0.0559	−0.057	[−0.073,0.074]	0.1908	−0.049	[−0.068,0.065]	0.2228
Unemployed	0.010	[−0.060,0.057]	0.7842	0.087	[−0.087,0.089]	0.1029	0.001	[−0.086,0.081]	0.9760
Employed	−0.072	[−0.045,0.042]	0.0050	−0.024	[−0.073,0.068]	0.5524	0.065	[−0.070,0.077]	0.1489
Household receives AFDC	0.030	[−0.029,0.029]	0.0939	0.022	[−0.041,0.037]	0.3606	−0.001	[−0.036,0.034]	0.9530
Receives food stamps	0.024	[−0.055,0.059]	0.4755	0.090	[−0.070,0.069]	0.0420	−0.044	[−0.065,0.062]	0.2428
Joint F-test:									
Statistic	1.7841			0.8716			0.6383		
p-value	0.0170			0.6883			0.8901		

Panel D. Female youth

	$q \leq 50$			$50 < q \leq 75$			$75 < q$		
	Mean diff.	90% C.I.	p-value	Mean diff.	90% C.I.	p-value	Mean diff.	90% C.I.	p-value
White	0.012	[−0.052,0.054]	0.7173	0.071	[−0.078,0.072]	0.1239	0.039	[−0.079,0.076]	0.3866
Black	0.019	[−0.050,0.049]	0.5514	−0.090	[−0.068,0.079]	0.0440	−0.030	[−0.070,0.066]	0.4765
19 to 21 years old	0.063	[−0.047,0.055]	0.0490	−0.043	[−0.073,0.076]	0.3616	0.035	[−0.071,0.071]	0.4196
< 10 years school	−0.037	[−0.050,0.050]	0.2298	0.061	[−0.066,0.062]	0.1189	−0.041	[−0.054,0.048]	0.1778
10 to 11 years school	0.011	[−0.048,0.046]	0.7193	0.047	[−0.067,0.070]	0.2517	−0.009	[−0.062,0.065]	0.8092
12 years school	0.024	[−0.051,0.046]	0.4565	−0.080	[−0.074,0.077]	0.0819	0.067	[−0.075,0.074]	0.1439
Never married	0.024	[−0.048,0.048]	0.3826	−0.024	[−0.067,0.066]	0.5445	−0.047	[−0.056,0.064]	0.2008
Married	−0.040	[−0.036,0.035]	0.0629	0.021	[−0.049,0.048]	0.4685	−0.005	[−0.044,0.041]	0.8551
Out of labor force	−0.039	[−0.050,0.059]	0.2368	0.024	[−0.079,0.068]	0.6024	−0.066	[−0.062,0.056]	0.0619
Unemployed	0.042	[−0.050,0.045]	0.1548	−0.078	[−0.069,0.076]	0.0799	0.040	[−0.076,0.071]	0.3666
Employed	−0.006	[−0.034,0.032]	0.7263	−0.001	[−0.069,0.065]	0.9830	0.054	[−0.064,0.071]	0.2068
Household receives AFDC	−0.006	[−0.050,0.053]	0.8422	0.006	[−0.067,0.065]	0.9121	−0.029	[−0.058,0.054]	0.3936
Receives food stamps	−0.040	[−0.051,0.053]	0.2278	0.031	[−0.074,0.075]	0.4685	−0.028	[−0.069,0.056]	0.4466
Joint F-test:									
Statistic	1.0014			1.3737			0.8010		
p-value	0.4296			0.1578			0.7273		

NOTE: Mean treatment and control differences, confidence intervals, and p-values for tests of the null that the difference equals zero. The final rows of each section give the test statistic and p-value for an F-test against the hypothesis that the entire vector of demographic variable mean differences (between treatment and control observations) equals zero in each quantile range. The demographic variables used are those shown in the left column of each table plus all site indicators accounting for at least 5% of observed individuals within each demographic group. All p-values are bootstrapped in exactly the manner described by Bitler, Gelbach, and Hoynes (2006, pp. 28–31); we choose, however, to bootstrap the distribution of a joint test F-statistic instead of a χ^2 statistic as they do (see their fn. 26, p. 31). Our choice allows us to exploit commonplace MANOVA statistical routines to construct and bootstrap the distribution of this F-statistic.

SOURCE: Authors' calculations using the SR Sample from the NJS data.

5
Evidence from the National Supported Work Demonstration

Sebastian Calónico
Jeffrey Smith

This chapter analyzes data from the National Supported Work (NSW) Demonstration. As in the other chapters, we examine the relationship between a survey-based participant evaluation measure and estimates of program impacts based on the two identification strategies outlined in Chapter 3. We also examine the determinants of a positive participant evaluation within the context of the multiple conceptual frameworks laid out in Chapter 2.

The NSW analysis provides additional perspective on the information content of participant evaluation measures. As we discuss in detail later in the chapter, the NSW measure closely resembles that from the JTPA data analyzed in Chapter 4, and the population served by the NSW overlaps with that served by JTPA. The NSW treatment, however, differs substantially from JTPA both in its nature and in its intensity and cost. Studying a more expensive and intensive treatment sheds some light on whether the lack of a relationship found in the JTPA context results from the relatively modest services typically provided by that program.

Empirically, we find that, like the participant evaluation measure in the JTPA study, the participant evaluation measure in the NSW study has a weak positive relationship to the estimated quantile treatment effects and no relationship to the experimental impacts based on subgroup variation. The NSW measure does correlate strongly with various proxies for impacts, which supports the lay scientist view laid out in Chapter 2.

The remainder of this chapter has the following structure: We start by describing the NSW program, the treatment it provided, and the evaluation whose data we use. We then describe the data and our analysis sample, as well as the participant evaluation measure employed in our analysis. Following that, we review the results of our investigation, starting with bivariate correlations between subgroup impacts and subgroup means of the participant evaluation measure, and continuing with the multivariate subgroup analysis, the quantile treatment effect analysis, our check on the restrictions implicit in the first decision theory viewpoint, and the analysis of the determinants of a positive participant evaluation. We end the chapter with a summary and some conclusions.

PROGRAM

The NSW program provided intensive work experience to individuals in the treatment group who chose to participate. Though the content of the program in terms of the type of work varied widely across sites, program designers required four features in all sites: First, the program was transitional, which means that participants had to leave the program if they reached the maximum program duration of 12 months at some sites and 18 months at others. Second, the program emphasized a context of peer group support; participants worked together in teams with other participants. Third, program staff knowledgeable about both the substance of the work and dealing with disadvantaged workers closely supervised the work. Fourth and finally, the NSW treatment provided an environment of graduated stress, in which the job-related expectations for participants increased over time. On the scale of social programs aimed at improving the employment outcomes of the disadvantaged, NSW lies at the expensive end, with a direct cost of around $15,000 per participant in current dollars. This substantially exceeds the average cost of the JTPA services considered in Chapter 4 and so allows a test, in a loose sense, of the effect of overall program intensity on the performance of participant evaluation measures.

The NSW demonstration focused on four target groups: 1) female long-term recipients of Aid to Families with Dependent Children (AFDC), 2) ex-addicts, 3) ex-convicts, and 4) young high-school dropouts ("youth"). AFDC is the predecessor of the current Temporary Assistance for Needy Families (TANF) program. The experimental evaluation of the NSW demonstration encompassed 10 out of a total of

15 program sites, all but one of them in urban areas. Most sites served two or three of the target groups, one served only one, and none served all four. We combine the San Francisco and Oakland sites in our empirical work, as they are located in the same labor market.

To be eligible, individuals in all of the groups had to be "unemployed" (defined as having worked no more than 10 hours per week in the four weeks prior to application) and had to have held a job for no more than three of the past six months. They also had to pass a screening interview with the local program operators, who had the right to determine which eligible applicants reached random assignment. Long-term AFDC recipients had to be women and had to have received AFDC benefits for 30 of the past 36 months, and their youngest child had to be age six or older. The ex-addict group included current enrollees in drug treatment programs along with those enrolled at some point in the preceding six months. The ex-convicts target group included only individuals incarcerated in the preceding six months as the result of a conviction. Ex-addicts and ex-convicts had to be at least 18 years old, while the high-school dropout target group included individuals ages 17 to 20 without a high school diploma or GED and not enrolled in school in the preceding six months. Half of the youth at each site serving youth had to have some record of delinquency. The population served by NSW overlaps with that served by JTPA and by Jobs First (see Chapter 6) but differs in important ways as well. The Jobs First program served only AFDC recipients. JTPA served many AFDC recipients and many dropouts, but relatively fewer ex-addicts and ex-convicts. The JTPA participant population, on average, faced fewer barriers to employment than those faced by the NSW participants.

Given the disparate nature of the four groups, combined with divergent experimental impacts (more on this below) and the lack of population weights to use in combining them, we conduct our analysis separately by target group. Note too that we use the four original target groups from the experiment as designed, not the reduced set of two groups (the AFDC women and the men from the other three target groups pooled together) used by LaLonde (1986) in his famous study.[1]

MDRC, which was founded for the purpose of running the NSW demonstration (and which was also heavily involved with the JTPA study considered in Chapter 4 and the Jobs First evaluation, whose data we examine in Chapter 6), ran the evaluation in cooperation with its subcontractors at Mathematica Policy Research and the Institute for Research on Poverty at the University of Wisconsin. The NSW evaluation represented one of the first major social experiments in the United States or, indeed, in the world. Hollister, Kemper, and Maynard (1984) summarize the experimental design and findings. Random assignment of eligible (and prescreened) applicants in the four target groups ran from April 1975 to August 1977. Overall, 6,616 individuals were randomly assigned to the treatment group, which could but did not have to participate in the NSW demonstration, and to the control group, which could not participate in NSW but could participate in other, less intensive (and less expensive) programs such as those operated under the Comprehensive Employment and Training Act (CETA, JTPA's predecessor). Not surprisingly, given the expensive and intensive services on offer from NSW, a very large fraction of the treatment group actually received services; at the same time, few control group members appear to have substituted into other programs. For example, for the AFDC target group, Masters and Maynard (1981, Table A.15) report a nine-month participation rate of 0.95 in the treatment group and a control group substitution rate of only 0.11. Given the low rates of dropout and substitution, and the low intensity of the substitutes, the experimental impact estimates provide relatively clean estimates of the impact of NSW versus no treatment over the relevant period. Put differently, in this case the intent-to-treat (ITT) parameter roughly coincides with the average treatment effect on the treated (ATET) parameter.

The experimental evaluation found substantial effects on earnings for the AFDC women, and some effects on crime for the ex-convict target group. Despite the high cost of the program, the data did not reveal any meaningful impacts for either the ex-addict or youth-dropout target groups.[2] Couch (1992) provides long-term earnings impacts based on Social Security administrative data.

DATA AND SAMPLE

The NSW evaluation relied primarily on survey data, along with administrative data from the demonstration's management information system. As the latter data source fed mainly into the evaluation's cost-benefit analysis, we use only the survey data in our work. Everyone randomly assigned had opportunities to complete three surveys: 1) a baseline survey around random assignment, 2) a follow-up survey around 9 months after random assignment, and 3) another around 18 months after random assignment. In addition, individuals who enrolled relatively early in the random assignment period had the opportunity to complete surveys at 27 months and, if they had enrolled very early, at 36 months after random assignment. Response rates to the follow-up surveys present a glass half full. Though the rates are not bad given the populations participating in the NSW, they are not great either, and they vary widely across subgroups and decline with the length of follow-up. Hollister (1984) describes a range from 83 percent for the AFDC target group at 18 months to 57 percent for ex-convicts at 36 months. The interviews collect data on participant demographics, employment history, job search, mobility, household income, housing, crime, drug use, and participation in other programs, as well as participant evaluation measures related to their NSW experience. Because of the declining response rates across follow-up surveys, we use only data from the baseline and the first two (i.e., the 9-month and 18-month) follow-up surveys in our work. Furthermore, although all of the follow-up surveys collected responses to (the same set of) participant evaluation questions, we restrict our attention to responses from the first follow-up survey in order to obtain the reactions of participants as soon as possible after they complete their participation in the program.

The public-use NSW data available from the Interuniversity Consortium for Political and Social Research (ICPSR) have an important limitation: they do not include the calendar dates of the interviews. This makes it impossible to calculate earnings relative to the month of random assignment. Following LaLonde (1986), we obtain the survey dates by matching unemployment-rate series (USDOL 1976) to the information included in the public-use data on local unemployment rates for each participant in the second, fifth, and eighth months prior to each interview. Using the survey dates obtained in this manner, we calculate real earnings for each quarter before and after random assignment. We convert nominal earnings to real earnings in 1982 dollars using the monthly CPI-W, the Consumer Price Index for Urban Wage Earners and Clerical Workers.[3]

In this paper, we use a sample of individuals with nonmissing quarterly earnings in each quarter of the four quarters before random assignment and the six quarters after that. We include individuals with zero earnings in any or all of the quarters. Meeting this criterion requires completion of the baseline survey and the first two follow-up surveys. In addition, we require a valid response to the participant evaluation question described in the next section. Appendix Table 5A.1 details the sample loss at each stage in our sample construction process. The extent of sample loss varies by target group, which follows directly from the differential nonresponse by target group already mentioned. We do not attempt to use weights to deal with the nonresponse.

PARTICIPANT EVALUATION MEASURE

Box 5.1 presents the participant evaluation survey question from the NSW's first follow-up survey; it forms the basis for our participant evaluation measure. Individuals in the treatment group who were "no shows" to the NSW treatment or who had participated in NSW for less than 30 days as of the interview date did not get asked this question. Inspired by the use of program dropouts as a participant evaluation measure in Heckman and Smith (1998) and Philipson and Hedges (1998), we code such individuals as "0" on our participant evaluation measure, and they remain in the treatment group for the purposes of constructing the impact estimates. Among those individuals who pass the screens and get asked the question, we code responses of "No" as "0" and responses of "Yes" as "1" for our participant evaluation measure.

The NSW participant evaluation measure bears a close resemblance to the measure we examined in the JTPA data in Chapter 4. The NSW question uses "preparation" for a job rather than "help" getting a job,

---

Box 5.1 NSW Participant Evaluation Survey Question

V0041   Has (specific SW program name) prepared you to get a regular job outside of the (specific SW program name) program? Yes/No

as in the JTPA study formulation. Preparation, though somewhat more precise, as it rules out an interpretation solely focused on job placement assistance, still leaves a lot of meaning for the respondent to fill in. Does preparation refer to the teaching of skills particular to a specific job or type of job, such as how to run a cash register, or to general skills related to employment, such as the ability to regularly show up sober and on time, or to the desire to take and hold a job, or to all of these? Can a program "prepare" one for a job without actually leading to employment? Like the JTPA question, the NSW question does not explicitly reference a counterfactual, leaving the respondent to determine some implicit counterfactual, such as receipt of services from a different program or continued job search, or simply not to have one at all. The latter interpretation suggests responses based on the treated outcome rather than the change in outcomes relative to the untreated counterfactual.

Table 5.1 tabulates the participant evaluation measure we analyze for the four target groups and the full sample. Two patterns of interest

Table 5.1 Distribution of the Participant Evaluation Measure

	AFDC		Ex-Addicts		Ex-Convicts		Youth		Total	
	N	%	*N*	%	*N*	%	*N*	%	*N*	%
Panel A: Self-Reported Participation Question										
No	314	42	288	47	452	51	277	57	1,331	49
Yes	376	50	205	34	278	31	157	32	1,016	37
Refused	50	7	84	14	88	10	41	8	263	10
Don't know	12	2	28	5	66	7	7	1	113	4
Missing	1	0	3	0	2	0	3	1	9	0
No. Obs.	753		608		886		485		2,732	
Panel B: Participant Evaluation Measure										
No	335	50	293	64	408	66	252	67	1288	61
Yes	336	50	164	36	213	34	126	33	839	39
Sample size	671		457		621		378		2,127	

NOTE: In the top panel, the "Refused" category includes valid skips associated with the "no-shows." As described in the text, we code the no-shows as "No" in the lower panel. The top panel uses the full sample of 2,732 observations, while the bottom panel uses our analysis sample of 2,127 observations.

SOURCE: Authors' calculations using the NSW data.

emerge from the values in Table 5.1. First, the four target groups differ meaningfully in their responses: the AFDC group has the highest fraction, with a positive evaluation at 0.50, followed by the ex-addicts at 0.36, the ex-convicts at 0.34, and then the youth dropouts at 0.33. Second, the NSW treatment group members, despite a much more intensive treatment than that provided under JTPA, as well as much higher take-up rates and a participant evaluation question with similar wording, do not have consistently higher fractions with a positive participant evaluation. The last finding puzzles us, but we have no good explanation for it.

EMPIRICAL RESULTS

Descriptive Statistics

Table 5.2 presents descriptive statistics for the four target groups in our analysis sample of 2,127 individuals. The characteristics vary among the target group in predictable ways: The AFDC recipients are all women, the ex-addicts and ex-convicts mostly men. The youth are the youngest and the AFDC recipients the oldest. The ex-addicts have the highest mean earnings prior to random assignment, the AFDC women the lowest, and so on. Overall, as expected given the eligibility criteria, the NSW served a very disadvantaged population even relative to the JTPA study. In addition, within target groups, the average characteristics differ very little between the treatment groups and the corresponding control groups, indicating that random assignment worked its magic and effectively balanced the observed characteristics. Appendix Table 5A.2 presents the same statistics as Table 5.2 but for the full experimental sample of 6,529 individuals. It shows that, across the four target groups, the average characteristics of our analysis sample differ remarkably little from those of the full experimental sample.

Outcomes and Experimental Impacts

We consider eight outcome variables: four of them measure earnings over various periods after random assignment, and four of them measure employment over the same periods after random assignment.

Table 5.2 Descriptive Statistics of the Main Covariates for the Four Target Groups in the Analysis Sample

	AFDC		Ex-Addicts		Ex-Convicts		Youth	
	Treatment	Control	Treatment	Control	Treatment	Control	Treatment	Control
Sex (male)	0.00	0.00	0.79	0.80	0.95	0.94	0.87	0.85
Age (yrs.)	33.58	33.71	27.75	27.82	25.48	25.11	18.24	18.35
Years of school	10.36	10.21	10.49	10.48	10.44	10.38	9.69	9.65
High school dropouts	0.69	0.69	0.70	0.73	0.74	0.74	0.99	1.00
Married	0.02	0.04	0.21	0.24	0.13	0.11	0.04	0.04
Black	0.84	0.82	0.78	0.77	0.84	0.84	0.80	0.77
Hispanic	0.11	0.13	0.09	0.07	0.08	0.10	0.15	0.17
Real earnings 1 yr. before RA ($)	392	422	2007	2221	982	997	1359	1459
Real earnings 2 yrs. before RA ($)	840	868	3993	4581	2622	2803	1615	1657
Hours worked 1 yr. before RA	86	97	335	346	186	177	302	323
Hours worked 2 yrs. before RA	180	178	565	634	416	413	358	390
Month of assignment (Jan.'78 = 0)	−12.20	−12.24	−17.84	−17.61	−15.83	−15.59	−14.38	−14.39
Number of observations	671	653	457	427	621	715	378	426

NOTE: The analysis sample consists of all program participants with valid earnings information (in the four quarters prior to random assignment and the first six quarters after random assignment) and a complete set of covariates, including the participant evaluation measure. RA = random assignment.

SOURCE: Authors' calculations using the NSW data.

The outcome variables all rely on the self-reported information from the follow-up surveys. For all of the measures, the first month "after" random assignment corresponds to the month of random assignment. In each group (whether "earnings" or "employment"), the first outcome (i.e., "Earnings One" or "Employ One") covers all 18 months after random assignment, the second covers months 10–18, the third, months 7–9, and the fourth, months 16–18. Our choice of periods builds on the upper limit on NSW participation, which equals 9 months at most sites, and the timing of the first two follow-up surveys at around 9 and 18 months after random assignment. Thus, the second and fourth measures include only months in which all or almost all respondents will have left supported employment, and the first, second, and fourth measures capture periods that end right around the time of the second follow-up survey. Though the participant evaluation question in the NSW evaluation refers to employment, we consider both employment and earnings in order to better capture (in a crude way) employment duration, as well as wage rates and differences between full-time and part-time employment.

Two of the four measures refer to periods after most of our sample members will have responded to the survey questions we use to construct our participant evaluation. This might seem odd, but we are keen to focus mainly on earnings other than those from the Supported Work job. Given the strong correlation over time in labor market outcomes, we hope that outcomes measured in the months shortly after the first follow-up survey will provide a better guide to labor market outcomes (as the respondent perceives them at the time of the participant evaluation) than do measures (such as our first earnings measure) that include the Supported Work job. Our later earnings measures also omit (helpfully, in our view) differences across sites in the wages paid on the Supported Work job (to account for local differences in cost of living) and variation across sites and individuals in the time spent in the program.

Table 5.3 presents descriptive statistics on our outcome variables for the analysis sample, while Table 5A.3 presents the corresponding table for the full experimental sample. Recall that we report values in 1982 dollars. Both tables also present differences in means between the treatment and control group samples (i.e., experimental impact estimates) along with p-values from a test of the null that this difference equals zero in the population. Within the analysis sample, three notable

Table 5.3 Descriptive Statistics of the Outcome Variables for the Four Target Groups in the Analysis Sample

	AFDC				Ex-Addicts				Ex-Convicts				Youth			
	Treatment	Control	Exper. impact	p-value	Treatment	Control	Exper. impact	p-value	Treatment	Control	Exper. impact	p-value	Treatment	Control	Exper. impact	p-value
Earnings One	9,133 (4,607)	2,884 (4,695)	6,249 (256)	0.000	8,590 (6,017)	5,071 (7,456)	3,519 (454)	0.000	9,254 (9,229)	5,401 (7,042)	3,852 (446)	0.000	7,829 (4,611)	4,170 (5,390)	3,659 (356)	0.000
Earnings Two	3,541 (3,130)	1,798 (3,243)	1,743 (175)	0.000	3,499 (4,193)	2,840 (4,533)	659 (294)	0.025	3,736 (4,714)	3,105 (4,672)	631 (257)	0.014	3,029 (3,199)	2,453 (3,369)	577 (233)	0.013
Earnings Three	1,756 (964)	445 (855)	1,311 (50)	0.000	1,458 (1,359)	789 (1,649)	669 (101)	0.000	1,539 (2,665)	789 (1,329)	750 (113)	0.000	1,323 (1,129)	616 (1,278)	708 (86)	0.000
Earnings Four	890 (1,266)	670 (1,169)	221 (67)	0.001	998 (1,620)	979 (1,683)	19 (111)	0.868	1,195 (1,761)	1,061	134	0.158	914 (1,215)	897 (1,247)	17 (87)	0.848
Employ One	0.97 (0.18)	0.50 (0.50)	0.46 (0.02)	0.000	0.96 (0.19)	0.66 (0.47)	0.30 (0.02)	0.000	0.97 (0.17)	0.73 (0.44)	0.24 (0.02)	0.000	0.99 (0.11)	0.77 (0.42)	0.22 (0.02)	0.000
Employ Two	0.77 (0.42)	0.40 (0.49)	0.37 (0.03)	0.000	0.64 (0.48)	0.52 (0.50)	0.13 (0.03)	0.000	0.65 (0.48)	0.56 (0.50)	0.09 (0.03)	0.001	0.67 (0.47)	0.59 (0.49)	0.08 (0.03)	0.015
Employ Three	0.82 (0.38)	0.28 (0.45)	0.54 (0.02)	0.000	0.69 (0.46)	0.37 (0.48)	0.32 (0.03)	0.000	0.65 (0.48)	0.39 (0.49)	0.26 (0.03)	0.000	0.70 (0.46)	0.40 (0.49)	0.29 (0.03)	0.000
Employ Four	0.41 (0.49)	0.35 (0.48)	0.05 (0.03)	0.053	0.39 (0.49)	0.40 (0.49)	0.00 (0.03)	0.897	0.48 (0.50)	0.45 (0.50)	0.03 (0.03)	0.291	0.46 (0.50)	0.47 (0.50)	-0.01 (0.04)	0.695
Number of Obs.	671	653			457	427			621	715			378	426		

NOTE: Earnings One: total self-reported earnings in the first six quarters after random assignment. Earnings Two: total self-reported earnings in the fourth through sixth quarters after random assignment. Earnings Three: total self-reported earnings in the third quarter after random assignment. Earnings Four: total self-reported earnings during the sixth quarter after random assignment. Employ One to Four correspond to indicator variables for when earnings in the respective periods are greater than zero. Values in parentheses represent standard deviations in the treatment and control columns, and standard errors in the experimental impact columns.

SOURCE: Authors' calculations using the NSW data.

patterns emerge: First, we find substantively large and strongly statistically significant impacts on the "Earnings One" and "Employ One" measures, which capture outcomes over the full 18 months after random assignment. Second, the employment and earnings impacts decline with time relative to random assignment for all four target groups. This decline reflects the near-complete take-up of Supported Work employment among treatment group members, followed by, in many cases, little or no employment and earnings after the Supported Work job. Third, looking at the "Earnings Four" and "Employ Four" outcomes for the sixth quarter after random assignment reveals very small and statistically insignificant impacts for the ex-addicts and the youth, modest but statistically insignificant impacts for the ex-convicts, and meaningful and statistically significant impacts for the AFDC women. These same qualitative patterns emerge for the full sample in Table 5A.3; at the same time, that table indicates clear positive selection into the analysis sample based on outcome levels.

Couch (1992) presents estimates of long-term impacts using administrative data for the two groups considered by LaLonde (1986): 1) the AFDC women and 2) all of the men from the ex-addict, ex-convict, and dropout groups pooled together. Consistent with the short-term impacts we present, he finds persistent long-term earnings impacts for the AFDC women and persistent zeros for the men. Heckman, LaLonde, and Smith (1999, Table 19) consider the long-term cost-benefit performance of Supported Work and find that, under certain reasonable assumptions but not others, it passes a cost-benefit test for the AFDC women.

Impact Variance

Appendix Table 5A.5 provides our estimate of the lower bound on the impact standard deviation, calculated using the quantile treatment effects for every percentile of the outcome distribution, as in Heckman, Smith, and Clements (1997); we discuss the QTEs themselves later in the chapter. For self-reported earnings in the 18 months after random assignment (i.e., "Earnings One"), we obtain a lower bound on the standard deviation of impacts for the AFDC subgroup of $2,639. The corresponding values for the ex-convicts, ex-addicts, and youth dropouts equal $2,092, $1,553, and $1,350, respectively. Not surprisingly, we find lower (but still substantively meaningful) bounds on the impact standard deviations for the earnings outcomes that combine a smaller number of months. Appendix Table 5A.5 also provides the fraction of positive predicted impacts (and of nonnegative predicted impacts) for each combination of target group and earnings outcome.

As in Chapter 4, we test the null of the common-effect model (i.e., the null that the variance of the impacts equals zero in the population) using the experimental control group, following the procedure in Appendix E of Heckman, Smith, and Clements (1997). Comparing the estimated lower bound to the cutoffs provides a p-value range from a test of the null of a zero-impact variance, along the lines discussed in Chapter 3. For the AFDC subgroup, we easily reject the common-effect null at the 1 percent level; we also reject the null at that level for the youth high-school dropouts. For the ex-convicts, we can reject only at the 10 percent level, while for the ex-addicts, we only come *close* to rejecting at the 10 percent level. Overall, we take this as relatively strong evidence against the common-effect null in the NSW data, implying that the data contain treatment-effect heterogeneity for us to capture.

Bivariate Correlations

Table 5.4 displays the fraction with a positive participant evaluation, along with experimental impacts on earnings and employment for the four target groups from the NSW experiment. As in Chapter 4, we arrange the table with the target groups as rows and the outcome variables as columns (recall that we do not have UI earnings for NSW participants). The first column shows the fraction positive, the next four contain estimated impacts on self-reported earnings, and the final four columns contain impacts on self-reported employment, defined here as positive earnings. The penultimate row of the table displays the correlation, at the target-group level, between the fraction with a positive participant evaluation and the estimated impact on the outcome variable in each column, while the final row presents p-values from tests of the nulls that these correlations equal zero.

The same basic picture emerges for all eight outcomes: a substantially larger impact for the AFDC target group than for the other three target groups (which do not vary much among themselves on either the participant evaluations or the impacts), combined with a substantially

Table 5.4 Bivariate Results for the Relationship between Experimental Impacts and Positive Participant Evaluation, by Group

	Percent positive participant evaluation	Earnings One	Earnings Two	Earnings Three	Earnings Four	Employ One	Employ Two	Employ Three	Employ Four
AFDC	0.501	6249	1743	1311	221	0.465	0.369	0.541	0.052
		(256)	(175)	(50)	(67)	(0.021)	(0.025)	(0.023)	(0.027)
Ex-Addicts	0.359	3519	659	669	19	0.302	0.128	0.319	−0.004
		(454)	(294)	(101)	(111)	(0.024)	(0.033)	(0.032)	(0.033)
Ex-Convicts	0.343	3852	631	750	134	0.242	0.093	0.261	0.029
		(446)	(257)	(113)	(95)	(0.019)	(0.027)	(0.026)	(0.027)
Youth	0.333	3659	577	708	17	0.217	0.083	0.292	−0.014
		(356)	(233)	(86)	(87)	(0.022)	(0.034)	(0.034)	(0.035)
Correlation with positive participant evaluation		0.978	0.997	0.976	0.814	0.981	1.000	0.988	0.794
		[0.022]	[0.003]	[0.024]	[0.186]	[0.019]	[0.000]	[0.012]	[0.206]

NOTE: Values in the table are means of the binary participant evaluation variable along with experimental impacts for the eight outcomes. The values in parentheses are standard errors, and the values in square brackets are p-values. "Percent positive participant evaluation" is calculated as the mean of the binary indicator in the treatment group.

SOURCE: Authors' calculations using the NSW data.

higher fraction with a positive participant evaluation for the AFDC target group. This pattern leads to large, positive, and statistically significant correlations in the bottom row. Keeping in mind the lack of independence between the eight measures (i.e., they do not provide eight separate bits of information), and keeping in mind that we consider correlations based on only four categories, this table provides some modest evidence in support of this particular participant evaluation measure. Given the large standard errors on the correlations, and their relative lack of variation across outcomes, we cannot say much about how the timing of the outcome measure relates to the strength of the association with the participant evaluations.

Spurred on by the tempting findings in Table 5.4, we decided to dig deeper into bivariate relationships between subgroup impacts and participant evaluations. Tables 5.5 through 5.8 present estimates for subgroups defined by race/ethnicity, age, education, and site within each of the four target groups (we omit age and schooling for the youth dropout target group because of lack of variation). Within each table, the rows denote the variable used to define a particular set of subgroups, with the table notes (or Appendix 5A) providing details. Each value in the table is the correlation between the fraction with a positive participant evaluation and the experimental impacts for subgroups defined using the row variable and for impacts on the column variable. For example, in Table 5.5, the second row corresponds to subgroups defined by age. In particular, as described in the table notes, we divide the individuals in the AFDC target group addressed in Table 5.5 into four subgroups: 1) ages less than 22, 2) ages 22 to 25, 3) ages 26 to 34, and 4) ages 35 and above. We then calculate the fraction with a positive participant evaluation and the experimental impacts on the eight outcomes separately for each of these subgroups. The value of 0.933 in the "Earnings 3" column indicates the correlation between participant evaluations and impacts for the age subgroups for the "Earnings Three" outcome. The bottom row of each table summarizes the obtained correlations, indicating the number of positive and negative correlations and the number statistically significant at the 5 and 10 percent levels.

The findings here look much like those in the corresponding tables in Chapter 4 for the JTPA data. In particular, we find roughly equal numbers of positive and negative estimates, leaning a bit more positive for the ex-convicts and youth dropouts. Each table features a small

Table 5.5 Bivariate Correlations between Experimental Impacts and Participant Evaluations for Eight Outcomes, AFDC

	Earnings One	Earnings Two	Earnings Three	Earnings Four	Employ One	Employ Two	Employ Three	Employ Four
Race	0.906	−0.400	0.989	0.711	0.981	−0.962	0.886	0.722
	[0.279]	[0.738]	[0.095]	[0.497]	[0.125]	[0.176]	[0.308]	[0.486]
Age category	0.378	−0.271	0.933	−0.025	−0.263	0.881	0.651	−0.169
	[0.622]	[0.729]	[0.067]	[0.975]	[0.737]	[0.119]	[0.349]	[0.831]
Education category	−0.314	−0.976	−0.679	−0.396	−0.994	0.467	−0.434	−0.921
	[0.797]	[0.141]	[0.525]	[0.741]	[0.069]	[0.691]	[0.714]	[0.254]
Site	0.114	0.525	0.405	−0.261	0.122	−0.173	−0.060	−0.533
	[0.807]	[0.475]	[0.425]	[0.671]	[0.795]	[0.827]	[0.910]	[0.355]

Positive correlations:
  Overall: 15 of 32 (47%); significant at 0.10: 2 of 32 (6%); significant at 0.05: 0 of 32 (0%).
Negative correlations:
  Overall: 17 of 32 (53%); significant at 0.10: 1 of 32 (3%); significant at 0.05: 0 of 32 (0%).

NOTE: Values in the table are correlations between the mean positive participant evaluation and the experimental impacts at the subgroup level. The values in square brackets are *p*-values. Fraction positive participant evaluation is the mean of the binary participant evaluation variable in the treatment group. The categories are defined as the following. Race: Black, Hispanic, and others. Age: less than 22 years, 22–25 years, 26–34 years, and 35+ years. Education: under 10 years, 10–11 years, 12 years, 13+ years. Site: nine site categories.
SOURCE: Authors' calculations using the NSW data.

Table 5.6 Bivariate Correlations between Experimental Impacts and Participant Evaluations for Eight Outcomes, Ex-Addicts

	Earnings One	Earnings Two	Earnings Three	Earnings Four	Employ One	Employ Two	Employ Three	Employ Four
Race	0.870	-0.365	0.948	0.600	0.071	-0.943	0.897	0.717
	[0.328]	[0.762]	[0.207]	[0.591]	[0.955]	[0.216]	[0.291]	[0.491]
Age	-0.385	-0.058	-0.751	0.737	-0.960	-0.806	0.310	-0.263
category	[0.615]	[0.942]	[0.249]	[0.263]	[0.040]	[0.194]	[0.690]	[0.737]
Education	-0.913	-0.056	-0.022	0.673	-0.473	-0.984	-1.000	-0.365
category	[0.267]	[0.964]	[0.986]	[0.530]	[0.687]	[0.113]	[0.008]	[0.762]
Site	0.159	0.987	0.664	0.265	-0.105	-0.437	-0.121	-0.506
	[0.734]	[0.013]	[0.151]	[0.666]	[0.823]	[0.563]	[0.820]	[0.384]

Positive correlations:

Overall: 13 of 32 (41%); significant at 0.10: 1 of 32 (3%); significant at 0.05: 1 of 32 (3%).

Negative correlations:

Overall: 19 of 32 (59%); significant at 0.10: 2 of 32 (6%); significant at 0.05: 2 of 32 (6%).

NOTE: Values in the table are correlations between the mean positive participant evaluation and experimental impacts at the subgroup level. The values in square brackets are *p*-values. Fraction positive participant evaluation is the mean of the binary participant evaluation variable in the treatment group. The categories are defined as the following. Race: Black, Hispanic, and others. Age: less than 22 years, 22–25 years, 26–34 years, and 35+ years. Education: under 10 years, 10–11 years, 12 years, 13+ years. Site: nine site categories.

SOURCE: Authors' calculations using the NSW data.

Table 5.7 Bivariate Correlations between Experimental Impacts and Participant Evaluations for Eight Outcomes, Ex-Convicts

	Earnings One	Earnings Two	Earnings Three	Earnings Four	Employ One	Employ Two	Employ Three	Employ Four
Race	0.915	0.480	0.216	-0.742	0.991	0.599	0.999	-0.691
	[0.264]	[0.681]	[0.861]	[0.468]	[0.085]	[0.591]	[0.024]	[0.514]
Age	-0.776	0.788	0.394	-0.473	-0.895	-0.189	-0.946	0.691
category	[0.224]	[0.212]	[0.606]	[0.527]	[0.105]	[0.811]	[0.054]	[0.309]
Education	0.065	0.774	-0.158	-0.991	0.989	-0.767	0.769	0.221
category	[0.958]	[0.436]	[0.899]	[0.085]	[0.095]	[0.443]	[0.441]	[0.858]
Site	0.424	0.423	0.125	-0.721	0.592	0.723	-0.308	-0.425
	[0.343]	[0.577]	[0.813]	[0.169]	[0.162]	[0.277]	[0.552]	[0.475]

Positive correlations:

Overall: 19 of 32 (59%); significant at 0.10: 3 of 32 (9%); significant at 0.05: 1 of 32 (3%).

Negative correlations:

Overall: 13 of 32 (41%); significant at 0.10: 2 of 32 (6%); significant at 0.05: 0 of 32 (0%).

NOTE: Values in the table are correlations between the mean positive participant evaluation and experimental impacts at the subgroup level. The values in square brackets are p-values. Fraction positive participant evaluation is the mean of the binary participant evaluation variable in the treatment group. The categories are defined as the following. Race: Black, Hispanic, and others. Age: less than 22 years, 22–25 years, 26–34 years, and 35+ years. Education: under 10 years, 10–11 years, 12 years, 13+ years. Site: nine site categories.
SOURCE: Authors' calculations using the NSW data.

Table 5.8 Bivariate Correlations between Experimental Impacts and Participant Evaluations for Eight Outcomes, Youth

	Earnings One	Earnings Two	Earnings Three	Earnings Four	Employ One	Employ Two	Employ Three	Employ Four
Race	0.993	0.119	0.767	−0.685	0.130	−0.689	1.000	−0.571
	[0.076]	[0.924]	[0.444]	[0.520]	[0.917]	[0.516]	[0.000]	[0.613]
Site	0.401	0.867	0.495	0.084	0.128	−0.466	−0.492	−0.673
	[0.373]	[0.133]	[0.318]	[0.893]	[0.784]	[0.534]	[0.321]	[0.213]

Positive correlations:
Overall: 10 of 16 (63%); significant at 0.10: 2 of 16 (13%); significant at 0.05: 1 of 16 (6%).
Negative correlations:
Overall: 6 of 16 (38%); significant at 0.10: 0 of 16 (0%); significant at 0.05: 0 of 16 (0%).

NOTE: Values in the table are correlations between the mean positive participant evaluation and experimental impacts at the subgroup level. The values in square brackets are *p*-values. Fraction positive participant evaluation is the mean of the binary participant evaluation variable in the treatment group. The categories are defined as the following. Race: Black, Hispanic, and others. Site: nine site categories.
SOURCE: Authors' calculations using the NSW data.

number of estimates statistically distinguishable from zero; these estimates have no clear sign pattern, and their number roughly equals what
one would expect from sampling variation alone. In short, we do not
find very much at all. Looking at the tables along other dimensions,
none of the particular subgroup variables or of the particular outcomes
stand out for having consistent positive correlations. Taken together,
the results on bivariate correlations estimated using subgroups within
the four target groups serve mainly to diminish our enthusiasm for the
positive findings using the target-group-level correlations in Table 5.4.

Subgroup Impacts

We now turn to the multivariate analysis using predicted impacts
based on subgroup variation. As described in detail in Chapter 3, we
first construct predicted impacts by estimating Equation (3.1) and then
applying Equation (3.2) separately for each target group. We then estimate the model in Equation (3.4) using only the experimental treatment group observations. This relates the predicted impacts, on the left-
hand side of the equation, to the participant evaluation measure, on the
right-hand side, with individuals rather than subgroups as the unit of
observation.

For the NSW analysis, we include indicators for subgroups defined
by the following variables measured at baseline: age (four categories),
schooling (four categories), marital status (two categories), and site
(nine categories). Appendix 5A provides precise definitions for the
categories. We selected these variables based on subgroups commonly
employed in other evaluations and based on a priori notions of importance. We do not choose a second set based on stepwise regression, as in
Chapter 4, because we concluded from that exercise that it did not add
much substantively to the findings.

Table 5.9 has eight rows (corresponding to our eight labor-market
outcomes) and four columns (one for each target group). Each value in
the table comes from a separate regression using the predicted impacts
on the row outcome and the observations in the column target group.
For example, the value of -0.5 in the "Employment 1" row and the "Ex-
addicts" column indicates that switching from a "0" to a "1" response
on the participant evaluation variable decreases the expected predicted
impact on employment over the 18 months after random assignment by

**Table 5.9 Relationship between Predicted Impacts and Participant
Evaluations for Eight Outcomes, by Group**

	AFDC	Ex-Addicts	Ex-Convicts	Youth
Earnings One	−234.3	−36.1	387.5	−123.0
	(125.5)	(118.5)	(243.2)	(89.3)
Earnings Two	−142.4	123.4	118.2	−102.1
	(62.4)	(117.2)	(61.3)	(79.0)
Earnings Three	−29.1	−51.4	58.0	7.1
	(25.7)	(45.2)	(38.1)	(20.4)
Earnings Four	−61.0	3.9	48.5	−44.7
	(22.9)	(54.8)	(30.7)	(34.0)
Employ One	−1.11	−0.5	1.0	−2.3
	(0.8)	(0.9)	(0.8)	(0.9)
Employ Two	0.4	−1.2	1.1	−2.5
	(0.8)	(0.8)	(1.1)	(1.4)
Employ Three	0.0	0.0	1.3	0.0
	(1.0)	(1.5)	(0.6)	(0.7)
Employ Four	−2.5	−1.1	0.6	−4.1
	(1.0)	(1.3)	(1.3)	(1.9)
Positive (all / 0.10 / 0.05)	(1/0/0)	(3/0/0)	(8/2/1)	(1/0/0)
Negative (all / 0.10 / 0.05)	(7/4/3)	(5/0/0)	(0/0/0)	(7/3/2)

NOTE: Each cell in the table presents the coefficient estimate from a regression of
the estimated impacts for each individual, based on subgroup variation as the dependent variable and the participant evaluation indicator as the independent variable. The
regression is estimated using the experimental treatment group. Heteroskedasticity-
consistent standard errors appear in parentheses. Estimated coefficients and standard
errors for the employment outcomes are multiplied by 100 for ease of presentation.
The bottom two rows give counts of the number of cells in each column with positive
or negative estimates and, among those, the fractions statistically significant at the
0.10 and 0.05 levels. Subgroups are defined by age, marital status, schooling, race,
and site.
SOURCE: Authors' calculations using the NSW data.

0.5 percentage points among ex-addicts. Heteroskedasticity-consistent
estimated standard errors appear in parentheses below each coefficient
estimate; the −0.5 estimate has an estimated standard error of 0.9. The
final two rows of the table summarize the estimates by sign and statistical significance level.

The findings from the multivariate analysis differ somewhat from
those in the bivariate analysis just discussed. For the AFDC and youth

groups, we find negative relationships for seven of the eight outcomes, with several of them attaining statistical significance. For the ex-convicts, we find some modest evidence of a positive relationship between predicted impacts and participant evaluations, with all eight coefficients turning out positive and two of them significant at least at the 10 percent level. The results for the ex-addicts, on the other hand, look much like those from the bivariate analysis, with a rough balance between positive and negative and no statistically significant estimates.

Taken together, we find mixed but generally negative evidence from our multivariate subgroup analysis. Although we find more meaningful correlations than we did in the JTPA data considered in Chapter 4, more often than not those correlations have a negative sign.

Quantile Treatment Effects (QTEs)

This section presents evidence on the relationship between quantile treatment effects and participant evaluations. We estimate the QTEs as in Equation (3.3) and interpret them in light of the rank preservation assumption discussed in Chapter 3. We estimate the fraction with a positive participant evaluation at a particular quantile j by taking the average of the participant evaluations for individuals within a window defined by the $j + 5$ and $j - 5$ percentiles. In formal terms, we estimate the local average participant evaluation using a uniform kernel with a bandwidth of 10 percentiles. We estimate both quantities for every fifth percentile from the 5th through the 95th.

Figures 5.1A to 5.1D present our estimates in graphical form. The horizontal axis corresponds to percentiles of the outcome distribution. The solid line presents the predicted impacts on self-reported earnings in the 18 months after random assignment as a function of the percentile, while the dotted line presents the participant evaluations as a function of the percentile. The corresponding numerical values appear in Table 5.10. In Table 5.10, we have a pair of columns for each of the four target groups. The columns labeled "Effect" contain the predicted impacts, and the columns labeled "Evaluation" contain the estimated fractions with a positive participant evaluation. The penultimate row in Table 5.10 presents the correlation between the impacts and participant evaluations, along with the p-value from a test against the null of a zero correlation. The final row presents the slope coefficient from a

**Figure 5.1 Quantile Treatment Effects and Percentage Reporting
Positive Participant Evaluation**

Panel A: AFDC

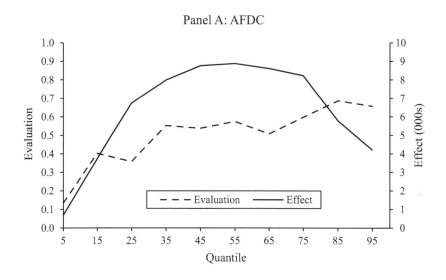

Panel B: Ex-Addicts

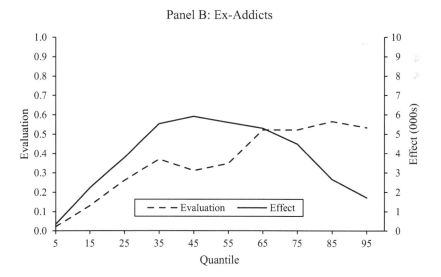

NOTE: The solid line presents the predicted impacts on self-reported earnings in the 18
  months after random assignment; the dotted line presents the participant evaluations.
SOURCE: Authors' calculations using the NSW data.

Figure 5.1 (continued)

Panel C: Ex-Convicts

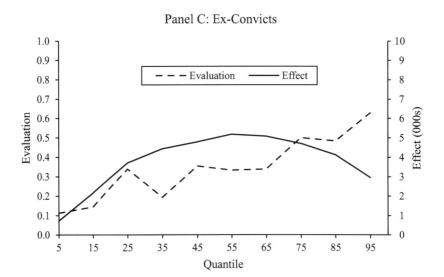

Panel D: Youth

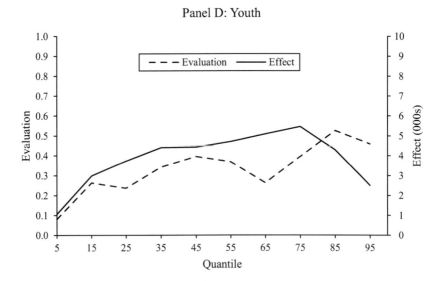

NOTE: The solid line presents the predicted impacts on self-reported earnings in the 18
    months after random assignment; the dotted line presents the participant evaluations.
SOURCE: Authors' calculations using the NSW data.

regression of the predicted impacts on the fraction with a positive participant evaluation for each group and its heteroskedasticity-consistent estimated standard error.

The figures reveal a similar pattern for each of the four target groups: the impacts first increase and then decrease, while the fraction with a positive participant evaluation increases fairly steadily over the entire range. Because the upward slope of the impact curve over the lower percentiles usually lasts longer than the downward slope at the highest percentiles, we end up with positive correlations in Table 5.10 for all four groups, with one of them statistically different from zero at the 10 percent level but not the 5 percent level. The magnitudes range from 0.370 for the ex-addicts to 0.592 for the AFDC women.

Table 5A.4 in the appendix presents the results from the Bitler, Gelbach, and Hoynes (2005) rank preservation test for the NSW data. Those tests provide some statistical evidence against rank preservation, though the magnitudes of the covariate imbalances suggest only minor departures. Taken all together, we interpret the analysis using the quantile treatment effects as providing rather modest, but not zero, evidence in support of the participant evaluation measures in the NSW data.

As an aside, note the absence of the range of zero QTEs at the lowest percentiles that we saw in the JTPA data, which resulted from the nontrivial proportion of both the treatment and control groups in that evaluation with zero earnings in the 18 months after random assignment. In the NSW context, because our "Earnings One" measure includes earnings the treatment group members received as participants in the Supported Work program, and because the program had a very high take-up rate, nearly everyone in the treatment group has positive earnings in the 18 months after random assignment. This implies a very limited number of zero QTE estimates at the low end of the outcome distribution for our first earnings measure.

Testing the Decision Theory Viewpoint

This subsection uses estimates of R_s and P_s from the NSW data to test whether the relationship in Equation (2.5) holds, under the assumption that $c = 0.5$. This represents a (weak) test of the first decision theory viewpoint advanced in Chapter 2. Estimates of R_s, the proportion with a positive participant evaluation, appear in the lower panel of Table 5.1

Table 5.10 Relationship between Quantile Treatment Effects for 18-Month Earnings and the Fraction with a Positive Participant Evaluation, by Group

Quantile	AFDC		Ex-Addicts		Ex-Convicts		Youth	
	Effect	Evalua-tion	Effect	Evalua-tion	Effect	Evalua-tion	Effect	Evalua-tion
5	696	0.13	354	0.02	734	0.11	1059	0.08
	(213)	(0.34)	(180)	(0.15)	(113)	(0.32)	(216)	(0.28)
15	3736	0.40	2226	0.13	2168	0.15	2985	0.26
	(322)	(0.49)	(191)	(0.34)	(119)	(0.36)	(159)	(0.45)
25	6736	0.36	3782	0.26	3713	0.34	3720	0.24
	(251)	(0.48)	(275)	(0.44)	(243)	(0.48)	(285)	(0.43)
35	7976	0.55	5531	0.37	4434	0.19	4396	0.34
	(118)	(0.50)	(397)	(0.49)	(376)	(0.40)	(348)	(0.48)
45	8756	0.54	5912	0.31	4784	0.35	4423	0.39
	(149)	(0.50)	(463)	(0.47)	(447)	(0.48)	(432)	(0.50)
55	8871	0.57	5597	0.35	5172	0.33	4705	0.37
	(256)	(0.50)	(537)	(0.48)	(521)	(0.48)	(500)	(0.49)
65	8605	0.51	5301	0.52	5073	0.34	5089	0.26
	(462)	(0.50)	(593)	(0.51)	(547)	(0.48)	(504)	(0.45)
75	8217	0.60	4489	0.52	4703	0.50	5463	0.39
	(497)	(0.49)	(716)	(0.51)	(688)	(0.50)	(566)	(0.50)
85	5783	0.69	2653	0.57	4119	0.48	4291	0.53
	(526)	(0.47)	(1000)	(0.50)	(700)	(0.50)	(634)	(0.51)
95	4219	0.66	1711	0.53	2957	0.63	2506	0.46
	(620)	(0.48)	(1809)	(0.50)	(1299)	(0.49)	(899)	(0.51)
Correlation with frac-tion positive participant evaluation	0.592 [0.090]		0.370 [0.308]		0.407 [0.357]		0.501 [0.202]	
Coefficient on fraction positive participant evaluation	9,762* (5,055)		3,873 (3,555)		3,574 (3,656)		5,250 (3,776)	

NOTE: The left column of the upper panel for each group presents estimated quantile treatment effects at 10 quantiles. Standard errors appear in parentheses. The right column of the upper panel for each group presents the fraction with a positive participant evaluation in a window of width 0.10 around the corresponding quantile, calculated using the treatment group. The first row of the lower panel contains correlations between the treatment effect estimates and the fractions with a positive participant evaluation by quantile and, in square brackets, the p-value from a test of the null that the correlation equals zero. The second row of the lower panel shows estimated coefficients from regressions of the quantile treatment effects on the fraction with a positive participant evaluation for 19 quantiles. Heteroskedasticity-consistent standard errors appear in parentheses.
SOURCE: Authors' calculations using the NSW data.

for the four NSW target groups. Based on these estimates, the bounds on the right-hand side of Equation (2.5) equal [0.2500, 0.7500] for the AFDC women, [0.1794, 0.6794] for the ex-addicts, [0.1715, 0.6715] for the ex-convicts, and [0.1972, 0.6972] for the youth dropouts.

Table 5A.5 presents the fractions of positive impacts from both the subgroup analyses and the QTEs for each of the four earnings outcomes for each of the four target groups. Looking first at the "fraction positive" estimates from the subgroup analyses, we see that they nearly always well exceed the upper bounds in Equation (2.5), with the fourth earnings measure for ex-addicts and youth providing the exceptions. Turning to the QTEs, for the "Earnings One" outcome, all of the fractions lie outside the points. For the other three earnings outcomes, the fractions that are positive typically lie within the bounds (or, as with the AFDC women and the "Earnings Two" outcome, just above the upper bound). However, the distinction between "fraction positive" and "fraction nonnegative" matters for these three outcomes, which have many zero QTEs. Relying on fraction nonnegative consistently moves the estimates outside the bounds. Overall, we see the NSW data as providing at most very limited evidence in support of the first decision theory viewpoint.

Determinants of Positive Participant Evaluations

We now turn to an investigation of whether simple proxies for impacts predict positive participant evaluations, in line with the lay scientist view developed in Chapter 2. As described earlier in the chapter, NSW provided a much more homogeneous treatment than did JTPA; as a result, we do not attempt an analysis of service intensity. We do, though, examine both levels and changes in labor market outcomes in the period after random assignment.

Tables 5.11 and 5.12 present the results from earnings and employment levels, respectively. For the earnings outcomes in Table 5.11, the three panels correspond to three of the four earnings outcomes defined in Appendix 5A and used in our earlier analyses. We omit the earnings and employment outcomes "Earnings One" and "Employ One," which include the period during which the treatment-group members participated in Supported Work. The columns refer to the four target groups. Within each target group, we define indicator variables for zero earnings and quartiles of the nonzero distribution of the outcome variables,

Table 5.11 Logit Estimates of the Relationship between Earnings Outcomes and Positive Participant Evaluations, by Group

	AFDC	Ex-Addicts	Ex-Convicts	Youth
Earnings Two				
Quartile 1	0.204	0.064	0.087	0.114
	(0.064)	(0.072)	(0.057)	(0.073)
Quartile 2	0.232	0.239	0.067	0.082
	(0.053)	(0.060)	(0.058)	(0.072)
Quartile 3	0.286	0.191	0.233	0.196
	(0.055)	(0.062)	(0.055)	(0.066)
Quartile 4	0.360	0.244	0.263	0.194
	(0.057)	(0.060)	(0.047)	(0.078)
χ^2 Test 1: outcome	38.980	22.810	15.350	3.995
	0.000	0.000	0.009	0.319
χ^2 Test 2: covariates	4.796	12.440	33.440	4.701
	0.779	0.133	0.162	0.034
χ^2 Test 3: site indicators	16.270	9.282	11.760	10.390
	0.012	0.026	0.000	0.407
Earnings Three				
Quartile 1	0.169	0.197	0.059	0.151
	(0.084)	(0.072)	(0.063)	(0.076)
Quartile 2	0.280	0.246	0.143	0.276
	(0.059)	(0.069)	(0.064)	(0.065)
Quartile 3	0.373	0.382	0.259	0.211
	(0.057)	(0.053)	(0.051)	(0.068)
Quartile 4	0.388	0.386	0.301	0.346
	(0.064)	(0.058)	(0.043)	(0.081)
χ^2 Test 1: outcome	19.240	5.910	10.370	2.578
	0.789	0.000	0.240	0.000
χ^2 Test 2: covariates	4.697	47.170	48.080	22.340
	0.000	0.255	0.017	0.631
χ^2 Test 3: site indicators	43.520	10.140	13.850	4.229
	0.004	0.116	0.000	0.376
Earnings Four				
Quartile 1	0.053	0.027	0.088	0.172
	(0.072)	(0.079)	(0.059)	(0.077)
Quartile 2	0.051	0.054	0.177	0.224
	(0.068)	(0.085)	(0.061)	(0.064)
Quartile 3	0.206	0.168	0.085	0.205
	(0.052)	(0.073)	(0.069)	(0.070)

Table 5.11 (continued)

	AFDC	Ex-Addicts	Ex-Convicts	Youth
Earnings Four (cont.)				
Quartile 4	0.209	0.165	0.179	0.171
	(0.074)	(0.063)	(0.048)	(0.090)
χ^2 Test 1: outcome	4.135	9.846	11.920	16.710
	0.845	0.149	0.029	0.154
χ^2 Test 2: covariates	19.390	12.050	16.940	6.685
	0.005	0.043	0.155	0.002
χ^2 Test 3: site indicators	18.360	10.800	12.430	3.820
	0.001	0.013	0.002	0.431
Observations	671	457	621	375

NOTE: Each cell in columns 1 through 4 displays estimates from a separate logit model with the binary participant evaluation variable as the dependent variable and with the background variables in Table 5.2 plus the indicated measure of Y_1, the labor market outcome in the treated state, as independent variables. The cells report mean numerical derivatives, with the associated standard errors in parentheses. For earnings outcomes, we recode the underlying continuous variable into four indicators for quartiles of the nonzero earnings distribution and leave the zeros as the omitted category. All models are estimated using the treatment group. Test 1 corresponds to the null that the coefficients on all of the earnings outcomes equal zero, while Test 2 corresponds to the null that the coefficients on all of the background variables equal zero, and Test 3 corresponds to the null that the coefficients on all of the site indicators equal zero.
SOURCE: Authors' calculations using the NSW data.

and then estimate Equation (3.5), including four of the five indicators and the same baseline characteristics used to define the subgroups for the analysis in Table 5.9. In each case, zero earnings serves as the omitted category. A similar procedure yields the results for the employment outcomes in Table 5.12, with nonemployment (i.e., zero earnings) the implicit omitted category. Both tables also present three chi-squared statistics and the associated p-values. The first is from a test of the null that the coefficients on all of the earnings or employment indicators equal zero. The second one is from a test of the null that the coefficients on all of the background covariates equal zero, and the third one is from a test of the null that the coefficients on all of the site indicators equal zero.

We find very strong results with both the earnings and employment outcome levels, with the partial exception of the youth target group. With the earnings, all the estimates have the correct sign, and the mean

Table 5.12 Logit Estimates of the Relationship between Employment Outcomes and Positive Participant Evaluations, by Group

	AFDC	Ex-Addicts	Ex-Convicts	Youth
Employ Two	0.273	0.195	0.174	0.146
	(0.043)	(0.046)	(0.039)	(0.053)
χ^2 Test 1: outcome	32.840	16.050	17.640	7.156
	0.000	0.000	0.022	0.350
χ^2 Test 2: covariates	5.661	9.374	12.970	4.438
	0.685	0.125	0.000	0.426
χ^2 Test 3: site indicators	13.980	12.640	13.110	3.853
	0.030	0.025	0.113	0.007
Employ Three	0.326	0.330	0.230	0.242
	(0.050)	(0.048)	(0.039)	(0.055)
χ^2 Test 1: outcome	15.710	35.880	29.450	3.646
	0.713	0.047	0.018	0.000
χ^2 Test 2: covariates	5.411	10.320	13.620	3.774
	0.000	0.000	0.000	0.456
χ^2 Test 3: site indicators	34.870	7.934	12.100	16.760
	0.015	0.243	0.147	0.437
Employ Four	0.144	0.115	0.140	0.198
	(0.038)	(0.044)	(0.036)	(0.045)
χ^2 Test 1: outcome	5.008	11.900	13.780	16.270
	0.000	0.127	0.018	0.165
χ^2 Test 2: covariates	17.810	12.590	13.720	3.652
	0.757	0.011	0.131	0.455
χ^2 Test 3: site indicators	13.500	6.401	12.470	6.502
	0.007	0.008	0.000	0.000
Observations	671	457	621	375

NOTE: Each cell in columns 1 through 4 displays estimates from a separate logit model with the binary participant evaluation variable as the dependent variable and with the background variables in Table 5.2 plus the indicated measure of Y_1, the labor market outcome in the treated state, as independent variables. The cells report mean numerical derivatives, with the associated standard errors in parentheses. All models are estimated using the treatment group. Test 1 corresponds to the null that the coefficients on all of the employment outcomes equal zero, while Test 2 corresponds to the null that the coefficients on all of the background variables equal zero, and Test 3 corresponds to the null that the coefficients on all of the site indicators equal zero.

SOURCE: Authors' calculations using the NSW data.

derivatives often show a monotone relationship: the higher the earnings, the higher the probability of a positive participant evaluation response, conditional on observed demographic characteristics. We find a similar story for the employment outcomes: for all three measures, we find positive, substantively important, and highly statistically significant relationships between employment and the participant evaluations. These findings are consistent with the lay empiricist view that respondents use outcomes as a proxy for impacts.

The strength of the results comes as some surprise as, for most respondents, two of the four outcomes we consider come after the survey in which they give their participant evaluation. Future outcomes having an effect on current participant evaluations can arise because of the strong serial correlation in labor market outcomes over time (so that our outcomes measure outcomes around the time of the survey with only modest error). They can also arise from forward-looking respondents, who feel themselves more "employable," in the jargon of the job training literature, even if not yet more employed as of the time of the participant evaluation. The former interpretation comports with the lay empiricist view; the latter with the subjective rationality view.

Table 5.13 presents the results from our estimation of Equation (3.5) using variables that measure changes in labor market outcomes as the impact proxy. The top two panels in the table look at before-after changes in earnings, while the bottom two panels look at before-after changes in employment. For each outcome, the upper panel uses 12 months before random assignment as the "before" period, while the lower panel uses 24 months before random assignment as the "before" period. The columns, as usual, correspond to the four target groups. Estimation proceeds as in Tables 5.11 and 5.12 but with the before-after change variables as the proxies. One difference is that, in the case of earnings, we now include indicators for four out of the five quintiles of the within-group before-after changes, with the lowest quintile (those with the smallest before-after changes) as the omitted group. For employment, we include indicators for three of the four possible before-after employment status patterns: 1) not employed before and after, 2) not employed before and employed after, 3) employed before and not employed after, and 4) employed both before and after. Those employed both before and after random assignment serve as the omitted group.

Table 5.13 Logit Estimates of the Relationship between Before-After Outcome Changes and Positive Participant Evaluations, by Group

	AFDC	Ex-Addicts	Ex-Convicts	Youth
Panel A: Before-after earnings (12 months before)				
Quintile 2	0.458	0.086	0.044	−0.100
	(0.178)	(0.098)	(0.102)	(0.114)
Quintile 3	0.515	0.231	0.150	0.055
	(0.164)	(0.080)	(0.087)	(0.091)
Quintile 4	0.685	0.293	0.254	0.049
	(0.157)	(0.074)	(0.086)	(0.090)
Quintile 5	0.798	0.364	0.355	0.214
	(0.155)	(0.073)	(0.081)	(0.091)
χ^2 Test 1: outcome	50.490	5.123	12.280	3.119
	0.000	0.207	0.022	0.009
χ^2 Test 2: covariates	6.079	10.910	13.160	4.316
	0.638	0.000	0.000	0.538
χ^2 Test 3: site indicators	19.740	28.420	38.420	13.420
	0.003	0.163	0.139	0.365
Panel B: Before-after earnings (24 months before)				
Quintile 2	−0.152	0.029	−0.094	0.049
	(0.180)	(0.097)	(0.096)	(0.124)
Quintile 3	0.318	0.143	0.025	0.093
	(0.130)	(0.069)	(0.068)	(0.103)
Quintile 4	0.410	0.244	0.163	0.159
	(0.124)	(0.062)	(0.064)	(0.101)
Quintile 5	0.526	0.337	0.248	0.220
	(0.121)	(0.062)	(0.060)	(0.101)
χ^2 Test 1: outcome	6.031	31.130	12.590	7.700
	0.644	0.281	0.000	0.343
χ^2 Test 2: covariates	18.780	5.137	35.500	4.495
	0.000	0.000	0.028	0.615
χ^2 Test 3: site indicators	46.770	9.771	12.140	2.668
	0.005	0.162	0.145	0.103
Panel C: Before-after employment (12 months before)				
Employed before and not employed after	−0.314	−0.120	−0.062	−0.192
	(0.089)	(0.062)	(0.059)	(0.062)
Not employed before and employed after	−0.062	−0.019	0.046	−0.089
	(0.075)	(0.070)	(0.052)	(0.069)

Table 5.13 (continued)

	AFDC	Ex-Addicts	Ex-Convicts	Youth
Panel C: Before-after employment (12 months before) (cont.)				
Always not employed	0.168	−0.124	−0.142	0.265
	(0.073)	(0.058)	(0.052)	(0.060)
χ^2 Test 1: outcome	18.320	12.550	12.010	18.730
	0.000	0.008	0.022	0.000
χ^2 Test 2: covariates	5.508	11.790	16.390	6.237
	0.702	0.128	0.001	0.182
χ^2 Test 3: site indicators	17.260	6.479	13.140	4.397
	0.008	0.091	0.151	0.355
Panel D: Before-after employment (24 months before)				
Employed before and not	−0.231	−0.092	−0.115	−0.221
employed after	(0.069)	(0.054)	(0.047)	(0.054)
Not employed before and	−0.034	0.060	0.027	−0.115
employed after	(0.066)	(0.079)	(0.055)	(0.090)
Always not employed	−0.140	−0.110	−0.154	−0.213
	(0.063)	(0.061)	(0.053)	(0.066)
χ^2 Test 1: outcome	5.440	11.660	14.460	5.956
	0.001	0.009	0.002	0.202
χ^2 Test 2: covariates	16.320	7.082	12.610	4.174
	0.710	0.127	0.126	0.383
χ^2 Test 3: site indicators	17.150	12.570	13.200	17.910
	0.009	0.069	0.022	0.000
Observations	671	457	621	375

NOTE: Before-after participant-reported earnings changes consist of monthly self-reported earnings and employment-status changes over the 18 months after random assignment, compared to the same outcome in the 12 months prior to random assignment in Panels A and C, and the 24 prior months in Panels B and D. The before-after earnings changes enter in the form of indicator variables for being in the second, third, fourth, and fifth quintiles of the before-after earnings change distribution. The omitted category is the first quintile of the distribution. For employment, we consider four patterns (always employed, never employed, employed before but not after, and employed after but not before), and we include indicator variables for three of them, with "always employed" as the omitted category. Each cell in columns 1 through 4 displays estimates from a separate logit model, with the binary participant evaluation variable as the dependent variable and with the background variables in Table 5.2 plus a measure of earnings or employment change in the treated state as independent variables. We report mean numerical derivatives, with the associated standard errors in parentheses. All models are estimated using the treatment group. Test 1 corresponds to the null that the coefficients on all of the earnings or employment outcomes equal zero, while Test 2 corresponds to the null that the coefficients on all of the background variables equal zero, and Test 3 corresponds to the null that the coefficients on all of the site indicators equal zero.

SOURCE: Authors' calculations using the NSW data.

The estimates using the before-after earnings changes show a strong pattern. The more positive the change in earnings, the higher the probability of a positive participant-evaluation response. In general, we see a nice, monotone pattern of coefficients on the indicators for the quintiles of the before-after changes. The highest quintile, and usually one or two below that, is statistically distinguishable from the omitted lowest quintile. The results matter substantively as well. For example, in the column for the long-term AFDC recipients, a change from the lowest to the highest quintile increases the probability of a positive participant evaluation by over 0.79. These estimates clearly match what one would expect if respondents use before-after earnings changes as a simple proxy for impacts, as suggested by the lay scientist view (as well as what one would expect if before-after differences correlate with impacts).

The employment results paint a moderately different picture. The lower probabilities of a positive participant evaluation for those who lack employment in the relevant periods both before and after random assignment, and those employed before but not after random assignment, make sense in comparison with the omitted category of those with jobs both before and after random assignment. But we find only modest, statistically insignificant differences between those employed both before and after and those not employed before who become employed after. These results suggest that the participants pay more attention to negative changes than to positive changes.

SUMMARY AND CONCLUSIONS

In this chapter we examined a participant evaluation measure collected as part of the evaluation of the National Supported Work demonstration. Our findings here resemble those from our analysis of the (not dissimilar) participant evaluation measure from the National JTPA Study in Chapter 4.

First, we find very little evidence of a consistent, positive relationship between the participant evaluations and predicted impacts based on subgroup variation in experimental impacts, but some evidence of a positive relationship based on the quantile treatment effects interpreted under rank preservation. We would have preferred the reverse pattern, given that the QTEs rely on additional identifying assumptions beyond those required for the subgroup estimates, but the estimates taken as a whole provide a marginally more positive picture than in Chapter 4.

Second, we find strong positive relationships between participant evaluations and both outcome levels and before-after outcome changes. Though they could have other explanations as well, these quite strong patterns are consistent with the lay scientist view of how respondents approach the participant evaluation questions described in Chapter 2.

Notes

1. The data from the NSW experiment have achieved prominence of a sort as a result of their use by LaLonde (1986) in his widely cited paper, as well as by many subsequent authors such as Dehejia and Wahba (1999, 2002) and Smith and Todd (2005a,b), who rely on LaLonde's version of the NSW data for men (his data for women having been lost at some point). All these papers combine the NSW data with observational comparison-group data from the Current Population Survey and the Panel Study of Income Dynamics in order to examine the performance of alternative nonexperimental identification strategies and estimators against an experimental benchmark. Calónico and Smith (2017) go back to the raw data in order to replicate and extend LaLonde's (1986) analysis of the AFDC women target group.

2. See Hollister, Kemper, and Maynard (1984), and the individual target group reports cited therein, for more details on the impacts and cost-benefit performance of NSW.

3. Consumer price index figures come from the Social Security Administration's Office of the Actuary.

Appendix 5A

Sample

Table 5A.1 (p. 139) shows the sample loss at various stages as we move from the original sample to the analysis sample.

Box 5A.1 Variables Used in Construction of the Subgroup Impacts

The following variables were used in the construction of the subgroup impacts:

Race/ethnicity
      White
      Black
      Hispanic

Education
      Less than 10 years
      10 or 11 years
      12 years
      More than 12 years

Marital status
      Married
      Not married

Site

      Atlanta, GA
      Chicago, IL
      Hartford, CT
      Jersey City, NJ
      Newark, NJ
      New York, NY
      Oakland, CA, and San Francisco, CA
      Philadelphia, PA
      Fond du Lac and Winnebago Counties, WI

Box 5A.2 Outcome Variables

As noted in the text, the first quarter "after" random assignment includes the month of random assignment in all cases.

Earnings One: Total self-reported earnings in the first six quarters (i.e., first 18 months) after random assignment, in 1982 dollars.

Employ One: Indicator for any self-reported employment in the first six quarters (i.e., first 18 months) after random assignment. The variable equals one if self-reported earnings over that period are positive and zero otherwise.

Earnings Two: Total self-reported earnings in the fourth through sixth quarters (i.e., months 10 to 18) after random assignment, in 1982 dollars.

Employ Two: Indicator for self-reported employment in the fourth through sixth quarters (i.e., months 10 to 18) after random assignment. The variable equals one if self-reported earnings in that period are positive and zero otherwise.

Earnings Three: Total self-reported earnings in the fourth quarter (i.e., months 10 to 12) after random assignment, in 1982 dollars.

Employ Three: Indicator for any self-reported employment during the fourth quarter (i.e., months 10 to 12) after random assignment. This variable equals one if self-reported earnings over that period are positive and zero otherwise.

Earnings Four: Total self-reported earnings during the sixth calendar quarter (i.e., months 16 to 18) after random assignment, in 1982 dollars.

Employ Four: Indicator for any self-reported employment during the sixth quarter (i.e., months 16 to 18) after random assignment. This variable equals one if self-reported earnings in that period are positive and zero otherwise.

Table 5A.1 Sample Size

	AFDC		Ex-Addicts		Ex-Convicts		Youth		Total		All sample
	Treatment	Control	Treatment	Control	Treatment	Control	Treatment	Control	Treatment	Control	
Original sample	800	802	715	692	1,109	1,167	566	678	3,190	3,339	6,529
With valid earnings	684	654	487	431	691	718	390	433	2,252	2,236	4,488
With complete set of covariates	682	653	485	427	686	715	385	426	2,238	2,221	4,459
With participant evaluation measure	671		457		621		378		2,127		2,127

NOTE: See text for additional details. Blank = not applicable.
SOURCE: Authors' tabulations using the NSW data.

Table 5A.2 Descriptive Statistics of the Main Covariates for the Four Target Groups in the Experimental Sample

	AFDC		Ex-Addicts		Ex-Convicts		Youth	
	Treatment	Control	Treatment	Control	Treatment	Control	Treatment	Control
Sex (male)	0.00	0.00	0.83	0.83	0.94	0.94	0.89	0.87
Age (yrs.)	33.37	33.63	27.80	27.77	25.63	25.17	18.22	18.35
Years of school	10.30	10.27	10.48	10.45	10.34	10.32	9.62	9.68
High school dropouts	0.70	0.69	0.70	0.72	0.74	0.74	0.99	0.99
Married	0.02	0.04	0.23	0.25	0.12	0.11	0.05	0.04
Black	0.84	0.82	0.75	0.74	0.80	0.79	0.74	0.71
Hispanic	0.12	0.13	0.11	0.11	0.10	0.11	0.18	0.20
Real earnings 1 yr. before RA ($)	393	396	2,007	2,207	1,067	1,039	1,406	1,447
Real earnings 2 yrs. before RA ($)	856	898	3,938	4,585	2,639	2,663	1,603	1,620
Hours worked 1 yr. before RA	90	92	339	337	202	180	320	326
Hours worked 2 yrs. before RA	186	188	572	632	407	401	356	368
Month of assignment (Jan. '78 = 0)	-12.23	-12.26	-17.68	-17.77	-15.68	-15.53	-14.50	-14.16
Sample size	799	798	688	657	1,089	1,136	555	668

NOTE: RA = random assignment.
SOURCE: Authors' tabulations using the NSW data.

Table 5A.3 Descriptive Statistics of the Outcome Variables for the Four Target Groups in the Experimental Sample

	AFDC		Ex-Addicts		Ex-Convicts		Youth	
	Treatment	Control	Treatment	Control	Treatment	Control	Treatment	Control
Earnings One	8,322	2,555	6,558	3,570	6,749	3,869	6,169	3,210
	(4,903)	(4,451)	(6,027)	(6,443)	(8,213)	(6,132)	(4,886)	(4,818)
Earnings Two	3,097	1,575	2,472	1,946	2,492	2,099	2,269	1,856
	(3,217)	(3,142)	(3,817)	(3,987)	(4,216)	(4,063)	(3,109)	(3,133)
Earnings Three	1,752	447	1,437	745	1,505	839	1,297	631
	(963)	(859)	(1,349)	(1,559)	(2,446)	(1,376)	(1,153)	(1,232)
Earnings Four	898	697	989	952	1,135	1,013	898	927
	(1,287)	(1,199)	(1,596)	(1,661)	(1,721)	(1,668)	(1,220)	(1,272)
Employ One	0.91	0.46	0.80	0.50	0.79	0.56	0.85	0.62
	(0.28)	(0.50)	(0.40)	(0.50)	(0.41)	(0.50)	(0.36)	(0.48)
Employ Two	0.67	0.35	0.46	0.35	0.43	0.38	0.51	0.43
	(0.47)	(0.48)	(0.50)	(0.48)	(0.50)	(0.49)	(0.50)	(0.50)
Employ Three	0.82	0.28	0.67	0.36	0.63	0.41	0.68	0.40
	(0.38)	(0.45)	(0.47)	(0.48)	(0.48)	(0.49)	(0.47)	(0.49)
Employ Four	0.40	0.36	0.39	0.38	0.45	0.43	0.45	0.48
	(0.49)	(0.48)	(0.49)	(0.49)	(0.50)	(0.49)	(0.50)	(0.50)
Number of Observations	800	802	715	692	773	819	566	678

NOTE: Earnings One: total self-reported earnings in the first six quarters after random assignment. Earnings Two: total self-reported earnings in the fourth through sixth quarters after random assignment. Earnings Three: total self-reported earnings in the third quarter after random assignment. Earnings Four: total self-reported earnings during the sixth calendar quarter after random assignment. Employ One to Four correspond to indicator variables for when earnings in the respective periods are greater than zero. Values in parentheses represent standard deviations.

SOURCE: Authors' calculations using the NSW Data.

Table 5A.4 Treatment-Control Differences in Covariates at Selected Quantiles of the Outcome Distribution (Earnings 1)

	0–25th percentile		25th–75th percentile		75th–100th percentile	
AFDC	Mean difference	90% Confidence interval	Mean difference	90% Confidence interval	Mean difference	90% Confidence interval
Age	-1.074	[-1.183 ; 1.151]	-0.658	[-0.956 ; 0.899]	1.520*	[-1.228 ; 1.126]
Years of school	0.099	[-0.328 ; 0.351]	-0.140	[-0.217 ; 0.236]	0.249	[-0.321 ; 0.294]
High school dropout	-0.031	[-0.070 ; 0.070]	0.072*	[-0.055 ; 0.055]	0.003	[-0.083 ; 0.084]
Married	0.017	[-0.030 ; 0.025]	-0.037*	[-0.022 ; 0.020]	-0.031*	[-0.025 ; 0.024]
Black	-0.045	[-0.065 ; 0.066]	0.033	[-0.043 ; 0.047]	0.053	[-0.063 ; 0.061]
Hispanic	0.019	[-0.061 ; 0.055]	-0.002	[-0.037 ; 0.035]	-0.033	[-0.052 ; 0.052]
Real earnings 1 yr. before RA	117.7	[-134.7 ; 116.4]	-310.4*	[-153.4 ; 138.1]	-90.5	[-280.4 ; 234.1]
Real earnings 2 yrs. before RA	246.1	[-279.8 ; 207.3]	-241.0	[-289.6 ; 248.1]	-486.1*	[-446.8 ; 415.6]
Hours worked 1 yr. before RA	17.9	[-31.2 ; 29.5]	-62.8*	[-33.5 ; 31.7]	-34.8	[-49.2 ; 41.6]
Hours worked 2 yrs. before RA	63.4*	[-56.5 ; 45.2]	-27.3	[-57.7 ; 50.3]	-108.9*	[-84.1 ; 82.4]
Chi-squared test and *p*-value	15.1	0.130	29.5	0.001	28.8	0.001
Ex-Addicts						
Age	-1.093	[-1.535 ; 1.621]	0.805	[-1.045 ; 0.949]	0.234	[-1.086 ; 1.185]
Years of school	0.111	[-0.352 ; 0.329]	0.014	[-0.246 ; 0.264]	-0.094	[-0.355 ; 0.320]
High school dropouts	-0.019	[-0.084 ; 0.089]	-0.046	[-0.066 ; 0.067]	0.010	[-0.095 ; 0.103]
Married	-0.075	[-0.080 ; 0.083]	-0.026	[-0.061 ; 0.053]	-0.004	[-0.100 ; 0.091]
Black	-0.040	[-0.073 ; 0.084]	0.047	[-0.055 ; 0.062]	0.006	[-0.097 ; 0.100]
Hispanic	0.021	[-0.049 ; 0.042]	0.006	[-0.036 ; 0.036]	0.000	[-0.076 ; 0.063]
Real earnings 1 yr. before RA	561.6	[-639.7 ; 576.4]	-887.0*	[-505.1 ; 510.7]	-180.4	[-1,017.6 ; 841.1]
Real earnings 2 yrs. before RA	364.2	[-1,307.6 ; 1,143.1]	-1,002.9*	[-922.5 ; 841.3]	-1,422.4*	[-1,493.8 ; 1,306.8]
Hours worked 1 yr. before RA	154.8*	[-95.6 ; 91.6]	-123.8*	[-81.1 ; 72.0]	-35.0	[-126.1 ; 111.4]
Hours worked 2 yrs. before RA	22.6	[-150.3 ; 131.3]	-101.5	[-111.3 ; 97.0]	-189.5*	[-174.4 ; 149.0]
Chi-squared test and *p*-value	21.4*	0.019	16.5*	0.086	4.2	0.936

Ex-Convicts

Age	-1.006	[-1.124 ; 1.003]	0.784*	[-0.684 ; 0.723]	1.016	[-1.094 ; 1.158]
Years of school	0.102	[-0.299 ; 0.306]	-0.074	[-0.210 ; 0.209]	0.280	[-0.326 ; 0.322]
High school dropout	-0.004	[-0.075 ; 0.074]	0.033	[-0.054 ; 0.050]	-0.059	[-0.084 ; 0.079]
Married	-0.021	[-0.053 ; 0.054]	0.028	[-0.034 ; 0.036]	0.054	[-0.065 ; 0.062]
Black	-0.028	[-0.050 ; 0.056]	0.029	[-0.041 ; 0.044]	-0.025	[-0.063 ; 0.067]
Hispanic	0.036	[-0.053 ; 0.045]	-0.041*	[-0.037 ; 0.037]	-0.009	[-0.045 ; 0.044]
Real earnings 1 yr. before RA	-68.0	[-333.0 ; 319.7]	-160.3	[-252.4 ; 241.3]	297.5	[-454.4 ; 451.8]
Real earnings 2 yrs. before RA	526.0	[-600.0 ; 590.7]	-280.9	[-609.9 ; 612.7]	-786.9	[-996.5 ; 987.2]
Hours worked 1 yr. before RA	-15.3	[-54.2 ; 53.5]	-13.1	[-45.2 ; 41.6]	70.7*	[-71.7 ; 68.3]
Hours worked 2 yrs. before RA	46.1	[-96.9 ; 99.8]	-33.1	[-76.6 ; 79.0]	19.8	[-124.7 ; 126.9]
Chi-squared test and p-value	8.7	0.558	13.1	0.220	18.4	0.049

Youth

Age	-0.269*	[-0.257 ; 0.243]	0.074	[-0.181 ; 0.162]	-0.286*	[-0.223 ; 0.231]
Years of school	-0.337*	[-0.248 ; 0.261]	0.135	[-0.162 ; 0.157]	0.201	[-0.251 ; 0.248]
High school dropout	-0.001	[-0.022 ; 0.026]	-0.006*	[-0.005 ; 0.009]	0.000	[-0.011 ; 0.019]
Married	-0.027	[-0.035 ; 0.023]	0.034*	[-0.030 ; 0.029]	-0.033	[-0.045 ; 0.043]
Black	0.038	[-0.083 ; 0.091]	-0.002	[-0.064 ; 0.064]	0.080	[-0.092 ; 0.091]
Hispanic	-0.073	[-0.083 ; 0.070]	0.044	[-0.058 ; 0.058]	-0.119*	[-0.082 ; 0.081]
Real earnings 1 yr. before RA	12.8	[-387.0 ; 317.4]	-135.3	[-345.6 ; 322.0]	-142.4	[-566.7 ; 501.4]
Real earnings 2 yrs. before RA	-316.0	[-561.5 ; 462.9]	310.6	[-412.3 ; 389.0]	-472.8	[-649.1 ; 562.4]
Hours worked 1 yr. before RA	-12.3	[-84.2 ; 70.7]	-25.7	[-71.3 ; 62.1]	-18.0	[-117.8 ; 112.7]
Hours worked 2 yrs. before RA	-77.0	[-135.2 ; 105.5]	23.8	[-98.7 ; 88.9]	-96.5	[-134.2 ; 127.0]
Chi-squared test and p-value	16.1	0.097	17.1	0.072	15.1	0.129

NOTE: Bootstrap confidence intervals under the null appear in square brackets. * significant at the 0.10 level.
SOURCE: Authors' calculations using the NSW data.

Table 5A.5 Characterizing the Distribution of Impacts

	AFDC	Ex-Addicts	Ex-Convicts	Youth
Earnings One				
Impact standard deviation	2,639	2,092	1,553	1,350
Fraction positive (based on quantile analysis)	0.97	0.94	0.97	0.98
Fraction nonnegative (based on quantile analysis)	1.00	0.97	0.99	0.99
Fraction positive (based on subgroups analysis)	1.00	1.00	1.00	1.00
Earnings Two				
Impact standard deviation	1,229	793	592	656
Fraction positive (based on quantile analysis)	0.77	0.60	0.64	0.64
Fraction nonnegative (based on quantile analysis)	1.00	0.95	0.98	0.96
Fraction positive (based on subgroups analysis)	0.94	0.93	0.88	0.88
Earnings Three				
Impact standard deviation	864	866	764	712
Fraction positive (based on quantile analysis)	0.83	0.62	0.60	0.70
Fraction nonnegative (based on quantile analysis)	1.00	0.93	0.94	1.00
Fraction positive (based on subgroups analysis)	1.00	1.00	1.00	1.00
Earnings Four				
Impact standard deviation	317	125	196	103
Fraction positive (based on quantile analysis)	0.40	0.27	0.46	0.26
Fraction nonnegative (based on quantile analysis)	1.00	0.89	0.99	0.80
Fraction positive (based on subgroups analysis)	0.94	0.62	0.81	0.63

NOTE: The first three rows for each outcome present estimates of features of the distribution of impacts under the assumption of rank preservation for the four target groups. The final row for each outcome presents the fraction with a positive impact, based on the impact estimates using subgroup variation.
SOURCE: Authors' calculations using the NSW data.

6
Evidence from the Connecticut Jobs First Program

Tanya Byker
Jeffrey Smith

This chapter provides further evidence regarding the information content, if any, of participant evaluation survey questions by examining the data from the experimental evaluation of the Connecticut Jobs First welfare-to-work program. The analysis in this chapter differs in three important and interesting ways from the analyses presented in Chapters 4 and 5.

First, while the Job Training Partnership Act of 1982 (JTPA) and National Supported Work (NSW) Demonstration treatments aimed to change outcomes mainly by providing human capital to their participants, Jobs First aims to change outcomes by changing the budget constraints facing low-income single parents in Connecticut so as to alter their behavior in specific ways.

Second, the participant evaluation question differs in important ways from that considered in the JTPA and NSW cases. In particular, it refers to behavior under the control of the respondent, it focuses on a more concrete outcome, and the wording is more explicit in encouraging the respondent to think about the counterfactual of what would have happened without the Jobs First program.

Third, unlike the two preceding chapters, the participant evaluation responses in Jobs First do correlate with predicted impacts based on both of our identification strategies.

The chapter proceeds in the now-familiar (to those reading straight through the book) manner: We begin by describing the program or policy whose effects the participants are asked to evaluate, then we describe the data, our sample, and the particular participant evaluation question whose responses we analyze. Our empirical findings follow, starting with bivariate relationships with subgroup impacts and continuing with the multivariate subgroup analysis, the analysis based on quantile treatment effects, a look at the restrictions implicit in our first decision theory viewpoint, and the analysis of predictors of a positive participant evaluation. The final section summarizes our findings and places them into the broader context of the book.

PROGRAM

The Connecticut Jobs First welfare-to-work program began under one of the waivers issued to states by the federal government prior to national welfare reform (specifically, the Personal Responsibility and Work Opportunity Reconciliation Act of 1996). These waivers allowed states to modify their Aid to Families with Dependent Children (AFDC) programs. AFDC (now called Temporary Assistance for Needy Families, or TANF) provides cash assistance to low-income families (primarily single mothers) with children, as well as links to other programs and services. The waiver system required states to conduct a rigorous evaluation of their reforms; in the case of Jobs First, this took the form of a random-assignment evaluation conducted by MDRC (formerly the Manpower Demonstration Research Corporation) that compared the Jobs First program to the preexisting AFDC program.

Connecticut replaced AFDC with Jobs First in 1996 in all but two of its welfare offices. At those two sites, Manchester and New Haven, eligible AFDC recipients were randomly assigned either to continue in the preexisting AFDC program or to participate in Jobs First. New Haven, home to about three-quarters of our sample members, differs from Manchester in having a much higher concentration of poverty. Random assignment took place between January 1996 and February 1997. Starting in March 2001, individuals originally assigned to the AFDC group transitioned into the ongoing Jobs First program.

The Jobs First program had three main components. The first was relatively severe time limits on lifetime welfare receipt, which headlined the program. This aspect of the policy aimed to focus benefit recipients' minds on work. It imposed a limit of 21 months—far below the 60-month limit eventually adopted under national welfare reform; indeed, Connecticut relaxed this aspect of the policy after the evaluation. Even during the evaluation, the possibility of exemptions for individuals not available to work (e.g., because of caring for a sick relative) or with very young children softened the policy. The state also offered extensions for those reaching the time limit but with incomes below the maximum benefit level for their family composition and judged to have made a good-faith effort to find employment. Figure 2 of Bloom et al. (2002) shows what happened for a random subset of 100 cases from the evaluation that reached the time limit. Among the 100 cases, the state terminated 43 at the time limit, gave 55 an extension, and gave 2 an exemption. Though it might not seem so to readers unfamiliar with this policy area, this level of enforcement represents pretty strong medicine.

The second main component consisted of a change in the earnings disregard. Traditional AFDC programs, including the one in Connecticut, disregarded only a small portion of earned income when calculating payments. In contrast, Jobs First disregarded all earnings up to the federal poverty line. This allowed recipients to combine work with welfare and thereby substantially increase their total incomes, at least until they arrived at the time limit. Here the policy aimed to provide a strong incentive to work for a long-enough period that at least some recipients would develop strong ties to the labor market.

The third component of Jobs First centered on mandatory "work first" employment services. As described in Bloom et al. (2002), this aspect of the program ended up being only partially implemented because of administrative overload combined with not one but two changes in the organization of the service provision during the early years of the program. Jobs First also provided more traditional skills training (similar to that offered by JTPA) in a limited number of cases to recipients who had already looked hard for a job. The experimental data show that total receipt of any employment and training services (from whatever source—recall that JTPA is operating in the background) differs little between the treatment and control groups, but that service type tilts more toward job search–related activities in the treatment group. Failure to participate in the mandatory services or engage in other required employment-related activities could, and did, result in benefit sanctions for some clients.

Unlike the JTPA and NSW programs examined in Chapters 4 and 5, Jobs First represents primarily a change to the budget constraint, rather than a service. As a result, assuming sound implementation, it has 100 percent take-up essentially by definition. As mentioned above, Jobs First applied only to parents (mostly single mothers) collecting AFDC in Connecticut. This population overlaps somewhat with the populations treated in the JTPA and NSW evaluations. More precisely, a large fraction of the "adult women" subgroup in the JTPA evaluation consisted of AFDC recipients, and one of the four main subgroups in the NSW evaluation consisted of long-term AFDC recipients.

DATA AND SAMPLE

The MDRC experimental evaluation, whose data we use for our analysis, relied on four distinct data sources: 1) a baseline survey, 2) a follow-up survey (the "three-year client survey") administered around 36 months after random assignment, 3) administrative data on quarterly earnings from the Connecticut Unemployment Insurance (UI) system, and 4) monthly administrative data on AFDC/TANF benefits from the state's Eligibility Management System. We use information from all four of these data sources in our analysis. In particular, we use the baseline survey and the administrative data for background characteristics, the follow-up survey for our participant evaluation measure as well as for self-reported measures of service receipt, the UI data for pre-random-assignment employment history variables as well as earnings and employment outcomes, and the welfare data for pre-random-assignment AFDC receipt history variables. Bloom et al. (2002) describe the data sources in greater detail in their "Section V" of Chapter 1.

Later in the chapter, we discuss issues with the survey data that arise within particular contexts. In regard to the UI administrative data, a failure to cover employment and earnings outside Connecticut both before and after random assignment, as well as off-the-books (and some on-the-books) employment within Connecticut, represents the most important limitation. A similar limitation applies to the administrative data on welfare receipt. These limitations loom larger in Connecticut, a small state that overlaps in part with the greater New York City labor market, than they would elsewhere.

Our focus on the participant evaluation variable limits our sample to observations that 1) have valid administrative data from both sources, 2) completed the three-year client survey and provided enough information for us to construct our participant evaluation measure, and 3) completed the baseline survey. In general, the client survey imposes the binding constraint on the sample. As described in Appendix D of Bloom et al. (2002), for cost reasons, MDRC did not attempt to administer the client survey to everyone who underwent random assignment, but rather to a stratified random sample within the experimental population. Among those whom it attempted to survey, MDRC achieved a very good response rate of 82.0 percent in the treatment group and 78.7 percent in the control group.[1] In addition, MDRC excluded from the survey (and from its analysis and, by implication, our analysis) all child-only cases and two-parent cases, as well as some random-assignment errors, leaving only single-parent AFDC cases.

Of the 1,244 treatment group members who completed the client survey, all but 22 provided usable responses to the participant evaluation variable. As it turns out, all these individuals had usable data from the baseline survey and both administrative data sources as well, implying an analysis sample of 1,222. We add in 1,170 control-group members who completed the survey, for a total analysis sample of 2,392.[2] We deal with item nonresponse (other than on the participant evaluation question) on the baseline survey through indicator variables for missing values rather than "listwise deletion," the term the literature gives to deleting any observation with a missing value for any covariate. As a result, we do not suffer additional sample loss on this score. The appendix describes the sample construction in greater detail.[3]

PARTICIPANT EVALUATION MEASURE

Table 6.1 presents the survey question underlying the participant evaluation measure we use from the Jobs First data. It asks respondents whether they thought that they obtained employment sooner than they otherwise would have because of the time limit on AFDC benefit receipt they faced under the Jobs First program. A four-point Likert scale structures and orders the possible responses.

Table 6.1 Responses to Participant Evaluation Question: "(Because of the time limit) I went to work sooner than I would have."

Survey responses	Number of respondents	Percent
Agree a lot	220	17.68
Agree a little	115	9.24
Disagree a little	107	8.60
Disagree a lot	372	29.90
Don't know	1	0.08
No answer	21	1.69
Valid skip	408	32.80
Total	1,244	
Recoded participant evaluation indicator		
Agree	335	27.41
Do not agree	887	72.59
Total	1,222	

SOURCE: Authors' calculations using MDRC Jobs First Public Use File data.

In several important ways, this participant evaluation measure differs from those we considered from the JTPA evaluation in Chapter 4 and the NSW Demonstration in Chapter 5. First, while not asking the respondent to directly construct a counterfactual outcome, it does refer explicitly to the counterfactual state in which the respondent does not face a time limit on his or her AFDC benefit receipt. As we discuss in more detail in Chapter 7, prompting respondents to construct or at least think about the counterfactual may affect the performance of participant evaluation questions. Second, relative to the other two questions we consider, the Jobs First participant evaluation question focuses on a much more concrete object—i.e., how long it took the respondent to get a job—and on behavior under the control of the respondent—i.e., job search effort and job search acceptance. In the Jobs First context, some respondents may have consciously taken a job that they at least imagine they would not have taken without the time limits looming. This focus on a very specific, concrete behavior also largely eliminates concerns about respondents considering outcomes other than employment or aspects of the treatment (such as the helpfulness of their AFDC caseworkers) in devising their participant evaluations. More formally,

Assumption A1 (mutual outcome correspondence) from Chapter 2 likely holds true for this question, as it did not for the questions considered in Chapters 4 and 5. Finally, this question elicits responses on a four-point Likert scale rather than simple binary responses; we say more about that later in this section.

The top section of Table 6.1 presents the raw responses to the participant evaluation question for the treatment group. Some control group members also respond to this question, but we do not use their responses in our analysis. Unusually, the two extreme responses on the Likert scale attract the most responses. In all, 17.7 percent of respondents indicate that they "agree a lot" with the statement that they went to work sooner because of the time limit, while 29.9 percent indicate that they "disagree a lot" with that claim. This focus on extreme responses differs from the distribution of responses often observed with Likert scales in other contexts, in which the responses are concentrated in the center, rather than at the extremes. Many respondents in the Jobs First data clearly have strong beliefs about the effect of the time limits on their behavior.

In our analysis, we collapse the four-point Likert scale into a binary variable, with the responses "agree a lot" and "agree a little" coded as 1, indicating a positive participant evaluation, and the responses "disagree a lot" and "disagree a little" coded as 0, indicating a negative participant evaluation. Collapsing the four-point scale into a binary variable has both costs and benefits. On the cost side of the ledger, collapsing the responses throws out potentially useful information. Agreeing a lot rather than agreeing a little may represent a meaningful distinction, whose information content we fail to exploit. On the benefit side of the ledger, collapsing the responses allows this analysis to parallel the ones in Chapters 4 and 5 and also allows us to avoid the more complex and difficult-to-interpret econometric methods associated with multiple ordered responses. We discuss the sensitivity of our results to this coding below, in the context of the analysis using subgroup variation in impacts, but we leave a broader evaluation of this aspect of the Jobs First participant evaluation measure to future research.

Survey respondents were not asked the participant evaluation question under four conditions: 1) they reported that they did not believe themselves subject to a time limit on their AFDC benefit receipt, 2) they reported that they were uncertain about being subject to a time limit,

3) they did not receive AFDC in the period between random assignment and the survey, and 4) they did not work in the period between random assignment and the survey. These four conditions account for the 408 valid "skips" in Table 6.1. We code valid skips due to reasons (1) and (2) as 0 on the grounds that we do not expect respondents who do not perceive (or are uncertain about the presence of) a time limit on their AFDC benefit receipt to change their behavior even though they do, in fact, face such a time limit. Of course, this argument carries greater weight in case (1) than in case (2). We code valid skips due to reason (4) as 0 for the obvious reason that someone who did not work between random assignment and the survey date cannot have gotten a job sooner as a result of the time limits.[4]

We have also coded valid skips due to reason (3) as 0, though we remain less happy about this than about the other codings because we worry that one reason a recipient might get off AFDC and onto some other means of support (e.g., work or marriage) is that they want to preserve their AFDC eligibility for some future time when they may need it more. At the same time, this group also surely includes individuals who would have gotten off AFDC immediately had they ended up in the control group, along with individuals determined to be ineligible for AFDC after random assignment. If we could separate out the three types of individuals who did not get asked the participant evaluation question because of reason (3), we would code the first group as 1 and the second and third as 0. But because we cannot make this separation, we face the unhappy choice of either inducing some measurement error in one direction or another or reducing our sample size, limiting our external validity, and possibly inducing bias by dropping them from the analysis entirely. We chose a coding of 0 as the best choice among this set of options, as the text in Bloom et al. (2000, p. 18) suggests that the third, ineligible group predominates. Finally, we code the 21 "don't know" and "no answer" responses as "missing" and do not include them in any of our analyses.

The lower panel of Table 6.1 gives the distribution of responses after collapsing the four-point scale, recoding the valid skips and dropping the "don't know" and "no answer" responses. It shows that 27.4 percent of our analysis sample indicated that the program affected their time to employment, while the other 72.6 percent of the analysis sample indicated that it did not.

EMPIRICAL RESULTS

Descriptive Statistics

Table 6.2 presents descriptive statistics on our analysis sample. As with AFDC (or TANF) recipients in general, participants in the Jobs First evaluation had low average levels of education, employment, earnings, and marriage at the time of random assignment. A majority had received AFDC in the four quarters prior to random assignment.

Outcomes and Experimental Impacts

The outcomes we consider derive from UI administrative earnings data. The set of outcomes considered in this chapter differs from the set found in previous chapters because it includes measures related to the time to first employment after random assignment. We add these measures here because they correspond directly to the object of interest in the participant evaluation question we analyze. The appendix describes the outcome variables in greater detail.

Table 6.3 lists the outcome variables and presents descriptive statistics separately for the treatment and control groups, along with the difference between the two groups (an experimental impact of the program) and p-values from tests of the null of a zero difference. The outcomes we examine include indicators for any employment (defined as nonzero earnings) in the calendar quarter (we dispense with the qualifier "calendar" in what follows) of random assignment (hereafter, "quarter 0") or the first quarter after random assignment, in quarters 0 to 4, in quarters 0 to 12, or only in quarter 12. We also examine total UI earnings over quarters 0 to 4 and over quarters 0 to 12.

In addition, we consider a set of variables that try to get at employment status changes. The variable "Maintained or transitioned to employment in quarter 1" equals 1 for individuals employed in both quarters 0 and 1, or just in quarter 1, and it equals 0 otherwise. Similarly, the variable "Maintained or transitioned to employment in quarters 1 to 2" equals 1 for individuals employed in quarter 0 and at least one of quarters 1 and 2, and for individuals not employed in quarter 0 but employed in at least one of quarters 1 and 2, and 0 otherwise.

Table 6.2 Characteristics of Analysis Sample Members at Random Assignment

	AFDC (control)	Jobs First (treatment)	Full sample
Age			
Under 25	26.92	27.89	27.42
25–34	43.33	42.77	43.04
35 or over	29.74	29.34	29.54
Race/Ethnicity			
White, non-Hispanic	34.27	38.18	36.29
Black, non-Hispanic	41.20	40.43	40.80
Hispanic	22.48	19.37	20.88
Other	0.34	0.72	0.54
Missing	1.71	1.29	1.49
Marital status			
Never married	68.12	67.28	67.69
Married, living with spouse	0.77	0.80	0.79
Married living apart	11.88	12.46	12.18
Separated	6.15	6.43	6.30
Divorced	11.37	11.17	11.27
Widowed	1.28	1.13	1.20
Missing	0.43	0.72	0.58
Number of children under 7			
None	2.48	2.65	2.57
1	40.34	40.84	40.60
2	30.34	29.42	29.87
3 or more	26.84	27.09	26.97
Education			
GED	11.11	12.78	11.97
High school diploma	50.17	46.70	48.38
Technical/two-year college degree	3.08	4.34	3.73
Four-year (or more) college degree	1.62	1.29	1.45
None of the above	32.39	33.68	33.06
Missing	1.62	1.21	1.41

(continued)

Table 6.2 (continued)

	AFDC (control)	Jobs First (treatment)	Full sample
Prior AFDC receipt pattern (four calendar quarters prior to RA)			
NNNN	27.61	26.53	27.05
NNYY	1.97	2.97	2.49
NYYY	5.47	3.30	4.35
YYYY	59.32	62.30	60.85
Other	5.64	4.90	5.26
Prior employment pattern (four calendar quarters prior to RA)			
NNNN	45.73	51.85	48.88
NNNY or NNYY	11.62	8.20	9.86
YNNN	4.19	3.70	3.94
YYNN	6.24	6.11	6.17
YYYY	20.68	18.65	19.64
Other	11.54	11.50	11.52
Site			
New Haven	77.69	76.05	76.84
Manchester	22.31	23.95	23.16
Sample size	1,170	1,244	2,414

NOTE: These percentages are for the survey subsample who were interviewed approximately 36 months after random assignment. Differences from Table 1.4 in Bloom et al. (2002) are due to using the survey subsample and including individuals with missing values of some variables. Also note that the survey subsample oversampled individuals with some children under 7.
SOURCE: MDRC Jobs First Public Use File data.

The corresponding variable for quarters 1 to 4 has a similar definition. The variable "Number of quarters to first job" aims to capture exactly that, with a couple of twists defined shortly to deal with respondents employed at random assignment and respondents who never find a job in our data.

This set of outcomes reflects three design choices that merit a bit of discussion. Our desire to construct an outcome measure that captures time to employment, and so parallels the outcome considered in the participant evaluation measure, necessitates the first two choices: 1) how to measure employment at the time of random assignment and,

Table 6.3 Outcomes and Experimental Impacts for Treatment and Control Groups

	AFDC (control)	Jobs First (treatment)	Difference	p-value
Ever employed, Quarters 0 to 1	0.5282	0.5514	0.0232	0.2525
Ever employed, Quarters 0 to 4	0.6530	0.7211	0.0681***	0.0003
Number of quarters to first job	4.1197	3.5225	−0.5972***	0.0029
Maintained or transitioned to employment in:				
Quarter 1	0.4346	0.4743	0.0397	0.0776
Quarters 1 to 2	0.5128	0.5732	0.0603***	0.0029
Quarters 1 to 4	0.6128	0.6921	0.0793***	0.0000
Ever employed, Quarters 0 to 12	0.8120	0.8545	0.0425***	0.0050
Employed, Quarter 12	0.5812	0.6238	0.0426**	0.0325
Earnings, Quarters 0 to 4	4895	4770	−124	0.6567
Earnings, Quarters 0 to 12	18189	18580	391	0.6463

NOTE: These are outcomes and impacts for the survey subsample who were interviewed approximately 36 months after random assignment. *significant at the 0.10 level; **significant at the 0.05 level; ***significant at the 0.01 level.
SOURCE: MDRC Jobs First Public Use File data.

not unrelated but still distinct, 2) what to do with individuals who have nonzero earnings in quarter 0. The third choice concerns what to do in our "time to employment" outcome with individuals who never find a job during the time period covered by our data.

Starting with the first choice, we have two measures of employment at the time of random assignment: 1) UI earnings in the calendar quarter that includes random assignment and 2) a variable from the baseline survey on employment at random assignment. The variable directly measuring employment at random assignment would seem at first blush to be the obvious choice, but for two things. First, it is missing for 459 individuals for whom we have UI earnings in quarter 0. Thus, we take a sample size hit. Second, it often disagrees with the UI earnings variable. We expect some disagreement because an individual could work in the quarter of random assignment without being employed at the time of random assignment and, in the other direction, because the UI data do not capture all types of employment. But the amount of disagreement seemed too large to us to be due to these factors, particularly in the number of individuals coded as employed at random assignment but with zero UI earnings. On the other hand, the obvious problem with the UI earnings for quarter 0 is the potential inclusion of up to three months of earnings prior to random assignment. We performed the analysis using both definitions of employment at random assignment and decided to present the results with the UI earnings measure of employment in quarter 0 as our main results to keep the sample consistent across outcomes. This choice does not affect the qualitative findings.

Now let us turn to the second choice: what to do with individuals employed at random assignment. Here we see two obvious options: 1) drop such individuals or 2) alter the outcome measure to include maintaining employment as well as finding a job. The former is mildly problematic once we decide to use UI earnings in quarter 0 to measure employment at random assignment, because some of the earnings are post–random assignment rather than pre–random assignment. The former also requires changing the sample relative to that for the other outcomes we consider. Thus, we went with the latter. Doing it the other way does not change the qualitative findings.

Finally, recall that the third choice is what to do about individuals who never find employment when coding up our time-to-employment measure. We could simply drop such individuals, but because the treatment affects this behavior, doing so would induce a selection problem, which we would then have to solve in some way. Instead, we decided to simply code individuals who do not find a job within 12 quarters after random assignment to a value of 13. Given that we assign these individuals a number, the qualitative results do not depend on the particular number within a reasonable range.

In brief, the experimental impact estimates in Table 6.3 reveal substantively and statistically significant effects on employment over the four years following random assignment. For example, the probability of employment in quarters 0 to 4 for the treatment group exceeded that in the control group by almost seven percentage points, while the probability of employment in the 12th quarter after random assignment differed by about four percentage points in the same direction. Despite these employment differences, the data reveal no real earnings differences; given the program's cap on the earnings disregard at the poverty level, this is perhaps not surprising. Bloom et al. (2002) provide much greater detail on many dimensions.[5]

Impact Variance

Appendix Table 6A.2 displays our estimate of the lower bound on the impact standard deviation, calculated using the quantile treatment effects for every percentile of the outcome distribution, as in Heckman, Smith, and Clements (1997); we consider the QTEs themselves a bit later on. For earnings in quarters 0 to 4, the estimates range from 606, for the 24–34 age group, to 1,797, for those 35 and above. Similarly, the estimates for earnings in quarters 0 to 12 range from 1,830 for the 24–34 age group to 4,422 for those 35 and above. The relatively large lower bounds on the impact standard deviations indicate substantial variation in impacts for us to try and capture with our covariates.

Table 6A.2 also provides cutoff values based on the distribution of the impact variance under the null constructed using the experimental control group, as in Appendix E of Heckman, Smith, and Clements (1997). Comparing the estimated lower bound to the cutoffs provides a p-value range from a test of the null of a zero impact variance (i.e., of the common effect model), along the lines discussed in Chapter 3. For the full sample, we can reject this null at the 10 percent level; the smaller sample sizes for the subgroups, combined with the high variance of earnings at the individual level in our population, conspire to prevent us from rejecting the common-effect null at conventional levels for the subgroups.

Bivariate Correlations

Table 6.4 displays the bivariate relationships between subgroup impacts and various outcomes of interest for three subgroups defined by age. In particular, we divide the sample into those aged 23 and below at random assignment, those aged 24–34, and those aged 35 and above. As the overwhelming majority of AFDC recipients in Connecticut (and, indeed, in all other states) are women, it makes little sense to divide the data by sex. Unlike the JTPA and NSW evaluations, the experimental analysis summarized in Bloom et al. (2002) devotes only its Table 5 to subgroup impacts. It then presents such impacts only for one set of subgroups, defined by a measure of economic disadvantage that combines high school or GED completion, welfare histories, and employment experience. Bloom et al. present all of their remaining results for

Table 6.4 Bivariate Results for the Relationship between Experimental Impacts and Positive Participant Evaluation, by Age Group

	Fraction agree time limit led to job sooner	Ever employed		Number of quarters to first job	Maintained or transitioned to employment in:			Ever employed		Earnings	
		Q0 to Q1	Q0 to Q4		Q1	Q1 to Q2	Q1 to Q4	Q0 to Q12	Q12	Q0 to Q4	Q0 to Q12
Under 24	0.3158	0.0128	0.0580*	−0.3672	0.0285	0.0681*	0.0794**	0.0120	0.0276	−682	−1100
		(0.0387)	(0.0339)	(0.3266)	(0.0388)	(0.0384)	(0.0352)	(0.0225)	(0.0371)	(491)	(1469)
24–34	0.2710	0.0225	0.0644**	−0.5507*	0.0398	0.0556	0.0661**	0.0324	0.0150	159	494
		(0.0307)	(0.0284)	(0.3004)	(0.0310)	(0.0308)	(0.0292)	(0.0223)	(0.0303)	(429)	(1279)
Over 34	0.2388	0.0332	0.0801**	−0.8429**	0.0369	0.0584	0.0958***	0.0823**	0.0945**	−6	1656
		(0.0375)	(0.0364)	(0.4082)	(0.0368)	(0.0374)	(0.0368)	(0.0325)	(0.0372)	(543)	(1729)
Full sample	0.2741	0.0232	0.0681***	−0.5972**	0.0358*	0.0603***	0.0793***	0.0425***	0.0426**	−124	391
		(0.0203)	(0.0188)	(0.2001)	(0.0203)	(0.0203)	(0.0193)	(0.0151)	(0.0199)	(279)	(852)
Correlation with "Agree that time limits led to job sooner" [p-value]		−0.9929 [0.0760]	−0.9455 [0.211]	0.9748 [0.1432]	−0.7767 [0.4337]	0.7978 [0.4120]	−0.4692 [0.6891]	−0.9457 [0.2107]	−0.7207 [0.4876]	−0.8164 [0.3919]	−1.000** [0.0024]**

NOTE: The first column presents the fraction of each group with a positive participant evaluation. The remaining columns of the first four rows present experimental impacts for the ten outcomes we consider. Estimated standard errors appear in parentheses. The bottom row presents correlations between the subgroup impacts and the fraction with a positive participant evaluation. *p*-values are from a test of the null that the correlation equals zero appear in square brackets. The sample sizes are as follows: Under 24: 662; 24–34: 1039; and Over 34: 713.
*significant at the 0.10 level; **significant at the 0.05 level; ***significant at the 0.01 level.
SOURCE: Authors' calculations using MDRC Jobs First Public Use File data.

the full treatment and control groups. Without strong guidance from the underlying experimental evaluation, and with a preference for subgroups based on a single underlying variable, we chose to use age to define the subgroups for the bivariate analysis.

The first column of the first three rows of Table 6.4 presents the fraction of each subgroup offering a positive participant evaluation; the number of observations in each subgroup appears in the table notes. This fraction varies substantially across our three age groups, from a high of 0.32 for the youngest group to a low of 0.24 for the oldest group. The fourth row presents the corresponding values for the full sample. The remaining columns present the subgroup impacts for each of the outcome variables and, in the fourth row, the full sample impacts. The final row of the table gives the estimated correlations (based on just three subgroup observations) between the subgroup fractions with a positive participant evaluation and the subgroup impacts.

What we find is not too surprising, and it is consistent with the results in the preceding chapters. The experimental impact estimates reveal modest but not trivial variation among the subgroups. For 8 of the 10 outcome variables, the subgroup impacts correlate negatively with the fraction with a positive participant evaluation. Given the small number of subgroups, the estimated correlations lack precision and, thus, statistical significance.

Subgroup Impacts

We now turn to the multivariate analysis of subgroup impacts based on Equation (3.4). The appendix describes the subgroup variables in greater detail. Briefly, they include marital status (seven categories, including "missing"), number of children (four categories), race/ethnicity (five categories, including "missing"), highest degree attained (six categories, including "missing"), AFDC patterns prior to random assignment (four categories), employment patterns prior to random assignment (five categories), and binary variables for ever having been employed in the eight quarters prior to random assignment, ever having received AFDC in the two years prior to random assignment, and site. When using the full sample, we also include subgroups corresponding to the three age categories. Treating missing values on particular variables as a separate category allows us to retain individuals in the data who would be dropped if we did listwise deletion of item non-responders. For this chapter, we selected the variables used to define the subgroups based on a priori notions of relevance and based on subgroups commonly analyzed in other evaluations.

We depart from the norm somewhat by defining the subgroups based on the employment and AFDC histories using strings of binary statuses. In doing so, we take our inspiration from Card and Sullivan (1988), Heckman and Smith (1999), and, more recently, Dolton and Smith (2011). In the case of the AFDC history, we first code a binary indicator to "Y" or "N" for each of the four calendar quarters prior to the month of random assignment, where "Y" denotes any receipt of AFDC in that quarter and "N" no receipt of AFDC. We then concatenate the four indicators to produce strings such as "YYNN" or "NYNY." We create subgroups for the four most common patterns (YYYY, NNYY, NYYY, and NNNN) and relegate all the remaining strings to an "other" subgroup. We apply a similar scheme to create subgroups defined by strings of quarterly employment indicators.

Table 6.5 displays the results from our multivariate analysis using the subgroup impacts. We examine the same outcomes as in the bivariate analysis of Table 6.4, but now we arrange the results with the outcomes as rows and the subgroups (or full sample) as columns. Each entry in the table represents the coefficient estimate on the participant evaluation variable from a regression like that in Equation (3.4). The final row of the table summarizes the estimates by showing the number having the expected sign (positive for all the outcomes other than quarters to first employment), and the number having the expected sign and differing statistically from zero at either the 10 percent or the 5 percent level.

The findings in Table 6.5, though inconsistent, still stand in marked contrast to the corresponding findings in Chapters 4 and 5. For the oldest of the age-based subgroups, the estimates have the expected sign for all 10 of the outcomes, and they achieve statistical significance at the 10 percent level or better in three cases. For the middle age group, again all 10 of the coefficient estimates have the expected sign, with two statistically distinguishable from zero at conventional levels. Oddly, the results for the youngest age group are quite weak, with only two estimates in the expected direction and no statistically significant estimates in either direction. The estimates for the full sample resemble those for

Table 6.5 Regression Results for the Relationship between Predicted Impacts and Participant Evaluations for 10 Outcomes, by Age Group

	Under 24	24–34	Over 34	Full sample
Ever employed, Quarters 0 to 1	−0.0089	0.0230	0.0272	0.0111
	(0.0330)	(0.0166)	(0.0231)	(0.0076)
Ever employed, Quarters 0 to 4	0.0110	0.0219	0.0310	0.0138**
	(0.0227)	(0.0158)	(0.0203)	(0.0068)
Number of quarters to first job	0.1633	−0.2171	−0.4173*	0.0171
	(0.2403)	(0.1375)	(0.2314)	(0.0135)
Maintained or transitioned to employment in:				
Quarter 1	−0.0077	0.0361	0.0221	0.0169**
	(0.0301)	(0.0223)	(0.0231)	(0.0078)
Quarters 1 to 2	−0.0144	0.0345	0.0416*	0.0201**
	(0.0277)	(0.0210)	(0.0227)	(0.0081)
Quarters 1 to 4	0.0090	0.0284	0.0337	0.0202***
	(0.0226)	(0.0210)	(0.0216)	(0.0075)
Ever employed, Quarters 0 to 12	−0.0249	0.0108	0.0369*	0.0019
	(0.0156)	(0.0100)	(0.0217)	(0.0054)
Ever employed, Quarter 12	−0.0054	0.0274*	0.0375	0.0148**
	(0.0206)	(0.0157)	(0.0307)	(0.0072)
Earnings, Quarters 0 to 4	−18	612**	312	235**
	(343)	(246)	(332)	(112)
Earnings, Quarters 0 to 12	−104	796	962	547*
	(1117)	(605)	(1140)	(304)
Positive (overall/0.10/0.05)	3/0/0	9/2/1	9/2/0	10/7/6
Negative (overall/0.10/0.05)	7/0/0	1/0/0	1/1/0	0/0/0
Expected sign (overall/0.10/0.05)	2/0/0	10/2/1	10/3/0	9/7/6

NOTE: Each cell in the table is the coefficient estimate from a regression of individual predicted impacts based on subgroup variation on individual participant evaluations estimated using the experimental treatment group. Heteroskedasticity-consistent standard errors appear in parentheses. A test of the null of equal coefficients for the three age subgroups was rejected at a 0.05 significance level for 5 of the 10 outcomes. The p-values for this test for the remaining outcomes are as follows: Ever employed, Quarters 0–4: 0.077; Maintained or transitioned to employment in Quarters 1–2: 0.1470; Maintained or transitioned to employment in Quarters 1–4: 0.096; and Ever employed, Quarter 12: 0.2615. The values in the bottom three rows are counts of the number of estimates in each column that are positive, negative, or the expected sign, and, within each set of estimates, the number that are statistically different from zero at the 10 percent and 5 percent levels. *significant at the 0.10 level; **significant at the 0.05 level; ***significant at the 0.01 level.

SOURCE: Authors' calculations using MDRC Jobs First Public Use File data.

the middle age group, with nine estimates in the expected direction but with more statistically significant results, presumably due to the larger sample size.

Even taking into account the fact that we do not have 10 independent estimates but rather 10 correlated estimates, the Jobs First data present a much different picture than the JTPA and NSW data examined in the two preceding chapters. Here we have some real but not overwhelming evidence of a positive association between the participant evaluation measure and program impacts obtained using subgroup variation. Appendix Tables 6A.3 and 6A.4 demonstrate that these findings persist when we change the link between the Likert scale responses and the binary participant evaluation measure. At the end of the chapter, we consider possible reasons for the relatively strong performance of the Jobs First participant evaluation measure.

Quantile Treatment Effects

Tables 6.6, 6.7, and 6.8 present the quantile treatment effect estimates based on Equation (3.3). As discussed in Chapter 3, these estimates derive from differences in percentiles of the treatment and control outcome distributions. Under the assumption of rank preservation, we can interpret these estimates as impacts for individuals with particular values of the untreated outcome and then combine the impact estimates with simple nonparametric estimates of the fraction with a positive participant evaluation for those same individuals. Figures 6.1 to 6.6 display some of the estimates in graphical form.

As in the preceding chapters, our quantile treatment effect analysis focuses on earnings as the outcome variable rather than employment, as quantiles do not provide much additional information in the case of binary variables. In each table, the three pairs of columns correspond to the three subgroups defined by age. The rows (other than the last row) correspond to particular quantiles of the earnings distribution. The left column in each pair presents the QTE for earnings for that quantile, obtained through a simple quantile regression on the treatment indicator. The right column in each pair presents the average, within a window around the percentile in that row, of the binary participant evaluation variable. The window width equals 0.05 for Tables 6.6 and 6.8 and 0.10 for Table 6.7. The final row of each table gives the correlation between the QTE estimates and the fractions with positive participant

Table 6.6 Relationship between Quantile Treatment Effects for Earnings in First Four Quarters and the Percentage with a Positive Participant Evaluation (5% quantile windows)

	Under 24		24–34		Over 34	
	Quantile treatment effects	Fraction positive participant evaluation	Quantile treatment effects	Fraction positive participant evaluation	Quantile treatment effects	Fraction positive participant evaluation
5th	0	0.247	0	0.291	0	0.200
25th	100	0.471	0	0.291	0	0.200
	(103)	(0.125)				
50th	200	0.200	800	0.333	1,500	0.444
	(458)	(0.092)	(522)	(0.098)	(647)	(0.121)
75th	−1,400	0.200	0	0.360	200	0.500
	(761)	(0.107)	(717)	(0.098)	(1,071)	(0.139)
95th	−3,800	0.167	−2,100	0.160	−3,000	0.056
	(1,600)	(0.090)	(1,966)	(0.075)	(2,513)	(0.056)
Correlation with "Agree that time limits led to job sooner"	0.4978		0.2797		0.458	
[p-value]	[0.0301]		[0.2462]		[0.0486]	

NOTE: The values in the left column of the upper panel for each age group are estimated quantile treatment effects on earnings in the first four quarters after RA for selected quantiles. Bootstrap standard errors (based on 1,000 replications) appear in parentheses. The values on the right column of the upper panel for each age group are the means of the participant evaluation variable for treatment group members within a window of width 0.05 around the corresponding quantile of the outcome distribution. The first row of the lower panel displays correlations between the estimated quantile treatment effects and the fraction with a positive participant evaluation, calculated using estimates from 20 quantiles. p-values from tests of the null hypothesis that the population correlation equals zero appear in square brackets.
SOURCE: Authors' calculations using MDRC Jobs First Public Use File data.

evaluations constructed using the estimates (not all of them presented in the table) at every fifth percentile.

Table 6.6 and Figures 6.1 to 6.3 provide a baseline analysis for earnings from the quarter of random assignment to the fourth quarter after

Table 6.7 Relationship between Quantile Treatment Effects for Earnings in First Four Quarters and the Percentage with a Positive Participant Evaluation (10% quantile windows)

	Under 24		24–34		Over 34	
	Quantile treatment effects	Fraction positive participant evaluation	Quantile treatment effects	Fraction positive participant evaluation	Quantile treatment effects	Fraction positive participant evaluation
10th	0	0.247	0	0.291	0	0.200
30th	300	0.500	200	0.380	0	0.200
	(159)	(0.090)	(139)	(0.069)		
50th	200	0.290	800	0.229	1,500	0.389
	(437)	(0.083)	(507)	(0.061)	(652)	(0.082)
70th	−700	0.353	300	0.255	1,000	0.353
	(811)	(0.083)	(764)	(0.062)	(934)	(0.083)
90th	−1,200	0.235	−600	0.173	−2,000	0.176
	(1,933)	(0.074)	(1,119)	(0.053)	(1,951)	(0.066)
Correlation with "Agree that time limits led to job sooner"	0.5802		0.3995		0.5398	
[p-value]	[0.1014]		[0.2868]		[0.1336]	

NOTE: See note for Table 6.6. The only differences from Table 6.6 are that the window width is increased from 0.05 to 0.10 and we use 10 deciles to contruct the correlations.
SOURCE: Authors' calculations using MDRC Jobs First Public Use File data.

random assignment (quarters 0 to 4). At the low end of the earnings distribution, we see the familiar pattern of zero impact estimates resulting from the mass point at zero earnings in both the control and treatment groups. About 27 percent of the treatment group individuals with zero earnings in quarters 0 to 4 indicate that the time limit led them to find a job sooner. These seemingly anomalous responses may result from respondents' finding a job not covered by UI, or finding a job more than 12 months after random assignment but before responding to the participant evaluation question in the follow-up survey around three years after random assignment, or simply from confusion.

Table 6.8 Relationship between Quantile Treatment Effects for Quarters 1 to 12 Earnings and the Percentage with a Positive Participant Evaluation (5% quantile windows)

	Under 24		24–34		Over 34	
	Quantile treatment effects	Fraction positive participant evaluation	Quantile treatment effects	Fraction positive participant evaluation	Quantile treatment effects	Fraction positive participant evaluation
5th	0	0.233	0	0.194	0	0.130
25th	1,100	0.200	1,600	0.400	700	0.118
	(904)	(0.107)	(804)	(0.100)	(488)	(0.081)
50th	−800	0.588	1,700	0.231	7,200	0.316
	(2,014)	(0.123)	(2,255)	(0.084)	(2,279)	(0.110)
75th	−1500	0.444	−900	0.308	5,400	0.375
	(3,324)	(0.121)	(2,492)	(0.092)	(3,572)	(0.125)
95th	−6,500	0.222	−2,600	0.200	−4,900	0.222
	(4,528)	(0.101)	(3,412)	(0.082)	(7,216)	(0.101)
Correlation with "Agree that time limits led to job sooner"	0.1803		0.6609		0.6261	
[p-value]	[0.4601]		[0.0021]		[0.0041]	

NOTE: See note for Table 6.6. The only difference from Table 6.6 is that the outcome measure changes from earnings in the first 4 quarters after RA to earnings in the first 12 quarters after RA.
SOURCE: Authors' calculations using MDRC Jobs First Public Use File data.

Over the remainder of the income distribution, all three age groups show a hill-shaped pattern of impact estimates that peaks around the median and then turns negative (and surprisingly large) for the highest quantiles. The participant evaluations exhibit a similar hill-shaped pattern but with their peak further up the distribution. The fairly large standard errors that accompany the point estimates suggest not putting too much weight on their exact values, but the appearance of the hill-shaped pattern for both the earnings and the participant evaluation variables for all three subgroups is rather striking. Bitler, Gelbach, and Hoynes (2006) find the same hill-shaped pattern in their analyses of earnings impacts in the Jobs First data; see their Figures 3 and 4. They also provide a compelling economic explanation for this pattern of impacts.

Figure 6.1 Quantile Treatment Effects and Participant Evaluations, Earnings Quarters 0 to 12: Under 24

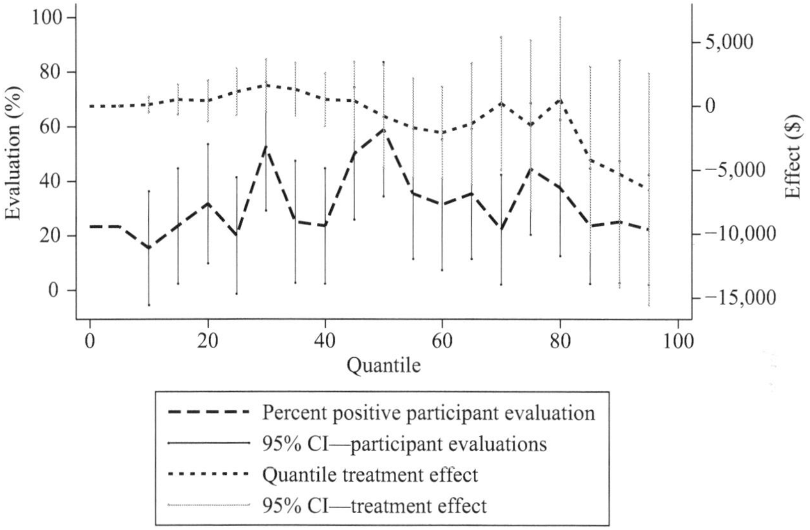

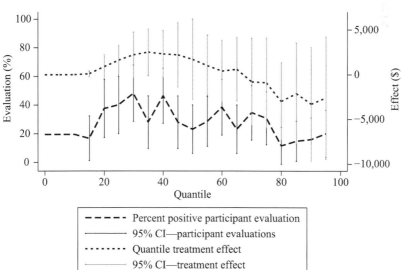

SOURCE: Authors' calculations using MDRC Jobs First Public Use File data.

Figure 6.2 Quantile Treatment Effects and Participant Evaluations, Earnings Quarters 0 to 12: Ages 24 to 34

SOURCE: Authors' calculations using MDRC Jobs First Public Use File data.

Figure 6.3 Quantile Treatment Effects and Participant Evaluations, Earnings Quarters 0 to 12: Ages 35 and Over

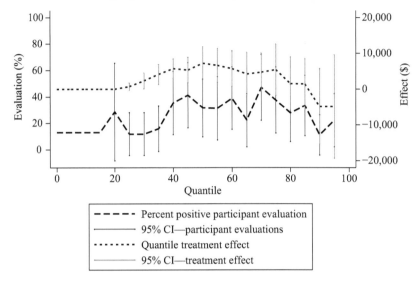

SOURCE: Authors' calculations using MDRC Jobs First Public Use File data.

Figure 6.4 Quantile Treatment Effects and Participant Evaluations, Earnings Quarters 0 to 4: Under 24

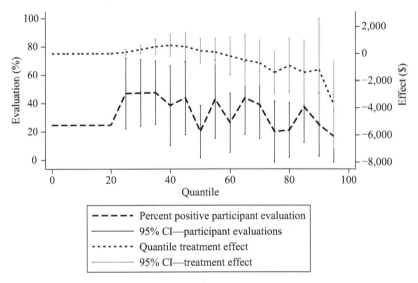

SOURCE: Authors' calculations using MDRC Jobs First Public Use File data.

Figure 6.5 Quantile Treatment Effects and Participant Evaluations, Earnings Quarters 0 to 4: Ages 24 to 34

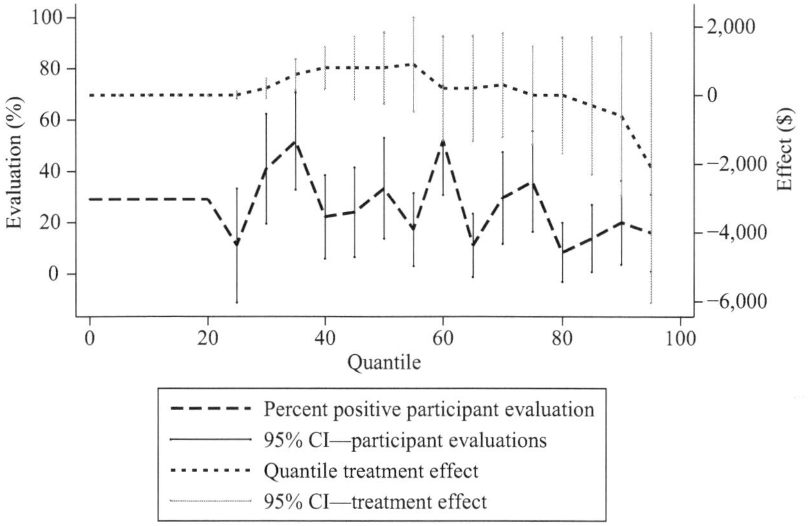

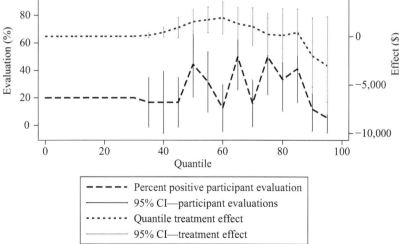

SOURCE: Authors' calculations using MDRC Jobs First Public Use File data.

Figure 6.6 Quantile Treatment Effects and Participant Evaluations, Earnings Quarters 0 to 4: Ages 35 and Over

SOURCE: Authors' calculations using MDRC Jobs First Public Use File data.

In relating earnings impacts to the time it takes for a respondent to find a job, two factors push in opposite directions. All else being equal, individuals who find a job sooner should earn more because they should spend more time employed. But a standard search and matching model of the labor market would indicate that all else is not in fact equal, and that individuals who find a job sooner will end up less well matched to their jobs, and so stay in them a shorter time. A priori, we cannot tell which effect will predominate in the data.

With these interpretational issues in mind, consider the correlations in the bottom row of Table 6.6. All three estimates exceed 0.25, with substantial correlations of 0.50 and 0.46 for the youngest and oldest groups, respectively. Moreover, these two estimates are both statistically different from zero at the 1 percent level. These positive and (mostly) statistically significant correlations reinforce the evidence from the subgroup analysis in support of the proposition that the participant evaluations in the Jobs First data have real content. In the Jobs First context, the participant evaluation responses correlate with impacts based on both of our identification strategies.

We vary the QTE analysis along two dimensions in order to learn about the sensitivity of our findings. First, we vary the number of quantiles at which we calculate estimates. Table 6.7 relies on estimates for every decile of the distribution of earnings in the first four quarters after random assignment rather than every ventile. In addition, in order to obtain more precise estimates of the fraction with a positive participant evaluation, we increase the window width used to calculate this fraction from 0.05 to 0.10 (i.e., 0.05 on either side of each decile). While the estimated standard errors do indeed decline as expected, the basic story does not change.[6]

Second, we change the dependent variable from earnings in quarters 0 to 4 to earnings in quarters 0 to 12. Qualitatively, the findings in Table 6.8 and Figures 6.4 to 6.6 for quarters 0 to 12 strongly resemble those already described for quarters 0 to 4. The hill-shaped patterns for both the quantile treatment effects and the fraction with a positive participant evaluation reappear, though with the peaks now at different points in the distribution for the three subgroups. The QTEs for earnings remain imprecisely estimated while the point estimates (not surprisingly when adding two additional years of earnings to the outcome variable) increase in absolute value. The correlations change substantially for the two younger subgroups, with a decrease for the youngest group and an increase for the middle group, but only modestly increase for the oldest group. All three estimated correlations remain positive and, for the two older groups, statistically different from zero at conventional levels.

As in Chapters 4 and 5, we undertake the test of (an implication of) the rank preservation assumption proposed in Bitler, Gelbach, and Hoynes (2005). Chapter 3 describes the test procedure and the intuition behind the test in greater detail, and Appendix Tables 6A.5 and 6A.6 display the test results using the distributions of earnings in quarters 0 to 4 and 0 to 12, respectively. The Jobs First data yield mixed results. Many of the joint tests reject the rank preservation null for both earnings measures, but almost all of the individual tests fail to reject, and when they do reject, the underlying difference in means is often substantively small. We read these results as suggesting that rank preservation fails, but not so badly as to render the QTE results uninformative or uninteresting.

Testing the Decision Theory Viewpoint

In this subsection, we again consider the (weak) test of the first decision theory viewpoint advanced in Chapter 2. In particular, we use estimates of R_s and P_s from the Jobs First data to test whether or not the relationship in Expression (2.5) holds, under the assumption that $c = 0.5$. Estimates of R_s, the proportion with a positive participant evaluation, appear in the first column of Table 6.4 for the subgroups defined by age and the full sample. Based on these estimates, the bounds on the right-hand side of Expression (2.5) equal [0.1579, 0.6579] for the under-24 age group, [0.1355, 0.6355] for the 24–34 age group, [0.1194, 0.6194] for the over-34 age group, and [0.1371, 0.6371] for the full sample.

Looking first at the "fraction positive" estimates from the subgroup analysis in the top panel of Table 6A.2, the estimates for time to first job lie comfortably inside the interval implied by the decision theory viewpoint in all cases. In contrast, the estimates of the fraction positive for the other outcomes (such as the employment transition measures along with earnings and employment over various intervals) often exceed the upper bound of the intervals. Using the estimates of the fraction positive based on the QTE analysis, where we have estimates only for earnings over quarters 0 to 4 and 0 to 12, we obtain findings similar to those for the same outcomes with the subgroups, namely that they lie near the upper end of the relevant interval or just above it. Overall, recalling that the participant evaluation question refers directly to how long it takes the respondent to find a job, we conclude that the Jobs First data do not provide strong evidence against the first decision theory viewpoint.

Determinants of Positive Participant Evaluations

We now turn to the determinants of a positive participant evaluation in the Jobs First context. Because of the positive associations described above between the participant evaluation measure and impacts on labor market outcomes, we focus here on background characteristics and on measures of service intensity. In particular, we include background variables related to race/ethnicity, marital status, highest educational credential, AFDC receipt histories, employment histories, and site (see Appendix 6A for more details). In addition, we examine two proxy measures, both from the follow-up survey. One measures receipt of job search assistance (e.g., job club or classes in how to look for a job) after random assignment, and the other captures receipt of other training, including skills training. As described above, most Jobs First participants had to participate in job search assistance unless they found a job very early after random assignment. In contrast, individuals typically received skills training only after the failure of a lengthy prior job-search effort.

Several issues complicate the interpretation of the proxies based on service intensity in the Jobs First context relative to the JTPA context in Chapter 4. First, all treatment group members should have received job search assistance, other than those exempt from the Jobs First requirements and those who found a job very quickly after random assignment. As a result, this variable may function in part as a proxy for exemption. Second, as just noted, skills training recipients typically had long and unsuccessful job search experiences prior to receiving their training. As a result, this variable may proxy for unobserved factors related to job market success. Third, as with the JTPA evaluation in Chapter 4, both job search assistance and training may have treatment effects of their own on the time it takes a participant to find a job; we worry about this in particular with job search assistance, which has proven to have sub-stantively small but quite robust employment effects in a large number of evaluations of welfare-to-work programs.

Finally, these self-reported service receipt variables come from a survey administered around three years after random assignment. We know from Smith and Whalley (2020) that respondents in the JTPA study often failed to recall job search assistance only 18 months after random assignment. We would expect even poorer recall at three years and, perhaps, selective recall that in and of itself represents something of a participant evaluation. Put differently, we might expect individuals to recall job search assistance three years on only if it made a particular impression on them at the time, perhaps because they learned a lot from it or found a job quickly or found a better job than what they would have expected. All of these factors complicate a "lay theory" interpretation along the lines of the one we advanced in Chapter 4, whereby respon-dents reason that because they received job search assistance they must have become better at finding a job and so found one more quickly, or because they received (relatively more) expensive skills training they must have become more desirable in the labor market and so found a job more quickly than they otherwise would have.

Table 6.9 contains mean derivatives from logit estimates of Equa-tion (3.5), with the binary participant evaluation measure as the depen-dent variable for the three age subgroups and the full sample. Table 6.10 presents the results of chi-squared tests of nulls that groups of related variables in the logit model have zero coefficients. A test of the null of common coefficients for the three age subgroups fails to reject the null with a p-value of 0.97, but that may represent more of a testament to imprecision than anything else. Empirically, we do not find much in the way of strong patterns from the background variables but do find some evidence related to the service receipt measures. The one factor among the background variables that matters somewhat consistently is the AFDC histories. In particular, individuals new to AFDC (i.e., with a history of "NNNN" indicating no AFDC receipt in the four quarters prior to random assignment) have a lower probability of a positive par-ticipant evaluation in all three age subgroups and in the full sample. The estimates range from −0.04 to −0.11 and differ statistically from zero at the 0.10 level (or better) for the youngest and oldest age groups and in the full sample. Our overall lack of predictors may reflect the relative

Table 6.9 Logit Estimates of the Determinants of a Positive Participant Evaluation, by Age Group

	Under 24	24–34	Over 34	Full sample
Marital status:	−0.093	−0.016	−0.021	−0.023
Ever married	(0.071)	(0.045)	(0.048)	(0.030)
	[0.198]	[0.727]	[0.659]	[0.440]
Race: Black	−0.042	−0.008	0.010	−0.006
	(0.062)	(0.048)	(0.055)	(0.031)
	[0.489]	[0.870]	[0.849]	[0.839]
Race: Hispanic	0.053	0.019	−0.006	0.025
	(0.082)	(0.058)	(0.069)	(0.039)
	[0.515]	[0.736]	[0.926]	[0.523]
Other races	−0.021	−0.068	0.192	0.033
	(0.181)	(0.131)	(0.185)	(0.097)
	[0.895]	[0.638]	[0.377]	[0.744]
Education: GED	0.018	−0.035	0.118	0.024
	(0.081)	(0.057)	(0.094)	(0.043)
	[0.820]	[0.552]	[0.237]	[0.579]
Education: high school diploma	−0.046	−0.089	−0.027	−0.054
	(0.055)	(0.041)	(0.049)	(0.027)
	[0.401]	[0.034]	[0.598]	[0.048]
Education: college and	0.234	−0.084	0.092	0.011
advanced degrees	(0.176)	(0.076)	(0.111)	(0.062)
	[0.21]	[0.272]	[0.421]	[0.865]
Number of children:	0.039	0.028	0.038	0.029
(1 to 7 years old): 2	(0.066)	(0.050)	(0.059)	(0.032)
	[0.555]	[0.581]	[0.524]	[0.383]
Number of children:	−0.096	0.027	0.048	0.011
(1 to 7 years old): 3	(0.074)	(0.051)	(0.059)	(0.033)
	[0.186]	[0.601]	[0.436]	[0.734]
Job search assistance	0.086	0.070	0.117	0.079
	(0.06)	(0.045)	(0.059)	(0.030)
	[0.172]	[0.140]	[0.050]	[0.014]
Other education or training	−0.015	0.032	0.044	0.021
	(0.078)	(0.076)	(0.112)	(0.048)
	[0.847]	[0.668]	[0.692]	[0.662]
Prior AFDC pattern:	−0.110	−0.041	−0.098	−0.089
NNNN	(0.056)	(0.055)	(0.054)	(0.030)
	[0.040]	[0.460]	[0.060]	[0.006]

Table 6.9 (continued)

	Under 24	24–34	Over 34	Full sample
Prior AFDC pattern:	0.326	0.135	0.086	0.185
NNYY	(0.137)	(0.140)	(0.183)	(0.087)
	[0.022]	[0.342]	[0.649]	[0.039]
Prior AFDC pattern:	−0.017	0.099	−0.108	0.005
NYYY	(0.137)	(0.122)	(0.152)	(0.078)
	[0.903]	[0.384]	[0.489]	[0.947]
Prior AFDC pattern:	0.125	−0.035	−0.047	0.010
Other	(0.126)	(0.087)	(0.117)	(0.063)
	[0.313]	[0.696]	[0.726]	[0.878]
Prior employment pattern:	−0.057	−0.076	0.037	−0.042
NNNY or NNYY	(0.086)	(0.056)	(0.107)	(0.044)
	[0.534]	[0.180]	[0.741]	[0.351]
Prior employment pattern:	0.108	0.070	−0.145	0.032
YNNN	(0.134)	(0.130)	(0.093)	(0.075)
	[0.413]	[0.573]	[0.117]	[0.665]
Prior employment pattern:	−0.008	0.092	−0.180	−0.014
YYNN or YYYN	(0.099)	(0.108)	(0.067)	(0.058)
	[0.941]	[0.392]	[0.007]	[0.815]
Prior employment pattern:	0.072	0.057	−0.072	0.020
YYYY	(0.090)	(0.074)	(0.080)	(0.046)
	[0.396]	[0.456]	[0.401]	[0.668]
Prior employment pattern:	−0.008	0.072	−0.129	0.003
Other	(0.072)	(0.069)	(0.080)	(0.043)
	[0.912]	[0.303]	[0.114]	[0.937]
Employed in Year 2, prior to RA	−0.024	−0.112	0.069	−0.039
	(0.058)	(0.046)	(0.077)	(0.032)
	[0.671]	[0.023]	[0.386]	[0.240]
AFDC in Year 2, prior to RA	0.008	0.073	0.007	0.020
	(0.078)	(0.098)	(0.101)	(0.050)
	[0.918]	[0.468]	[0.946]	[0.695]
Site: Manchester	−0.114	−0.040	0.017	−0.039
	(0.061)	(0.044)	(0.062)	(0.031)
	[0.067]	[0.376]	[0.785]	[0.222]
Under 24				0.060
				(0.036)
				[0.101]

(continued)

Table 6.9 (continued)

	Under 24	24–34	Over 34	Full sample
Over 34				−0.023
				(0.030)
				[0.456]

NOTE: Columns report the results from a logit model where the participant evaluation indicator variable is the dependent variable and the categorical variables listed in the row headings are the independent variables. The model is estimated using the experimental treatment group. The values in the table are mean numerical derivatives, with estimated standard errors in parentheses and p-values in square brackets. Indicator variables for missing values of the independent variables are also included in the regressions, but the corresponding estimates are not reported, to save space. The omitted category for marital status is "never married" and the included indicator is for "ever married" or "missing information on marital status." The omitted category for race is "white." The omitted category for education is "no degree." The omitted category for number of children aged 1 to 7 is "one or none." The omitted site is New Haven. The omitted prior AFDC pattern is YYYY, and the omitted prior employment pattern is NNNN. When estimating the regression on the full treatment group, the omitted age group is 24 to 35. The null hypothesis that the three age subgroups have the same coefficients in the logit model cannot be rejected; the p-value from the test equals 0.969. Blank = not applicable.
SOURCE: Authors' calculations using MDRC Jobs First Public Use File data.

homogeneity of the Jobs First participants compared to those in JTPA and NSW.

For the proxy variables, we find large positive effects of self-reported job search assistance for all three subgroups and the full sample; the estimates attain conventional levels of statistical significance for the oldest subgroup and the full sample. The mean derivatives vary from 0.07 to 0.12. For the reasons already described, we hesitate to treat this as strong evidence in favor of a "lay theorist" interpretation, particularly given that we find only quantitatively small, imprecise effects of mixed signs for the self-reported skills training variable. We suspect that these estimated effects have more to do with the sorting into the different types of services and/or selective recall than with individuals using service receipt or service intensity as a proxy for impacts on time to first employment.

**Table 6.10 Test Statistics from Logit Models of the Determinants of
Positive Participant Evaluation, by Demographic Group**

	Under 24	24–34	Over 34	Full sample
Marital status	1.41	0.12	0.19	0.57
	[0.234]	[0.729]	[0.665]	[0.452]
	$R^{*2} = 0.34$	$R^{*2} = 0.02$	$R^{*2} = 0.05$	$R^{*2} = 0.04$
Race	2.00	0.47	1.10	0.88
	[0.572]	[0.926]	[0.777]	[0.829]
	$R^{*2} = 0.48$	$R^{*2} = 0.08$	$R^{*2} = 0.34$	$R^{*2} = 0.06$
Education	3.13	4.76	6.16	7.46
	[0.537]	[0.313]	[0.188]	[0.114]
	$R^{*2} = 0.77$	$R^{*2} = 0.74$	$R^{*2} = 1.51$	$R^{*2} = 0.96$
Kids	2.25	0.40	0.79	0.85
	[0.325]	[0.818]	[0.674]	[0.654]
	$R^{*2} = 0.53$	$R^{*2} = 0.07$	$R^{*2} = 0.21$	$R^{*2} = 0.39$
Training	2.25	2.91	5.22	8.13
	[0.324]	[0.233]	[0.074]	[0.017]
	$R^{*2} = 0.54$	$R^{*2} = 0.47$	$R^{*2} = 1.28$	$R^{*2} = 0.56$
AFDC	13.04	4.35	3.45	16.75
	[0.023]	[0.500]	[0.631]	[0.005]
	$R^{*2} = 2.86$	$R^{*2} = 0.67$	$R^{*2} = 0.92$	$R^{*2} = 1.40$
Employment	2.43	7.42	5.60	2.93
	[0.877]	[0.284]	[0.470]	[0.818]
	$R^{*2} = 0.50$	$R^{*2} = 1.33$	$R^{*2} = 1.38$	$R^{*2} = 0.54$
Site	2.80	0.74	0.08	1.43
	[0.094]	[0.389]	[0.778]	[0.233]
	$R^{*2} = 0.64$	$R^{*2} = 0.13$	$R^{*2} = 0.02$	$R^{*2} = 0.45$
Age category				5.18
				[0.075]
				$R^{*2} = 0.35$

NOTE: Columns report the results from a logit model where the binary participant
evaluation variable is the dependent variable and the categorical variables summarized in the row headings are the independent variables. The values in the table are
chi-square statistics for joint tests of the null that all of the coefficients equal zero for
a given group of variables, with the p-values in brackets. The values for R^{*2} are the
partial pseudo r-squared × 100 of the group of covariates in the row. The regression
is estimated using the experimental treatment group sample. Indicator variables for
missing values for the independent variables are also included in the regressions.
SOURCE: Authors' calculations using MDRC Jobs First Public Use File data.

CONCLUSION

In this chapter, we have examined evidence on the relationship between impacts estimated using two different identifying assumptions and participant evaluations using data from the Connecticut Jobs First evaluation. We also examined correlations between participant evaluations and both observed participant characteristics and measures of service intensity. Unlike the JTPA and NSW data examined in Chapters 4 and 5, we find some evidence of a correlation between both sets of predicted impacts and participant evaluations, particularly for the oldest subgroup of participants and particularly for outcomes closely related to the participant evaluation measure. In contrast, we find only limited evidence of variation in participant evaluations by observed participant characteristics or impact proxies based on service intensity. In the latter case, while having received job search assistance predicts having a positive participant evaluation, institutional features of the Jobs First context make us hesitant to interpret this as evidence of lay theorists at work.

What to make of these findings? As discussed above, the Jobs First participant evaluation measure differs in several ways from the ones we considered for JTPA and NSW: it asks about a more precise outcome, it asks about behavior the respondent has some control over, and it refers more explicitly to a counterfactual. The Jobs First case also differs from the JTPA and NSW cases in other ways, most notably because the primary treatment in Jobs First consists of a change in the budget set rather than some sort of training, though many participants did receive job search assistance. To really pin down the factor or factors driving the notable difference in findings from the Jobs First data would require us to vary some of the factors while holding the others constant. We cannot do that within the context of the three preexisting data sets available to us. As such, we do not draw any strong conclusions here, but in the next chapter we do suggest a research agenda on participant evaluation.

Notes

1. Bloom et al. (2002), Appendix D, provide a detailed analysis of survey non-response.

2. We suffer a very minor loss of balance between the two experimental samples, as we cannot delete control group members who would have failed to provide a usable response to the participant evaluation question, had they been asked it. Given the small number of such observations in the treatment group, we do not expect that this issue affects our results.

3. MDRC produced weights designed to account for the stratified sampling done in the client survey from which we draw our participant evaluation measure. We do not use those weights in our analysis for three interrelated reasons: First, our primary interest is methodological, so we are less interested in generalizing to larger populations than we would be in other contexts. Second, MDRC indicates that use of the weights did not affect its results very much; we have run all of the models other than the quantile regression models both with and without weights and find the same thing. Finally, the software package we used does not allow weights with its quantile regression function; paying the fixed cost of porting the data to another package for one analysis did not seem to us to pass a cost/benefit test. Our failure to use the weights puts a modest damper on the robustness and generalizability of our results. Bloom et al. (2002, Appendix D) describe the survey weights in greater detail.

4. Some 987 control-group members got asked the participant evaluation question because they indicated that they believed themselves subject to a time limit on their AFDC benefit receipt. Some of them, who had moved out of the sites into other parts of the state, were correct; others were just confused. Of the 987 respondents, 237 (24.0 percent) received a 1 in our binary coding, 739 (74.9 percent) received a 0, and 11 (1.1 percent) responded with "don't know" and so were coded as missing. We do not use these responses in our analysis but note that they do affect the interpretation of the experimental impact estimate, as they suggest that some control group members (like some treatment group members) imagined themselves subject to the other arm of the experiment.

5. More broadly, the literature contains a number of surveys and even meta-analyses of the many evaluations of state welfare-to-work programs. See, e.g., Grogger and Karoly (2005).

6. As they should be, the QTEs at the median (the 50th percentile) are the same in Tables 6.6 and 6.7. The standard errors differ because the standard errors for the two tables rely on different bootstrap samples.

Appendix 6A

Sample

Table 6A.1 shows how we get from the raw data to our analysis sample.

Table 6A.1 Estimation Sample

	Jobs First	Control
Full experimental sample	2,396	2,407
Exclusions		
Not included in three-year survey	−1,153	−1,237
Response to participant eval. question: "Don't know" or no answer	−21	
Estimation sample	1,222	1,170

SOURCE: Authors' tabulations using MDRC Jobs First Public Use File data.

Box 6A.1 Variables Used in Construction of Subgroup Impacts

The following variables were used in constructing the subgroup impacts:

Marital status (all indicators)
  Married and together
  Married and not together (but not legally separated)
  Married and legally separated
  Divorced
  Widowed
  Not married (omitted category)
  Marital status missing

Number of children (all indicators)
  Zero (omitted category)
  One
  Two
  Three or more

(continued)

Box 6A.1 (continued)

Race/ethnicity (all indicators)
  White (omitted category)
  Black
  Hispanic
  Other ethnic groups
  Race information missing

Highest degree earned (all indicators)
  No degree (omitted category)
  GED
  High school diploma
  Technical/AA/other two-year degree
  BA/BS
  Degree information missing

AFDC receipt history pattern in four quarters prior to RA (all indicators)
  YYYY (omitted category)
  NNNN
  NNYY
  NYYY
  Any other AFDC pattern

Employment pattern in four quarters prior to RA (all indicators)
  NNYY
  YNNN
  YYNN or YYYN
  YYYY
  NNNN (omitted category)
  Any other employment pattern

Employed in quarters 5–8 prior to RA (indicator)
  Yes
  No (omitted category)

Received any AFDC in quarters 5–8 prior to RA (indicator)
  Yes
  No (omitted category)

(continued)

Box 6A.1 (continued)

Site (one indicator)
  Manchester
  New Haven (omitted category)

Age (full sample only, all indicators)
  Under 24
  24–34 (omitted category)
  Over 34

Box 6A.2 Outcome Variables

We examine the following outcome variables. In all cases, "earnings" refers to UI earnings, "quarter" refers to calendar quarter, and "RA" indicates random assignment. The notation "Q#" refers to the quarter indicated by "#."

Ever employed Q0 or Q1: This is an indicator variable for nonzero earnings in the quarter of RA or the first quarter after RA.

Ever employed Q0 to Q4: This is an indicator variable for nonzero earnings in the quarter of RA or the first four quarters after RA.

Number of quarters to first job: Number of quarters to the first quarter of nonzero earnings following RA. The variable is coded 1 for individuals with nonzero earnings in the quarter of RA and is coded to 13 if there are zero earnings in the quarter of RA and in the first 12 quarters after RA.

Maintained or transitioned to employment in Q1: This is an indicator equal to 1 for individuals with nonzero earnings in the quarter of RA and the first quarter after RA or with zero earnings in the quarter of RA and nonzero earnings in the first quarter after RA and equal to zero otherwise.

Maintained or transitioned to employment in Q1 or Q2: This indicator variable equals 1 for individuals with nonzero earnings in the quarter of RA and either of the first two quarters after RA and for individuals with

(continued)

Box 6A.2 (continued)

zero earnings in the quarter of RA and nonzero earnings in either of the first two quarters after RA.

Maintained or transitioned to employment in Q1 to Q4: This indicator variable is defined in the same way as the preceding one, but through Q4.

Ever employed in Q0 to Q12: This is an indicator variable for nonzero earnings in the quarter of RA or at least 1 of the first 12 quarters after RA.

Ever employed in Q12: This is an indicator variable for nonzero earnings in quarter 12 after RA.

Earnings Q0 to Q4: Total earnings (in $100 increments) in the quarter of RA and in the four quarters after RA.

Earnings Q0 to Q12: Total earnings (in $100 increments) in the quarter of RA and the 12 calendar quarters after RA.

Table 6A.2 Fractions of Positive Predicted Impacts and Impact Variance Lower Bounds

	Under 24	24–34	Over 34	Full sample
Subgroup analysis: fraction positive				
Ever employed, Quarters 0 to 1	0.669	0.575	0.685	0.682
Ever employed, Quarters 0 to 4	0.778	0.703	0.773	0.818
Number of quarters to first job	0.329	0.261	0.236	0.211
Maintained or transitioned to employment in:				
Quarter 1	0.692	0.592	0.668	0.703
Quarters 1 to 2	0.758	0.641	0.721	0.762
Quarters 1 to 4	0.798	0.703	0.770	0.808
Ever employed, Quarters 0 to 12	0.579	0.722	0.742	0.761
Employed in Quarter 12	0.617	0.581	0.710	0.710
Earnings Quarters 0 to 4	0.510	0.628	0.605	0.584
Earnings Quarters 0 to 12	0.568	0.600	0.658	0.629

(continued)

Table 6A.2 (continued)

	Under 24	24–34	Over 34	Full sample
Quantile analysis:				
Earnings, Quarters 0 to 4				
Fraction positive	0.323	0.535	0.495	0.414
Fraction nonnegative	0.576	0.848	0.879	0.707
Impact standard deviation,	1,392	606	1,797	1,057
lower bound	(654)	(373)	(575)	(316)
Cutoff value for $p = 0.50$	1,151	629	1,021	523
Cutoff value for $p = 0.40$	1,298	699	1,120	576
Cutoff value for $p = 0.30$	1,447	781	1,240	639
Cutoff value for $p = 0.20$	1,642	878	1,411	716
Cutoff value for $p = 0.10$	1,933	1,012	1,719	838
Cutoff value for $p = 0.05$	2,193	1,133	2,198	943
Cutoff value for $p = 0.01$	2,786	1,383	3,095	1,166
Earnings, Quarters 0 to 12				
Fraction positive	0.455	0.566	0.657	0.646
Fraction nonnegative	0.556	0.697	0.869	0.788
Impact standard deviation,	2,453	1,830	4,422	2,355
lower bound	(1,103)	(1,067)	(1,552)	(712)
Cutoff value for $p = 0.50$	2,609	1,690	2,915	1,360
Cutoff value for $p = 0.40$	2,884	1,830	3,191	1,483
Cutoff value for $p = 0.30$	3,210	1,997	3,522	1,628
Cutoff value for $p = 0.20$	3,629	2,217	3,976	1,813
Cutoff value for $p = 0.10$	4,241	2,596	4,777	2,108
Cutoff value for $p = 0.05$	4,802	3,007	6,038	2,381
Cutoff value for $p = 0.01$	6,101	3,849	8,825	2,961

NOTE: The fraction with positive predicted impacts based on the subgroup analysis is only among the Jobs First treatment group. For the earnings outcomes based on the quantile analysis, the fraction with positive predicted impacts, as well as the impact standard deviation lower bounds based on the Fréchet-Höffding lower-bound distribution, are calculated using impacts at all 100 percentiles of the outcome distribution. In parentheses are the bootstrapped standard errors of the impact standard deviation lower bound. The cutoff values for the distribution of those standard errors and the standard errors themselves are obtained using a procedure like that in Djebbari and Smith (2008).

SOURCE: Authors' calculations using MDRC Jobs First Public Use File data.

Table 6A.3 Regression Results for the Relationship between Predicted Impacts and Participant Evaluations for 10 Outcomes, by Age Group

Alternative coding of participant evaluation Likert scale, Strongly agree = 1; all other responses = 0

	Under 24	24–34	Over 34	Full sample
Ever employed, Quarters 0 to 1	−0.0070	0.0297*	0.0507	0.0144*
	(0.0358)	(0.0172)	(0.0347)	(0.0086)
Ever employed, Quarters 0 to 4	0.0109	0.0118	0.0587**	0.0125
	(0.0240)	(0.0180)	(0.0292)	(0.0079)
Number of quarters to first job	0.1539	−0.2642*	−0.7824**	−0.1018
	(0.2514)	(0.1475)	(0.3376)	(0.0828)
Maintained or transitioned to employment in:				
Quarter 1	0.0026	0.0284*	0.0501	0.0140
	(0.0351)	(0.0172)	(0.0324)	(0.0086)
Quarters 1 to 2	0.0129	0.0297*	0.0720**	0.0166**
	(0.0320)	(0.0172)	(0.0321)	(0.0087)
Quarters 1 to 4	0.0113	0.0068	0.0467*	0.0111
	(0.0249)	(0.0192)	(0.0257)	(0.0084)
Ever employed, Quarters 0 to 12	−0.0295*	0.0241**	0.0662**	0.0007
	(0.0166)	(0.0104)	(0.0326)	(0.0063)
Ever employed, Quarter 12	−0.0148	−0.0055	0.0776*	0.0074
	(0.0243)	(0.0143)	(0.0435)	(0.0083)
Earnings, Quarters 0 to 4	178	310	558	126
	(369)	(223)	(485)	(125)
Earnings, Quarters 0 to 12	354	−122	2659*	238
	(1237)	(499)	(1464)	(330)
Positive (overall/0.10/0.05)	7/0/0	7/3/1	9/3/3	9/3/0
Negative (overall/0.10/0.05)	3/1/0	1/1/0	1/0/1	1/0/0
Expected sign (overall/0.10/0.05)	6/1/0	8/8/1	10/3/4	10/2/0

NOTE: Each cell in the table is the coefficient estimate from a regression of individual predicted impacts, based on subgroup variation on individual participant evaluations estimated using the experimental treatment group. Heteroskedasticity-consistent standard errors appear in parentheses. The values in the bottom three rows are counts of the number of estimates in each column that are positive, negative, or the expected sign, and, within each set of estimates, the number that are statistically different from zero at the 10 percent and 5 percent levels. * significant at the 0.10 level; ** significant at the 0.05 level; *** significant at the 0.01 level.

SOURCE: Authors' calculations using MDRC Jobs First Public Use File data.

Table 6A.4 Regression Results for the Relationship between Predicted Impacts and Participant Evaluations for 10 Outcomes, by Age Group

Alternative coding of participant evaluation Likert scale, Strongly disagree = 0; all other responses = 1

	Under 24	24–34	Over 34	Full sample
Ever employed, Quarters 0 to 1	0.0043	0.0122	0.0187	0.0093
	(0.0297)	(0.0157)	(0.0209)	(0.0072)
Ever employed, Quarters 0 to 4	0.0226	0.0114	0.0327*	0.0134**
	(0.0207)	(0.0148)	(0.0180)	(0.0064)
Number of quarters to first job	0.0004	−0.1313	−0.4186**	−0.0892
	(0.2229)	(0.1297)	(0.2070)	(0.0686)
Maintained or transitioned to employment in:				
Quarter 1	0.0064	0.0144	0.0136	0.0091
	(0.0294)	(0.0154)	(0.0199)	(0.0073)
Quarters 1 to 2	0.0088	0.0170	0.0339*	0.0139*
	(0.0275)	(0.0146)	(0.0198)	(0.0074)
Quarters 1 to 4	0.0210	0.0111	0.0117	0.0119*
	(0.0214)	(0.0154)	(0.0181)	(0.0069)
Ever employed, Quarters 0 to 12	−0.0115	0.0107	0.0456**	0.0015
	(0.0152)	(0.0095)	(0.0189)	(0.0051)
Ever employed, Quarter 12	0.0004	0.0160	0.0580**	0.0126*
	(0.0194)	(0.0142)	(0.0272)	(0.007)
Earnings, Quarters 0 to 4	−60	511**	187	179*
	(319)	(232)	(316)	(104)
Earnings, Quarters 0 to 12	−18	468	858	345
	(1042)	(561)	(1056)	(289)
Positive (overall/0.10/0.05)	7/0/0	9/0/1	9/2/2	9/4/1
Negative (overall/0.10/0.05)	3/0/0	1/0/0	1/0/1	1/0/0
Expected sign (overall/0.10/0.05)	6/0/0	10/0/1	10/2/3	10/4/1

NOTE: Each cell in the table is the coefficient estimate from a regression of individual predicted impacts, based on subgroup variation on individual participant evaluations estimated using the experimental treatment group. Heteroskedasticity-consistent standard errors appear in parentheses. The values in the bottom three rows are counts of the number of estimates in each column that are positive, negative, or the expected sign, and, within each set of estimates, the number that are statistically different from zero at the 10 percent and 5 percent levels. * significant at the 0.10 level; ** significant at the 0.05 level; *** significant at the 0.01 level.

SOURCE: Authors' calculations using MDRC Jobs First Public Use File data.

188

Table 6A.5 Rank Preservation Tests—Earnings in Quarters 0–4

Full sample	q ≤ 50			50 < q ≤ 75			q > 75		
	Mean diff	90% C.I.	p-value	Mean diff	90% C.I.	p-value	Mean diff	90% C.I.	p-value
Black	0.018	[−0.0414;0.0388]	0.4890	−0.023	[−0.0599;0.0637]	0.5489	−0.045	[−0.0622;0.0593]	0.2475
White	0.018	[−0.0381;0.0393]	0.4830	0.027	[−0.0617;0.0500]	0.4511	0.097	[−0.0589;0.0574]	0.0040
Hispanic	−0.031	[−0.0366;0.0382]	0.1717	−0.010	[−0.0402;0.0434]	0.7226	−0.055	[−0.0511;0.0491]	0.0719
Other ethnicity	0.005	[−0.0068;0.0048]	0.1876	−0.004	[−0.0140;0.0097]	0.6208	0.010	[−0.0103;0.0065]	0.0739
Never married	−0.016	[−0.0414;0.0355]	0.5289	−0.006	[−0.0500;0.0571]	0.8683	0.014	[−0.0575;0.0594]	0.7046
No degree	−0.019	[−0.0446;0.0455]	0.4830	−0.002	[−0.0562;0.0552]	0.9621	0.087	[−0.0546;0.0480]	0.0120
GED	−0.006	[−0.0275;0.0269]	0.7206	0.057	[−0.0445;0.0393]	0.0200	0.023	[−0.0416;0.0411]	0.3852
HS diploma	−0.007	[−0.0457;0.0410]	0.7525	−0.046	[−0.0579;0.0661]	0.2575	−0.079	[−0.0681;0.0593]	0.0519
Tech. diploma	0.030	[−0.0126;0.0135]	0.0020	0.013	[−0.0260;0.0190]	0.3613	−0.023	[−0.0308;0.0304]	0.2236
College degree	0.004	[−0.0106;0.0077]	0.5190	−0.017	[−0.0150;0.0127]	0.0479	−0.005	[−0.0189;0.0155]	0.6766
No children	0.011	[−0.0155;0.0143]	0.2535	−0.011	[−0.0183;0.0157]	0.3333	−0.004	[−0.0145;0.0127]	0.5868
One child	0.007	[−0.0410;0.0441]	0.7804	0.016	[−0.0608;0.0619]	0.6747	−0.010	[−0.0581;0.0654]	0.7884
Two children	−0.010	[−0.0380;0.0357]	0.7226	0.010	[−0.0580;0.0526]	0.7884	−0.027	[−0.0592;0.0487]	0.4172
Three+ children	−0.008	[−0.0405;0.0384]	0.7705	−0.015	[−0.0540;0.0555]	0.6228	0.040	[−0.0552;0.0480]	0.2076
Under 24	0.040	[−0.0403;0.0360]	0.0838	−0.011	[−0.0542;0.0667]	0.7625	−0.030	[−0.0508;0.0517]	0.3473
Age 24-34	−0.007	[−0.0444;0.0434]	0.7984	−0.040	[−0.0735;0.0544]	0.3134	0.029	[−0.0630;0.0656]	0.4172
Over 35	−0.034	[−0.0402;0.0401]	0.1697	0.051	[−0.0574;0.0576]	0.1437	0.001	[−0.0598;0.0489]	0.9741
Manchester	−0.032	[−0.0367;0.0325]	0.1158	0.085	[−0.0593;0.0544]	0.0120	0.048	[−0.0563;0.0601]	0.1677
Chi-square test:									
Statistic	32.614			29.271			33.207		
p-value	0.019			0.045			0.016		

Under 24	$q \leq 50$			$50 < q \leq 75$			$q > 75$		
	Mean diff	90% C.I.	p-value	Mean diff	90% C.I.	p-value	Mean diff	90% C.I.	p-value
Black	−0.017	[−0.0857;0.0742]	0.7645	0.024	[−0.1213;0.0976]	0.7425	−0.098	[−0.1231;0.1250]	0.2056
White	−0.047	[−0.0716;0.0759]	0.2555	−0.113	[−0.1138;0.1363]	0.1477	0.166	[−0.1342;0.1056]	0.0279
Hispanic	0.047	[−0.0788;0.0834]	0.3214	0.068	[−0.1006;0.0906]	0.2495	−0.055	[−0.0905;0.0847]	0.2894
Never married	−0.076	[−0.0430;0.0502]	0.0100	0.009	[−0.0714;0.0797]	0.8523	0.051	[−0.0766;0.0725]	0.3014
No degree	0.026	[−0.0868;0.0839]	0.6208	0.029	[−0.1223;0.1164]	0.7046	0.063	[−0.1081;0.0943]	0.3154
GED	0.028	[−0.0454;0.0474]	0.3034	0.110	[−0.0814;0.0771]	0.0240	0.085	[−0.0736;0.0670]	0.0439
HS diploma	−0.073	[−0.0848;0.0837]	0.1477	−0.082	[−0.1151;0.1121]	0.2595	−0.135	[−0.1126;0.1200]	0.0519
Tech. diploma	0.012	[−0.0189;0.0114]	0.1297	−0.002	[−0.0501;0.0357]	0.9461	−0.006	[−0.0534;0.0449]	0.8443
College degree	0.006	[−0.0126;0.0057]	0.2715	−0.038	[−0.0308;0.0235]	0.0459	0.012	[−0.0256;0.0118]	0.3733
No children	0.023	[−0.0516;0.0465]	0.4411	−0.040	[−0.0525;0.0426]	0.1557	0.009	[−0.0420;0.0353]	0.7605
One child	−0.003	[−0.0857;0.0825]	0.9381	−0.092	[−0.1136;0.0943]	0.1417	−0.004	[−0.1124;0.0951]	0.9421
Two children	−0.045	[−0.0770;0.0646]	0.2994	0.065	[−0.0957;0.0964]	0.2655	0.015	[−0.0896;0.0951]	0.8004
Three+ children	0.025	[−0.0523;0.0555]	0.4571	0.067	[−0.0643;0.0567]	0.0758	−0.019	[−0.0465;0.0460]	0.5309
Manchester	−0.088	[−0.0646;0.0659]	0.0279	−0.001	[−0.1114;0.1122]	0.9760	0.039	[−0.1181;0.1102]	0.5709
Chi-square test:									
Statistic	23.330			25.035			19.891		
p-value	0.077			0.049			0.176		

(continued)

190

Table 6A.5 (continued)

Age 24–34	q ≤ 50			50 < q ≤ 75			q > 75		
	Mean diff	90% C.I.	p-value	Mean diff	90% C.I.	p-value	Mean diff	90% C.I.	p-value
Black	0.011	[−0.0698;0.0632]	0.7964	−0.078	[−0.0955;0.1024]	0.1637	0.030	[−0.0999;0.1019]	0.5828
White	0.050	[−0.0750;0.0668]	0.2335	0.097	[−0.1074;0.0931]	0.1317	0.028	[−0.0871;0.0936]	0.5988
Hispanic	−0.045	[−0.0545;0.0581]	0.1916	−0.016	[−0.0689;0.0730]	0.7206	−0.050	[−0.0826;0.0726]	0.2655
Never married	0.021	[−0.0613;0.0542]	0.5409	0.008	[−0.0814;0.0834]	0.8583	0.026	[−0.0906;0.0805]	0.6208
No degree	−0.064	[−0.0660;0.0620]	0.0978	0.075	[−0.0889;0.0792]	0.1437	0.069	[−0.0736;0.0760]	0.1477
GED	0.000	[−0.0469;0.0418]	0.9920	0.063	[−0.0703;0.0713]	0.1397	−0.030	[−0.0735;0.0633]	0.4631
HS diploma	0.009	[−0.0677;0.0622]	0.8224	−0.119	[−0.0940;0.0875]	0.0319	0.015	[−0.0931;0.0936]	0.7784
Tech. diploma	0.037	[−0.0215;0.0220]	0.0100	0.013	[−0.0472;0.0372]	0.6168	−0.050	[−0.0504;0.0446]	0.0918
College degree	0.015	[−0.0198;0.0148]	0.1457	−0.033	[−0.0261;0.0224]	0.0220	−0.009	[−0.0331;0.0229]	0.6248
No children	0.007	[−0.0194;0.0149]	0.5309	−0.009	[−0.0240;0.0152]	0.3253	0.008	[−0.0160;0.0076]	0.3872
One child	0.068	[−0.0567;0.0584]	0.0599	0.079	[−0.0906;0.0863]	0.1477	−0.025	[−0.0837;0.0794]	0.6427
Two children	−0.048	[−0.0647;0.0615]	0.2096	0.024	[−0.0963;0.0889]	0.6527	−0.043	[−0.0901;0.0857]	0.4411
Three+ children	−0.027	[−0.0700;0.0650]	0.5210	−0.094	[−0.0926;0.0943]	0.0978	0.060	[−0.0890;0.0921]	0.3094
Manchester	0.012	[−0.0557;0.0600]	0.7385	0.120	[−0.0993;0.0794]	0.0240	0.018	[−0.0932;0.0872]	0.7305
Chi-square test:									
Statistic	20.652			20.034			18.091		
p-value	0.148			0.171			0.258		

Over 34	q ≤ 50			50 < q ≤ 75			q > 75		
	Mean diff	90% C.I.	p-value	Mean diff	90% C.I.	p-value	Mean diff	90% C.I.	p-value
Black	0.052	[−0.0811;0.0772]	0.3034	0.022	[−0.1117;0.1136]	0.7545	−0.104	[−0.0976;0.1088]	0.1038
White	0.012	[−0.0801;0.0702]	0.8164	0.053	[−0.1108;0.1286]	0.4291	0.177	[−0.1112;0.1054]	0.0040
Hispanic	−0.057	[−0.0665;0.0735]	0.1836	−0.074	[−0.0752;0.0615]	0.0739	−0.107	[−0.0843;0.0762]	0.0339
Never married	−0.024	[−0.0889;0.0878]	0.6427	−0.095	[−0.1173;0.1088]	0.1657	−0.001	[−0.1076;0.1101]	0.9820
No degree	−0.002	[−0.0778;0.0819]	0.9601	−0.027	[−0.1116;0.1013]	0.7006	0.040	[−0.0835;0.0814]	0.4511
GED	−0.044	[−0.0494;0.0449]	0.1277	−0.006	[−0.0669;0.0708]	0.8882	0.040	[−0.0850;0.0755]	0.3832
HS diploma	0.039	[−0.0801;0.0781]	0.4291	0.001	[−0.1145;0.1218]	0.9880	−0.098	[−0.1150;0.1117]	0.1637
Tech. diploma	0.032	[−0.0240;0.0216]	0.0299	0.021	[−0.0513;0.0440]	0.5130	0.019	[−0.0823;0.0664]	0.6467
College degree	−0.012	[−0.0230;0.0162]	0.3034	0.011	[−0.0230;0.0112]	0.3313	−0.001	[−0.0362;0.0325]	0.9242
No children	0.005	[−0.0174;0.0109]	0.6407	−0.012	[−0.0230;0.0112]	0.1497	−0.012	[−0.0349;0.0222]	0.4232
One child	−0.130	[−0.0824;0.0701]	0.0080	0.035	[−0.1232;0.1082]	0.5888	0.066	[−0.1125;0.1170]	0.3194
Two children	0.130	[−0.0798;0.0738]	0.0060	−0.097	[−0.1051;0.1013]	0.1198	−0.100	[−0.0893;0.1013]	0.0918
Three+ children	−0.005	[−0.0793;0.0750]	0.8982	0.074	[−0.0953;0.1054]	0.2595	0.046	[−0.1064;0.0995]	0.4471
Manchester	−0.043	[−0.0695;0.0617]	0.2715	0.045	[−0.1076;0.0879]	0.3952	0.159	[−0.1002;0.1008]	0.0140
Chi-square test:									
Statistic	26.903			10.953			25.891		
p-value	0.030			0.756			0.039		

NOTE: Mean treatment and control differences, confidence intervals, and p-values are from tests of the null of a zero difference. The final rows of each section give the p-values from Chi-squared tests of the joint null that all of the differences equal zero. Null distributions were derived using methods in Bitler, Gelbach, and Hoynes (2005), who follow Abadie, Angrist, and Imbens (2002). The method for the joint test is also as in Bitler, Gelbach, and Hoynes (2005). See the text for fuller explanation.
SOURCE: Authors' calculations using MDRC Jobs First Public Use File data.

Table 6A.6 Rank Preservation Tests—Earnings Quarters 0–12

Full sample	$q \leq 50$			$50 < q \leq 75$			$q > 75$		
	Mean diff	90% C.I.	p-value	Mean diff	90% C.I.	p-value	Mean diff	90% C.I.	p-value
Black	0.017	[−0.0413;0.0376]	0.5090	−0.065	[−0.0568;0.0654]	0.0838	0.002	[−0.0597;0.0587]	0.9701
White	−0.003	[−0.0435;0.0384]	0.9042	0.075	[−0.0586;0.0627]	0.0399	0.088	[−0.0654;0.0569]	0.0120
Hispanic	−0.020	[−0.0319;0.0385]	0.3573	0.001	[−0.0489;0.0425]	0.9641	−0.086	[−0.0413;0.0473]	0.0060
Other ethnicity	0.008	[−0.0053;0.0032]	0.0120	−0.007	[−0.0144;0.0125]	0.3733	0.006	[−0.0071;0.0064]	0.1657
Never married	−0.009	[−0.0398;0.0378]	0.6946	−0.055	[−0.0527;0.0681]	0.1377	0.047	[−0.0558;0.0559]	0.1876
No degree	−0.009	[−0.0447;0.0443]	0.7665	0.023	[−0.0582;0.0545]	0.4770	0.039	[−0.0472;0.0497]	0.2016
GED	−0.002	[−0.0272;0.0257]	0.9062	0.048	[−0.0404;0.0415]	0.0499	0.022	[−0.0384;0.0408]	0.3273
HS diploma	−0.016	[−0.0465;0.0427]	0.5729	−0.034	[−0.0656;0.0595]	0.3593	−0.073	[−0.0623;0.0624]	0.0539
Tech. diploma	0.025	[−0.0114;0.0121]	0.0020	−0.005	[−0.0238;0.0215]	0.7126	0.005	[−0.0321;0.0298]	0.7665
College degree	0.004	[−0.0088;0.0077]	0.3253	−0.024	[−0.0182;0.0157]	0.0299	0.002	[−0.0195;0.0157]	0.8483
No children	0.008	[−0.0138;0.0132]	0.3812	−0.002	[−0.0221;0.0187]	0.9082	−0.008	[−0.0147;0.0126]	0.3373
One child	0.026	[−0.0399;0.0455]	0.3253	−0.045	[−0.0602;0.0599]	0.2056	0.014	[−0.0512;0.0689]	0.7305
Two children	−0.004	[−0.0377;0.0395]	0.8982	0.026	[−0.0601;0.0563]	0.4671	−0.055	[−0.0594;0.0518]	0.0978
Three+ children	−0.030	[−0.0379;0.0394]	0.2136	0.021	[−0.0532;0.0448]	0.4890	0.050	[−0.0568;0.0551]	0.1397
Under 24	0.042	[−0.0393;0.0383]	0.0758	−0.048	[−0.0572;0.0532]	0.1497	0.003	[−0.0560;0.0541]	0.9222
Age 24–34	−0.001	[−0.0436;0.0417]	0.9741	0.006	[−0.0660;0.0596]	0.8762	−0.028	[−0.0589;0.0605]	0.4431
Over 34	−0.041	[−0.0398;0.0411]	0.0958	0.042	[−0.0479;0.0643]	0.2216	0.024	[−0.0563;0.0518]	0.4671
Manchester	0.010	[−0.0350;0.0354]	0.6447	0.014	[−0.0535;0.0516]	0.6667	0.033	[−0.0590;0.0524]	0.3014
Chi-square test:									
Statistic	34.553			23.016			31.003		
p-value	0.011			0.190			0.029		

Under 24	q ≤ 50			50 < q ≤ 75			q > 75		
	Mean diff	90% C.I.	p-value	Mean diff	90% C.I.	p-value	Mean diff	90% C.I.	p-value
Black	−0.017	[−0.0809;0.0703]	0.7186	−0.038	[−0.1300;0.1098]	0.5968	−0.030	[−0.1228;0.1082]	0.6607
White	−0.041	[−0.0732;0.0787]	0.3473	−0.003	[−0.1187;0.1168]	0.9581	0.040	[−0.1128;0.1110]	0.5808
Hispanic	0.035	[−0.0843;0.0739]	0.4232	0.032	[−0.0827;0.0792]	0.5569	0.003	[−0.1100;0.0927]	0.9401
Never married	−0.058	[−0.0450;0.0451]	0.0499	−0.014	[−0.0758;0.0820]	0.7745	0.034	[−0.0662;0.0748]	0.4491
No degree	0.026	[−0.0955;0.0877]	0.6128	−0.031	[−0.1081;0.1044]	0.6367	0.109	[−0.1119;0.1089]	0.1058
GED	0.029	[−0.0461;0.0425]	0.3214	0.107	[−0.0800;0.0735]	0.0220	0.088	[−0.0744;0.0690]	0.0399
HS diploma	−0.071	[−0.0834;0.0860]	0.1796	0.001	[−0.1135;0.1132]	0.9920	−0.218	[−0.1154;0.1303]	0.0060
Tech. diploma	0.012	[−0.0133;0.0115]	0.1457	−0.003	[−0.0518;0.0345]	0.8982	−0.004	[−0.0537;0.0349]	0.9162
College degree	0.005	[−0.0126;0.0057]	0.2275	−0.038	[−0.0380;0.0230]	0.0499	0.012	[−0.0256;0.0116]	0.4112
No children	0.011	[−0.0438;0.0413]	0.6946	0.006	[−0.0660;0.0563]	0.8862	−0.015	[−0.0523;0.0438]	0.5269
One child	0.029	[−0.0852;0.0790]	0.5469	−0.157	[−0.1211;0.1139]	0.0279	0.002	[−0.1181;0.0963]	0.9780
Two children	−0.030	[−0.0751;0.0704]	0.4611	0.052	[−0.1092;0.1000]	0.3992	−0.005	[−0.0849;0.0808]	0.9401
Three+ children	−0.011	[−0.0525;0.0459]	0.7665	0.100	[−0.0686;0.0688]	0.0140	0.018	[−0.0584;0.0560]	0.6447
Manchester	−0.039	[−0.0653;0.0664]	0.3493	−0.023	[−0.1061;0.1039]	0.7146	−0.035	[−0.1078;0.0927]	0.5768
Chi-square test:									
Statistic	18.58			20.83			16.46		
p-value	0.18			0.11			0.29		

Table 6A.6 (continued)

Ages 24–34	$q \leq 50$			$50 < q \leq 75$			$q > 75$		
	Mean diff	90% C.I.	p-value	Mean diff	90% C.I.	p-value	Mean diff	90% C.I.	p-value
Black	0.010	[−0.0682;0.0647]	0.8184	−0.103	[−0.0931;0.0944]	0.0639	0.061	[−0.1003;0.0917]	0.3014
White	0.044	[−0.0716;0.0710]	0.2914	0.068	[−0.1021;0.0876]	0.2255	0.067	[−0.0890;0.0915]	0.2295
Hispanic	−0.057	[−0.0537;0.0592]	0.1018	0.068	[−0.0862;0.0731]	0.1856	−0.112	[−0.0748;0.0731]	0.0180
Never married	0.003	[−0.0595;0.0592]	0.9341	−0.004	[−0.0852;0.0974]	0.9321	0.075	[−0.0921;0.0807]	0.1637
No degree	−0.032	[−0.0720;0.0653]	0.3932	0.043	[−0.0930;0.0767]	0.4052	0.030	[−0.0720;0.0784]	0.5230
GED	−0.018	[−0.0489;0.0405]	0.5269	0.100	[−0.0648;0.0643]	0.0200	−0.030	[−0.0743;0.0646]	0.4691
HS diploma	0.015	[−0.0675;0.0621]	0.7485	−0.109	[−0.0973;0.0981]	0.0699	0.000	[−0.1002;0.0878]	0.9880
Tech. diploma	0.026	[−0.0208;0.0184]	0.0419	−0.002	[−0.0416;0.0364]	0.9441	−0.011	[−0.0498;0.0440]	0.7265
College degree	0.007	[−0.0159;0.0147]	0.4172	−0.032	[−0.0322;0.0226]	0.0639	0.006	[−0.0337;0.0295]	0.7485
No children	0.011	[−0.0199;0.0149]	0.3613	−0.008	[−0.0244;0.0152]	0.4391	0.000	[−0.0238;0.0150]	0.8503
One child	0.069	[−0.0554;0.0628]	0.0619	0.034	[−0.0908;0.0758]	0.5070	0.021	[−0.0988;0.0911]	0.7365
Two children	−0.019	[−0.0584;0.0592]	0.6208	−0.003	[−0.0936;0.0944]	0.9561	−0.073	[−0.0971;0.0885]	0.2016
Three+ children	−0.061	[−0.0759;0.0619]	0.1337	−0.022	[−0.0815;0.0898]	0.6786	0.053	[−0.0945;0.1017]	0.3752
Manchester	0.047	[−0.0641;0.0559]	0.1996	0.019	[−0.0927;0.0810]	0.7345	0.048	[−0.0852;0.0787]	0.3513
Chi-square test:									
Statistic	12.08			19.00			25.15		
p-value	0.60			0.16			0.03		

Over 34	q ≤ 50			50 < q ≤ 75			q > 75		
	Mean diff	90% C.I.	p-value	Mean diff	90% C.I.	p-value	Mean diff	90% C.I.	p-value
Black	0.065	[−0.0819;0.0782]	0.1677	−0.027	[−0.1201;0.1201]	0.7186	−0.081	[−0.1147;0.1024]	0.2096
White	−0.015	[−0.0797;0.0741]	0.7625	0.127	[−0.1221;0.1037]	0.0659	0.154	[−0.1117;0.1147]	0.0319
Hispanic	−0.050	[−0.0633;0.0657]	0.2355	−0.110	[−0.0931;0.0752]	0.0259	−0.084	[−0.0760;0.0822]	0.0858
Never married	−0.039	[−0.0916;0.0821]	0.4411	−0.088	[−0.1071;0.1140]	0.2096	0.021	[−0.1232;0.1190]	0.7405
No degree	−0.028	[−0.0803;0.0804]	0.5689	0.018	[−0.1010;0.1003]	0.7425	0.049	[−0.0876;0.0858]	0.3633
GED	−0.032	[−0.0495;0.0418]	0.2575	−0.032	[−0.0736;0.0730]	0.4731	0.041	[−0.0750;0.0739]	0.3413
HS diploma	0.041	[−0.0787;0.0789]	0.4212	0.021	[−0.1216;0.1169]	0.7545	−0.121	[−0.1172;0.1211]	0.0938
Tech. diploma	0.044	[−0.0293;0.0209]	0.0060	−0.025	[−0.0521;0.0444]	0.3952	0.042	[−0.0749;0.0664]	0.3174
College degree	−0.012	[−0.0234;0.0162]	0.2754	0.011	[−0.0236;0.0217]	0.5369	−0.001	[−0.0359;0.0325]	0.9202
No children	0.005	[−0.0175;0.0109]	0.5868	−0.012	[−0.0233;0.0111]	0.1477	−0.012	[−0.0349;0.0220]	0.4371
One child	−0.117	[−0.0843;0.0758]	0.0180	0.096	[−0.1348;0.1205]	0.2156	−0.025	[−0.1206;0.1088]	0.7086
Two children	0.099	[−0.0694;0.0752]	0.0200	−0.044	[−0.1056;0.1107]	0.5110	−0.089	[−0.1019;0.1013]	0.1737
Three+ children	0.013	[−0.0805;0.0720]	0.7864	−0.040	[−0.1006;0.1044]	0.5349	0.125	[−0.1071;0.1049]	0.0459
Manchester	−0.020	[−0.0714;0.0574]	0.6148	0.086	[−0.1088;0.0906]	0.1497	0.070	[−0.1021;0.0913]	0.2116
Chi-square test:									
Statistic	24.90			10.43			18.22		
p-value	0.04			0.73			0.20		

NOTE: Mean treatment and control differences, confidence intervals, and p-values are from tests of the null of a zero difference. The final rows of each section give the p-values from Chi-squared tests of the joint null that all of the differences equal zero. Null distributions were derived using methods in Bitler, Gelbach, and Hoynes (2005), who follow Abadie, Angrist, and Imbens (2002). The method for the joint test is also as in Bitler, Gelbach, and Hoynes (2005). See the text for fuller explanation.

SOURCE: Authors' calculations using MDRC Jobs First Public Use File data.

7

Alternatives to Typical
Participant Evaluation Questions

What about the questions themselves—can they be improved? The previous three chapters paint a mostly pessimistic picture of the usefulness of some existing participant evaluation questions. But in those chapters, we have deeply interrogated the usefulness of just three measures, one from each of three program surveys. Perhaps other (better) participant evaluation questions can be found in the same surveys, or in surveys associated with the evaluations of other programs. Alternatively, perhaps we can recommend new and better questions for use in future program surveys or, at a minimum, suggest some desirable features of new questions.

Throughout earlier chapters we have, in passing, noted various features—both good and bad—of the participant evaluation questions we studied. We begin this chapter by bringing those notes together in one place, and then fleshing out the resulting list with other pertinent considerations drawn from the broader literatures in psychology, survey design, and economics. Ultimately, the most fruitful use of participant evaluations would be to provide useful information that the analyst *cannot come by otherwise*. This is the motivating spirit behind Manski's (2004) long-standing interest in the elicitation of expectations and beliefs—an interest long shared by social psychologists and experimental economists: e.g., Kelley and Stahelski (1970); Kuhlman and Wimberley (1976); McKelvey and Page (1990); and Offerman, Sonnemans, and Schram (1996). In technical language, one hopes, ultimately, that such survey responses could replace suspicious identifying assumptions with reliable and useful evaluative information.

While some of our considerations will overlap with other goals, our primary goal in this chapter is to specify question characteristics that lend themselves to *testing the method*: we desire a rigorous evaluation of participant evaluation questions. This requires questions that (we hope) produce results that the analyst can also produce by other means (e.g., subgroup impact estimates based on random assignment).

We attempted this in Chapters 4, 5, and 6, but our evaluations have required auxiliary assumptions—partly because of the characteristics of existing questions. In this chapter, we want to begin by specifying a list of desirable question characteristics—*desiderata*—which, if implemented, could obviate those auxiliary assumptions, thus permitting a cleaner evaluation of the promise of participant evaluation.

With desiderata in hand, we then critically examine existing participant evaluation questions found in a number of surveys. We include the program surveys examined in Chapters 4, 5, and 6 for completeness, but also because (in two of the three data sets) there are other participant evaluation measures we might have scrutinized instead. This puts the three questions we chose to scrutinize into broader perspective. It also illustrates what survey designers have come up with (largely, we think, in the absence of studies such as ours which attempt to provide theoretical guidance on, or empirical examination of, question formats and wordings). We hope readers will agree that we have not picked the "worst" among the available participant evaluation questions!

In the third section, we propose and discuss some alternative participant evaluation questions. Again, our focus will be on questions that will permit an evaluation of the questions themselves—we should be able to make the same measurement by other means, allowing a clean check on the usefulness of question responses. These questions build on our interpretations of our own empirical work, as well as our desiderata. By making these proposals, we hope to advance the literature both by engendering further discussion and by tempting some worthy evaluator out there to actually give new and better questions a try—and an evaluation—in a future program evaluation survey.

DESIDERATA FOR PARTICIPANT EVALUATION QUESTIONS

In Chapters 2 and 3, we discussed several ways of viewing responses to participant evaluation questions, and also some econometric methods for examining some of those views in a critical way. The *subjective rationality* view is, in essence, the worry that in the absence of clear specification of specific outcomes and time periods, respondents may well answer questions about outcomes or time periods that do not correspond to those available to the analyst (or do not interest the analyst). Subjective rationality problems are primarily violations of *mutual outcome correspondence* (Assumption A.1 in Chapter 2); our first desideratum seeks to make that assumption maximally plausible:

> *Desideratum 1: Questions should be clear and specific about both the outcomes and the precise time period the respondent should consider in her answer.*

The ultimate payoff from participant evaluation would come from questions that provide information the analyst cannot get by other means. Recall, however, that we want questions that lend themselves to *testing* participant evaluation methodology, so we desire answers to questions that analysts can check on by using some independent data and method. This leads us to a second desideratum:

> *Desideratum 2: The outcomes and time periods specified in questions should be chosen to correspond precisely to outcomes and time periods that the analyst will be able to estimate using other (independent) data and analysis.*

Note that the first and second desiderata rule out questions about outcomes over an open-ended future (e.g., "Do you think program X will help you achieve outcome Y in the future?"), which, as we will see later, are common in existing surveys.

Satisfaction of Desideratum 2 requires some real planning and thought. We begin by repeating Equation (2.7) from Chapter 2:

$$(7.1) \quad Cov[E(\Delta_i | Z_i), E(\Delta_i | X_i)] = Cov[E(\Delta_i | X_i) + u_i, E(\Delta_i | X_i)]$$
$$= Var[E(\Delta_i | X_i)] \geq 0 .$$

Equation (7.1) is true, provided that $X_i \subseteq Z_i$. Now, recall the interpretation of each term in Equation (7.1). $\Delta_i = Y_i(1) - Y_i(0)$ is the impact of treatment on respondent i, which is inherently unobservable. $E(\Delta_i | Z_i)$ is the conditional expectation of Δ_i given the information Z_i available to respondent i at survey time, and $E(\Delta_i | X_i)$ is the conditional expectation of Δ_i given the information X_i available to the analyst.

Consider the case in which the outcome of interest is continuous—for instance, earnings or months of employment over some time period. We believe that discrete response formats, such as simple yes/no questions, should mostly be avoided in these cases. That is, when Δ_i is continuous, asking respondents to answer questions of the form "Is $E(\Delta_i|Z_i) > k$?" (e.g., whether they think the expected treatment effect is good or not) causes nothing but mischief. This produces a binary yes/no response $R_1 = 1[E(\Delta_i|Z_i) > k]$ and, as extensively discussed in Chapters 2 and 3, substitution of R_1 for $E(\Delta_i|Z_i)$ makes Equation (7.1) false without further auxiliary assumptions. In general, the binary responses R_1 cannot correctly represent the underlying ordering of conditional expectation $E(\Delta_i|Z_i)$ of a continuous Δ_i. That is, the sign of $Cov[R_1, E(\Delta_i|X_i)]$ is not guaranteed to be the same as the sign of $Cov[E(\Delta_i|Z_i), E(\Delta_i|X_i)]$ without extra assumptions (above and beyond the most basic ones)—even if the respondent bases her response R_1 on an unbiased estimate or even a true value of $E(\Delta_i|Z_i)$. Since the nonnegativity of $Cov[E(\Delta_i|Z_i), E(\Delta_i|X_i)]$ is what we want to evaluate, binary responses derived from underlying continuous outcomes do not do the job.

In cases where the outcome of interest is binary or categorical, we cautiously endorse elicitation of beliefs as suggested by Manski (2004) and his collaborators. Such questions would ask participants to report a percentage chance, or perhaps a frequency out of so many cases. We will say more about these kinds of choices later. Again, the purpose is to have a continuous response that can fully represent the underlying expectation $E(\Delta_i|Z_i)$ that appears in $Cov[E(\Delta_i|Z_i), E(\Delta_i|X_i)]$, allowing a test of participant evaluations to proceed with fewer auxiliary assumptions. From these considerations, we can state a third desideratum:

Desideratum 3: Questions should avoid binary or categorical response formats. When the analyst's outcomes are continuous, questions should request a continuous report. When the analyst's outcomes are binary or categorical but the analyst's estimates from those outcomes will be probabilities, questions should request the report of probabilities, percentage chances, or relative frequencies.

Our discussion so far has assumed that participant i will be asked to report $E(\Delta_i|Z_i) = E[Y_i(1)|Z_i] - E[Y_i(0)|Z_i]$ or estimate this. For treated participants, the uncertainty (for both the analyst and participant i) frequently lies wholly with the counterfactual term $E[Y_i(0)|Z_i]$ embedded within $E(\Delta_i|Z_i)$: when "complete outcome resolution" (Assumption A.2 in Chapter 2) holds, the time period in question is wholly in the past and $Y_i(1)$, the treated participant's outcome, is known with certainty. In these cases, questions could ask participants to report either the expected treatment effect or just its counterfactual part $E[Y_i(0)|Z_i]$. Upon reflection, we think it will be most simple and straightforward to ask respondents to report $E[Y_i(0)|Z_i]$.

However, the questions must make it clear that a counterfactual judgment is part (or all) of what is required to respond appropriately. This is our fourth desideratum:

Desideratum 4: Questions should make the counterfactual nature of the desired judgment and response clear to respondents.

The fourth desideratum comes not so much from a priori reasoning as from our own experience reading existing participant evaluation questions. Many existing questions permit interpretations that have nothing at all to do with counterfactuals, and we will point out examples of this in the next section.

EXISTING QUESTIONS

We examine participant evaluation questions from seven completed evaluations in the United States.

These evaluations represent a convenience sample in the sense that we already had, or could easily obtain, the survey instruments for them; at the same time, our discussions with professional evaluators and researchers suggest that they effectively represent current practice.[1] Box 7.1 provides the questions from the experimental evaluation of the National Job Training Partnership Act (JTPA) Study, conducted by Abt Associates and MDRC (formerly Manpower Demonstration Research Corporation) and analyzed in Chapter 4.[2] Box 7.2 shows the questions from the experimental evaluation of the U.S. National Supported Work (NSW) Demonstration analyzed in Chapter 5.[3] Box 7.3 covers the questions from MDRC's experimental evaluation of Florida's Family Tran-

Box 7.1 U.S. National JTPA Study Survey Questions

The following questions were asked on the first follow-up survey (and on the second follow-up survey if the respondent did not complete the first follow-up survey):

(D7) According to (LOCAL JTPA PROGRAM NAME) records, you applied to enter (LOCAL JTPA PROGRAM NAME) in (MONTH/ YEAR OF RANDOM ASSIGNMENT). Did you participate in the program after you applied?

YES (SKIP TO D9)

NO (GO TO D8)

(D9) Do you think that the training or other assistance that you got from the program helped you get a job or perform better on the job?

YES

NO

sition Program (FTP) for welfare recipients. FTP combined time limits on welfare receipt with services and incentives that aimed to smooth the transition from welfare to work.[4] Box 7.4 gives the questions from the experimental evaluation of the Job Search Assistance (JSA) demonstrations conducted by Mathematica Policy Research in Florida and Washington, DC. This program provided structured job search assistance, individualized job search assistance, and individualized job search assistance with training to unemployment insurance claimants.[5] Box 7.5 displays the participant evaluation questions from the experimental evaluation of the U.S. New Chance program, which provided education, training, and other services to teen-mother high school dropouts.[6] The questions in Box 7.6 come from the experimental evaluation of the Connecticut Jobs First (CJF) program, analyzed in Chapter 6.[7] The participant evaluation questions from the U.S. National Job Corps Study (NJCS), conducted by Mathematica Policy Research, appear in Box 7.7. This experimental evaluation estimated the impacts of this intensive (and expensive) program of residential training in occupational and life skills for disadvantaged young people.[8] Box 7.8 presents the cus-

Box 7.2   U.S. National Supported Work Demonstration Survey Questions

This set of questions is asked in the 9-, 18-, 27-, and 36-month follow-up surveys. In these questions, "R" denotes the survey respondent and "SW" stands for "Supported Work."

V0041 Has (SPECIFIC PROGRAM NAME) prepared you to get a regular job outside of the (specific program name) program? **Yes/No**

How did (SPECIFIC PROGRAM NAME) prepare you to get a job? (Note: all **Yes/No**)

V0042 Taught new skills/new trade

V0043 Improved work habits/attitude towards work/got experience working
V0044 Gave R employment history/work record
V0045 Self-confidence/self-esteem
V0046 Provided information about available jobs
V0047 Contacted employers/set up interviews
V0048 Gave references to prospective employers
V0049 Taught how to take job interview/fill out application, etc.
V0050 Other

V0051 Are there any things you didn't like about working at (SPECIFIC PROGRAM NAME)? **Yes/ No**

What didn't you like about it? (Note: all **Yes/No**)
Probe: Anything else
Record R's exact words: code after interview:

V0052 Pay benefits too low
V0053 Didn't like the type of work
V0054 Work is too hard
V0055 No raises/promotions/bonuses
V0056 Hours too long/too much overtime/didn't like hours
V0057 Working conditions
V0058 Supervisor too strict/not understanding/not competent/too much supervision

(continued)

Box 7.2 (continued)

As a result of working at (SW PROGRAM NAME), what would you say (WAS/IS) the most important thing that happened to you?
(Note: all **Yes/No**)
Record R's exact words: code after interview:

V0059 Conflict with boss/staff
V0060 Couldn't get along with crew members/fellow workers
V0061 Didn't like working with ex-addicts/exoffenders/AFDC/youth
V0062 Didn't like the way program was run/politics
V0063 Didn't like attitude of program operators
V0064 Other
V0065 Learned new skills/new trade
V0066 Improved work habits/attitude toward work
V0067 Steady job/steady income/chance to work
V0068 Self-confidence/self-esteem/self-understanding/responsibility
V0069 Stayed out of trouble/off streets/off drugs
V0070 Opportunity for advancement
V0071 Helped get job/school/training after SW
V0072 Met new people/made friends
V0073 Didn't like SW/some type of bad experience with program
V0074 Nothing
V0075 Other

tomer satisfaction measures used as part of the performance standards system of the U.S. Workforce Investment Act (WIA).[9] Until replaced by the Workforce Innovation and Opportunity Act (WIOA) in 2015, WIA was the largest federal program providing employment and training services to the disadvantaged and the unemployed.

Though by no means exhaustive, we believe that our selection gives a reasonable overview of the types of questions favored by current practice. The remainder of this section provides a typology of these questions as well as theoretical and empirical comments on each type, and notes whether our four desiderata are satisfied by any of these questions.

Box 7.3 Florida Family Transition Program (FTP) Survey Questions

The following questions are asked on the 24-month follow-up survey. In these questions, "CM" stands for "Case Manager" while "PI" stands for "Project Independence."

L1pat   Participant of FTP?
L1a   Received health care services
L2a   Value of health care services
L1b   Received mental health service
L2b   Value of mental health service
L1c   Received help paying for child care
L2c   Value of help paying for child care
L1d   Received advice from FTP CM
L2d   Value of advice from FTP CM
L1e   Received advice from PI worker
L2e   Value of advice from PI worker
L1f   Received help paying for gas or bus fare
L2f   Value of help paying for gas or bus fare
L1g   Received help paying for car repairs
L2g   Value of help paying for car repairs
L1h   Received help looking for job
L2h   Value of help looking for job
L1i   Received education or training
L2i   Value of education or training
L1j   Received substance abuse services
L2j   Value of substance abuse services

NOTE: The received variables are binary, and the "value" variables range from 1 to 3, in which a response of "1" indicates "very valuable," a response of "2" indicates "somewhat valuable," a response of "3" indicates "not very valuable," and missing values are coded as "8."

Recall of Service Receipt

Several questions simply ask participants whether they remember participating in the program or receiving particular services within the program. Question D7 in the JTPA evaluation in Box 7.1 provides a prime example. Many of the questions from CJF fit into this category

Box 7.4   Florida and Washington, DC, Job Search Assistance Demonstration Survey Questions

The following questions are asked in the follow-up survey 12 months after enrollment:

<D8> According to [FILL IN DC/FL] Unemployment Insurance agency records, after you lost your job around [FILL IN CLAIM MONTH AND YEAR], you participated in a job search workshop which was conducted as part of a special unemployment program called the Job Search Assistance program.

In your opinion, was the job search workshop very useful, somewhat useful, or not useful to you in defining your job skills and goals?

PROBE: The workshop taught you how to look for a job.

<1>   VERY USEFUL
<2>   SOMEWHAT USEFUL
<3>   NOT USEFUL
<4>   DON'T KNOW WHAT YOU ARE TALKING ABOUT/
       NEVER HEARD OF JOB SEARCH ASSISTANCE/NEVER
       HEARD OF JSA [go to D13]

<8>   DON'T KNOW
<9>   REFUSED

<D9> Was the Job Search Workshop very useful, somewhat useful, or not useful to you in preparing your job resume?

<1>   VERY USEFUL
<2>   SOMEWHAT USEFUL
<3>   NOT USEFUL

<8>   DON'T KNOW
<9>   REFUSED

Box 7.4 (continued)

<D10> How about in looking for and finding job openings—was it very useful, somewhat useful or not useful to you in looking for and finding job openings?

<1>   VERY USEFUL
<2>   SOMEWHAT USEFUL
<3>   NOT USEFUL

<8>   DON'T KNOW
<9>   REFUSED

<D11> Was the workshop useful to you [FILL IN "at all/in any other ways"]?

<1>   YES
<2>   NO [go to D13]

<8>   DON'T KNOW
<9>   REFUSED

<D12> If <1>, ASK: How was it useful?

<1>   TO SPECIFY AND END WITH [specify]

<8>   DON'T KNOW
<9>   REFUSED

<D17> In general, would you say that the interview was very useful, somewhat useful, or not useful to you in planning your work future?

<1>   VERY USEFUL
<2>   SOMEWHAT USEFUL
<3>   NOT USEFUL

<8>   DON'T KNOW
<9>   REFUSED

(continued)

Box 7.4 (continued)

<D39> Would you say that the [Job Resource] Center was very useful, somewhat useful, or not useful to you in finding suitable job openings?

<1>   VERY USEFUL
<2>   SOMEWHAT USEFUL
<3>   NOT USEFUL

<8>   DON'T KNOW
<9>   REFUSED

<D40> Why wasn't it useful?

INTERVIEWER: CODE ONE ONLY

INTERVIEWER: IF MORE THAN ONE REASON, PROBE: What was the main reason?

<1>   DID NOT HAVE ANY JOB OPENINGS
<2>   DID NOT HAVE SUITABLE JOB OPENINGS/DID NOT HAVE JOB OPENINGS IN MY FIELD
<3>   DID NOT HAVE SUITABLE MATERIALS/ENOUGH MATERIALS
<4>   DID NOT HAVE SUITABLE SPACE/ENOUGH SPACE
<5>   DID NOT OFFER INDIVIDUAL ATTENTION/NEEDED INDIVIDUAL ATTENTION
<6>   OTHER [specify]

<8>   DON'T KNOW
<9>   REFUSED

<D45> In your opinion, how helpful were the Job Search Assistance program activities in finding a job? Would you say...

<1>   VERY HELPFUL
<2>   SOMEWHAT HELPFUL
<3>   NOT VERY HELPFUL
<4>   NOT HELPFUL AT ALL

<8>   DON'T KNOW
<9>   REFUSED

Box 7.5 U.S. New Chance Program Survey Questions

The following questions were asked on the Wave I survey:

Q.75 On the 0 to 10 scale, where 0 means "not at all" and 10 means "the most possible," how much do you think (ACTIVITY) at (INSTITUTION) will actually help your chances for employment in the long run?

00 — not at all
10 — The most possible
98 — Don't know
99 — No answer
Blank = inapplicable, coded 2 in Q.66a-e or coded 1 in Q.71 or coded 2 in col. 30, Card 01.

Q.76 On the 0 to 10 scale, if a friend of yours wanted to get similar (education/training) and could choose any program, how much would you encourage her to choose (ACTIVITY) at (INSTITUTION)?

00 — Not at all
10 — The most possible
98 — Don't know
99 — No answer
Blank = inapplicable, coded 2 in Q.66a-e or coded 1 in Q.71 or coded 2 in col. 30, Card 01.

Q. 89 Did a program called (New Chance/LOCAL NAME) help you locate this job?

1 — Yes
2 — No
8 — Don't know
9 — No answer
Blank = inapplicable, coded 2 in col. 16 or coded 2 in col. 29, Card 01.

The following questions were asked on the Wave II survey:

309. Using the 0 to 10 scale, where 0 is completely dissatisfied and 10 is completely satisfied, how satisfied were you overall with the (New Chance/LOCAL NAME) program?

(continued)

Box 7.5 (continued)

309. (continued)

00 — Completely dissatisfied
10 — Completely satisfied
97 — Refused
99 — No answer
Blank = inapplicable, coded 2 in col. 29, Card 01, or coded 9995 in cols. 71–74, Card 18.

314. What kind of an effect would you say the (New Chance/LOCAL NAME) program has had on your life? Would you say:

1 — Very positive
2 — Somewhat positive
3 — Somewhat negative
4 — Very negative
5 — No effect at all
9 — No answer
Blank = inapplicable, coded 2 in col. 29, Card 01, or coded 9995 in cols. 71–74, Card 18.

---

as well, though there is some ambiguity because it is not clear that all participants should have received all the services they ask about. Failure to recall one's own participation, or failure to recall a service one in fact received, might be a powerful evaluative statement in and of itself.

For instance, JTPA Question D7 is meant to be a gateway question for a subsequent participant evaluation question of the second type (D9, discussed in the following section). In the JTPA data, 25 percent of those treatment group members who enrolled in the program did not recall having participated in the program when responding to this question. Both Heckman and Smith (1998) and Philipson and Hedges (1998) use program dropout as a direct behavioral participant evaluation, and one could imagine using recall failures in a similar manner.

Still, both failure of recall and dropout are crude evaluative measures, because both will reflect factors other than a negative or indif-

Box 7.6 Connecticut Jobs First Program Survey Questions

The following questions were asked on the 36-month follow-up survey:

(2750–2759) **I-2.** I'm going to read you several statements about your experience with the welfare system since random assignment date (RAD). For each one, tell me whether you agree a lot, agree a little, disagree a little, or disagree a lot.

2750 **I-2a.** I received help that improved my long-term chances of getting or keeping a job. Do you:
   Range: 1 Agree a lot
       2 Agree a little
       3 Disagree a little
       4 Disagree a lot
       7 Don't know
       9 No answer
       Blank — If I-1 = 2, 7
   Rules: If missing (I-2a is blank and I-1 = 1), edit I-2a to 9 for "No answer."

2751 **I-2b.** The staff took the time to get to know me and my particular situation. Do you:
   See range and rules for I-2a.

2752 **I-2c.** The staff urged me to get education or training to improve my skills. Do you:
   See range and rules for I-2a.

2753 **I-2d.** The staff pushed me to get off welfare quickly. Do you:
   See range and rules for I-2a.

2754 **I-2e.** The staff urged me to get a job as quickly as possible. Do you:
   See range and rules for I-2a.

2755 **I-2f.** It was easy to stay on welfare without taking part in any activities to prepare for employment. Do you:
   See range and rules for I-2a.

(continued)

Box 7.6 (continued)

2756   **I-2g.** The staff gave me useful information about how to find child care. Do you:

<blockquote>
Range: 1 Agree a lot
       2 Agree a little
       3 Disagree a little
       4 Disagree a lot
       5 Does not apply
       7 Don't know
       9 No answer
Blank — If I-1 = 2, 7
Rules: If missing (I-2g is blank and I-1 = 1), edit I-2g to 9 for "No answer."
</blockquote>

2757   **I-2h.** The staff gave me useful information about how to pay for child care. Do you:
See range and rules for I-2g.

2758   **I-2i.** The staff told me that working would make me better off financially. Do you:
See range and rules for I-2g.

2759   **I-2j.** The staff told me I will be allowed to keep all or part of my welfare benefits if I find a job. Do you:
See range and rules for I-2a.

---

ferent evaluation of a program or service. Typical program participants have likely had many more interactions with local, state, and federal agencies and social service providers than readers of this book. Such participants may find it hard to call to mind any particular interaction with these agencies and providers. Additionally, recall from Chapter 2 that participants in social psychology experiments are frequently influenced by treatments they cannot or do not recall in retrospective debriefing (Nisbett and Wilson 1977). For all these reasons, we think nonrecall of provided services or participation is at best an extremely crude "evaluation."

Box 7.7 U.S. National Job Corps Study Survey Questions

Survey questions (baseline survey):

The baseline survey was administered "soon after" random assignment. Most interviews were by phone, but in-person interviews were attempted if there was no contact after 45 days.

E24. How much were you expecting to earn per hour after completing your Job Corps training?

E35. How much do you think that Job Corps could help provide training for a specific job? [Would you say a lot, a little, or not at all?]

A lot	01
A little	02
Not at all	03

Survey questions (12-month and 30-month follow-up surveys):

B72. Would you recommend that a friend go to Job Corps?

Yes	01
No	02
Don't know	03

B73. How strongly would you recommend that a friend go to Job Corps? Would you say very strongly or not so strongly?

Very strongly	01
Not so strongly	02

B74. Why would you not (strongly) recommend Jobs Corps to your friends?

NOTE: There are also a few questions about very specific parts of the program (i.e., if you had parenting classes, did these classes help you become a better parent?). These questions generally evaluate program components that we expect will be only very weakly correlated with program impacts on wages, employment, or earnings.

Box 7.8 Workforce Investment Act (WIA) Customer Satisfaction Survey Questions

The performance management system for WIA relied on the following questions:

1) Utilizing a scale of 1 to 10, where "1" means "Very dissatisfied" and "10" means "Very satisfied," what is your overall satisfaction with the services provided from [LOCAL PROVIDER NAME]?

Very dissatisfied								Very satisfied	
1	2	3	4	5	6	7	8	9	10

2) Considering all the expectations you may have had about the services, to what extent have the services met your expectations? "1" now means "Falls short of your expectations" and "10" means "Exceeds your expectations."

Falls short of expectations								Exceeds expectations	
1	2	3	4	5	6	7	8	9	10

3) Now think of the ideal program for people in your circumstances. How well do you think the services you received compare with the ideal set of services? "1" now means "Not very close to the ideal" and "10" means "Very close to the ideal."

Not close to ideal								Very close to ideal	
1	2	3	4	5	6	7	8	9	10

There is a sense in which some of these recall questions partially satisfy our first and second desiderata for questions (they are clear and specific, and they deal with events during a particular time). However, these recall questions are about memory of treatment variables, rather than outcomes of interest to an analyst or a policymaker. Moreover, they are binary and categorical judgments that do not satisfy our third desideratum (a continuous response format).

Questions about Program Value

The most common questions in our tables are broad subjective evaluation questions about the value of the program, usually (but not always) about whether a program or service helped the participant get or keep a job. Examples include Question D9 from the JTPA evaluation in Box 7.1, Question V0041 from the NSW evaluation in Box 7.2, Question D45 from the JSA evaluation in Box 7.4, Questions 75, 89, and 314 from the New Chance evaluation in Box 7.5, Question 2750 from the CJF evaluation in Box 7.6, and Questions E24 and E35 from the NJCS in Box 7.7.

Most of these questions have the same basic format as Question D9 from the JTPA study: they ask whether the program helped the respondent get or keep a job or, in the case of New Chance Question 75, increased the respondent's chances for employment in the long run. Four questions vary this theme. Job Corps Questions E24 and E35 are ex ante participant evaluations: respondents indicate, around the time of random assignment, what they expect to earn after completing Job Corps and whether they think that "Job Corps could provide training for a specific job." New Chance Question 89 asks treatment-group members who have been employed since the date of random assignment whether the program helped them get the specific postrandom assignment job they held. Finally, New Chance Question 314 takes a holistic (and rather optimistic) approach and asks about the overall effect of the program on the respondent's life.

Chapter 4 examined in some depth the relationship between responses to the combination of Questions D7 and D9 from the JTPA evaluation (Box 7.1) and experimental and econometric estimates of program impacts. We find essentially no relationship between estimated impacts and a participant evaluation variable equal to the product of the two responses. Our findings in Chapter 4 confirm the very limited analysis of the same questions in Heckman and Smith (1998). We do find variables that account for some of the variation in the participant evaluations. In particular, indicator variables for sites, service type, outcome levels, and before-after changes in outcomes all correlate with the participant responses. We interpret the effects of the sites as picking up variation in program organization and service quality among the 16 sites in the experiment. The service-type variable indicates a higher fraction of positive responses for services that cost more to provide. Respondents, acting as lay theorists, may think that more inputs mean a larger impact on their employment chances.

Finally, the effect of outcome levels (and of before-after changes) may reflect hindsight bias, as in Markman and McMullen (2003). In this case, respondents apply a simple "post hoc ergo propter hoc" line of reasoning and assume that if they have a job now, and they just participated in the program, the one must result from the other. A similar line of reasoning holds for respondents without a job (who thereby likely infer correctly, at least on average, that the program had little if any impact on their employment outcomes). Indeed, the one glimmer of a relationship found in Chapter 4 concerns adult women (ages 22 and above) with zero earnings in the 18 months after random assignment, who have a lower (but still surprisingly high) level of positive responses to the combination of Questions D7 and D9 (Box 7.1) than do women with some positive earnings.

We see two main problems with these kinds of questions. First, none of these questions *explicitly* ask participants about counterfactuals (thus, they do not satisfy our fourth desideratum). As tools for impact evaluation, this might be an important oversight, especially if there are plausible, natural-language interpretations of the questions having nothing to do with counterfactual reasoning. For instance, a respondent placed in a specific job as a clear consequence of some particular JTPA service can truthfully respond in the affirmative to both Questions D7 and D9 even if, *had she not participated in JTPA*, she would have gone to work in the family business instead. This respondent's actual employment impact equals zero, but Questions D7 and D9 have no unambiguous way to get at that: nothing compels participants to read Question D9 as a request for a counterfactual consideration. We will see more examples of violations of our fourth desideratum below. Later, we suggest alternative question formulations that attempt to compel counterfactual consideration.

Second, many of these questions are too general to substitute for formal impact estimates. Put differently, many of these questions fail our first and second desiderata: they are not about specific outcomes, over specific time periods, that the analyst will be able to estimate by other means. Perhaps holistic "whole life" effects of programs are important to some policymakers. If so, questions like New Chance Question 314 should remain in follow-up surveys. But these are the least likely substitutes for formal estimates of impacts on very specific employment and earnings outcomes precisely because they may reflect a large set of considerations—considerations that, moreover, likely vary substantially across participants. We will return to this theme below when we suggest some alternative question formulations.

Finally, almost all of these questions use a binary or categorical response format, so they cannot satisfy our third desideratum, which calls for continuous response formats. There is one clear exception, and that is question E24 in the Job Corps Study (Box 7.7), which asks respondents how much they expect to earn per hour after completing Job Corps. There are near exceptions, too: New Chance Question 75 in Box 7.5 reads, "On the 0 to 10 scale, where 0 means 'not at all' and 10 means 'the most possible,' how much do you think (ACTIVITY) at (INSTITUTION) will actually help your chances for employment in the long run?" While this kind of response format moves in the right direction, it is not actually a probability response (a percent chance or frequency) but rather an ordinal expression of degree of belief—in principle, not that different from asking for a report on some ordinal verbal belief scale (e.g., "very likely," "likely," "toss-up," "unlikely," or "very unlikely"). Within a given individual, such responses can show very good coherence and calibration (Wallsten, Budescu, and Zwick 1993). However, there is substantial variance *between* individuals in the use of such ordinal belief scales (Mosteller and Youtz 1990). In the absence of information about each individual's use of such scales, it is difficult for an analyst to combine their separate judgments onto a meaningful cardinal probability scale.

Customer Satisfaction

The third category consists of customer satisfaction questions. This category includes Question 309 from the New Chance evaluation in Box 7.5 as well as the WIA performance measures in Box 7.8. These sorts of questions draw on a large literature in business on how to measure customer satisfaction; see Vavra (1997) for an introductory book on the subject. The WIA questions come from a firm (with ties to the Ross School of Business at the University of Michigan) called CFI International, which also produces the American Customer Satisfaction Index.[10] As noted in Merz (2007), the WIA measures have two main advantages over simple binary satisfaction measures like that used in the New Chance evaluation. First, the use of 1-to-10 scales allows a much more nuanced response and so provides more information about the degree of satisfaction. Second, the use of multiple measures (which can then be combined psychometrically into a single "scale" of satisfaction) should increase *construct validity*—the degree to which the resulting single measure corresponds to the concept of interest. Although such scales are based on several ordinal categorical responses, they can and frequently are treated like cardinal and continuous measures, so multiple measures in these response formats do move in the direction of satisfying our third desideratum (continuous-response formats).

These customer-service questions exhibit the same two problems we discussed above. First, with the exception of the third WIA question, they do not satisfy our fourth desideratum. That is, they do not explicitly ask respondents to consider a counterfactual. Was the participant more satisfied with the program than his or her best alternative and, if so, by how much? Or instead: How satisfying would your best alternative use of the time have been? The third WIA question does ask about a counterfactual, but it asks about the respondent's ideal program, not his or her best real-world alternative activity, and so has limited relevance for an impact evaluation (though it might, of course, have relevance to other things). Second, we again see a failure to satisfy our first and second desiderata. The satisfaction questions are too general: they may reflect a number of outcomes and not necessarily those of interest to the evaluator. A program participant might be satisfied with the program for many reasons, both relevant (it got her a job) and irrelevant (she made new friends) to the formal evaluator or policymaker. Finally, we do not know of any research linking customer-satisfaction measures to econometric or experimental estimates of program impact.

Recommend to Others

The fourth category of participant evaluation questions asks the respondent whether he or she would recommend the program to other people. New Chance Question 76 in Box 7.5 asks the respondent whether he or she would recommend the program to a friend who wanted to obtain such services. In contrast, NJCS Questions B72 and B73 in Box 7.7 ask about whether the respondent would recommend the Job Corps to a friend, with no mention of whether the friend was interested in such things, and, if so, how strongly the respondent would recommend it.

We do not know of any research that links the responses on such questions to program impacts. Inspection of the questions reveals several important difficulties. First, the questions yield only a binary (or in the case of the NJCS questions, a trinary) evaluation of the program. Thus, they do not help with a cost-benefit calculation, and, moreover, they do not satisfy our third desideratum, which calls for continuous-response formats. Second, they do not ask the respondent to indicate the reason for recommending or not recommending the program. As ever, respondents might have many reasons for recommending or not recommending a program, only some of which have to do with the impacts on employment and earnings that constitute the usual concerns of evaluators. Third, the questions are (again) too general, leaving many policy-relevant details unspecified. In the case of the New Chance question, the respondent learns that his or her friend is interested in similar programs but has no opportunity to respond (as he or she might well do, given the general pattern of findings in the evaluation literature on programs for youth) that all such programs are a waste of time. In contrast, the NJCS question does not ask the respondent to condition his or her recommendation on the friend having expressed interest in such programs. As a result, the respondent may interpret the question as asking whether he or she would recommend it to a friend without any indication of interest from that friend. For shy or polite respondents, or respondents who have a lot of stable, happy, employed friends who do not have much reason to want the services that Job Corps provides, the answer may well be no, even if the respondent feels that he or she had a positive impact from the program.

Subjective Evaluation of Particular Program Components

The final category of participant evaluation questions asks respondents to provide their subjective evaluations of particular program components or of the effect of the program on specific areas of knowledge or activity. Examples include NSW Questions V0051–V0075 in Box 7.2, the second in every pair of FTP questions in Box 7.3, all of the JSA questions in Box 7.4 other than Question D45, CJF Questions 2751–2759 in Box 7.6, and a long list of questions in the NJCS that we have omitted from Box 7.7 for reasons of space.

Some of these questions seem straightforward, and we have no complaint about them other than that they cannot be used as a substitute for econometric or experimental estimates of program impact. For example, the CJF questions in Box 7.6 ask directly about whether the staff did and said certain things during the respondent's participation in the program. The particular things that may have been done or said are reasonably well defined, and the respondent will have perceived personally (and may remember) whether or not they occurred. We cannot complain about generality here. But at best these questions indicate whether the program's inputs (staff actions) were as intended by program designers. Participants are not asked whether those inputs had specific effects relevant to program evaluators and policymakers. The questions are not about outcomes at all, but rather they seek to address the important, but substantively distinct, issue of implementation fidelity—that is, they seek to measure whether or not participants experienced the program as its designers intended.

The FTP questions in Box 7.3 and the JSA questions in Box 7.4 are also about specific program services, but these ask participants to rate the subjective value, usefulness, or helpfulness of these services. To our mind, the FTP questions do not define "value" narrowly enough (valuable for what?) to avoid the common problem of overly general questions we have discussed above. A few of the JSA questions come close to being clear and specific, but, again, they ask whether some input was "useful" or "helpful" in performing some task that may (or may not) be important for getting or keeping a job. While we can see these as being of some diagnostic value for improving the moving parts of some programs, they are not about specific outcomes of interest to evaluators and policymakers, nor are specific time periods given: again, the questions fail to satisfy our first and second desiderata. Additionally, none of these questions satisfy our third desideratum (continuous-response format): the response formats are ordered categories (Likert scales) with verbal labels (e.g., "very helpful," "not very useful"), which may have problems of interpersonal comparability and lack of real-world anchoring that limit their usefulness in empirical work. In our view, such questions are not likely to be useful for impact evaluation, and we do not know of any studies that attempt to link responses to such questions to econometric or experimental impact estimates.

NEW QUESTIONS

Our attitude toward the existing questions is not wholly negative and dismissive. Our desired purpose, remember, is to find questions that allow us to *test* participant evaluation with very few auxiliary assumptions. Our four desiderata are for that purpose. As we have pointed out in several places, some of these questions may be useful for other purposes, such as refining program procedures or services or measuring implementation fidelity. But all the existing questions fail to satisfy one or more of our desiderata. In this section, we propose alternative question formats that satisfy all our desiderata.

Proposal A

Our first proposal consists of one relatively simple-looking survey question:

Question A: Suppose that you had not participated in the program. What do you think is the percent chance (what are the chances out of 100) that you would be employed today? "Employed today" means that you would have worked 35 or more hours per week, in all four of the last four weeks.

Question A satisfies our first and second desiderata. It concerns a specific outcome over a specific time period, and one that analysts and policymakers care about (employment). The specific outcome is chosen to be something the analyst will be able to estimate by other means when all the data are in—in the simplest case, by using the control group in an experimental evaluation. As simple as this may look, actual formulations of a question like this will require substantial planning and foresight on the part of a research team. What data will be available to the analyst at the time of data analysis? Given that available data, how will the analyst define "employment" as a dependent variable in some estimating equation? The wording of Question A presumes this was all settled in advance: "'Employed today' means that you would have worked 35 or more hours per week, in all four of the last four weeks." That presumes three things: 1) that the analyst will have weekly employment data for both treated and nontreated individuals, 2) that this employment data will use the same definition of employment (35 or more hours per week for all four weeks), and 3) that this is an outcome the analyst will want to focus on.

Question A also satisfies our third and fourth desiderata. It uses a continuous response format—in this case, a probability judgment in the "percent chance" form. Question A also very explicitly asks about the respondent's counterfactual employment outcome—what would be true today, had the respondent not participated in the program. In terms of our formal analysis, Question A directly elicits $E[Y_i(0)|Z_i]$, rather than attempting to elicit an expected treatment effect $E(\Delta_i|Z_i)$.

Participant evaluations of this sort can be compared to econometric estimates of the probability of employment given treatment based on the observed employment outcomes of the participants. More generally, the mean employment rate among participant respondents minus their mean "percent chance" response to Question A provides a "participant evaluation estimate" of the impact of participation on employment at follow-up. This can be compared directly and unambiguously to experimental or nonexperimental econometric impact estimates of $E(\Delta_i|X_i)$ and, in particular, the covariance property in Equation (7.1) can be tested without the auxiliary assumptions we needed in Chapters 4, 5, and 6.

Proposal B

To our knowledge, there have been no experimental studies (in either psychology or economics) examining elicitation of beliefs about outcomes conditioned on counterfactual events, though Manski (1999, Section 2.3) contains a brief conceptual discussion. However, there are phenomena suggesting that this may be a very difficult thing to do. For instance, the literature on "hindsight bias" (Fischhoff 1975) suggests that it is difficult to undo knowledge of actual outcomes and return oneself, so to speak, to an earlier state of uncertainty. There is also a long history of findings that question human facility with conditional probability reasoning such as Bayes's rule (e.g., Edwards 1968; Grether 1980). Therefore, we think it prudent to offer a second proposal that avoids an explicit counterfactual judgment but still produces a probabilistic judgment that can provide a test of the covariance proposition in Equation (7.1).

To provide necessary context for an illustrative example, suppose the participant is a 23-year-old Latina who was treated with service X in program Y two years prior to follow-up. The analyst will want to know whether X results in an increase in the likelihood of employment at follow-up, defined as working 35 hours or more per week in all of the last four weeks (for instance). The formal evaluator also plans to produce separate impact estimates for subgroups defined by age, sex, and ethnicity. Then the Proposal B question is as follows:

Question B: Please think about 100 Latinas between 21 and 25 years of age who applied to program Y and were accepted into it, just as you were. In other words, please think about 100 women similar to you.

However, imagine that program Y was unexpectedly canceled for these 100 women so that they did not receive service X as you did. That is, keep thinking that these 100 women are, in all other ways, similar to you—except that they didn't receive service X from program Y as you did.

How many of these 100 women do you think are employed today? "Employed today" means that they worked 35 or more hours per week, in all four of the last four weeks.

There are several similarities between Proposals A and B, but enumerating the similarities also reveals important differences. First, Question B resembles Question A in that it conditions on a control treatment not actually received by the participant. Yet Question B2 is not *literally* counterfactual, since there could well be 100 women similar to the participant who did not receive service X. Second, Questions A and B elicit a numerical judgment with a probabilistic interpretation. The difference is that Question A concerns the conditional probability of a unique event (something that has no frequentist interpretation), while Question B concerns the frequency of an outcome conditional on membership in a specific "reference class." Finally, both questions concern a very specific outcome. As noted, Question A concerns not only a counterfactual event but also a unique event. Question B relaxes this somewhat but still defines a very specific reference class of people similar to (and different from) the participant in precisely stated ways. In both questions, the definition of the outcome is very specific: 35 hours a week for the previous four weeks.

Besides avoiding an explicitly counterfactual judgment, Question B incorporates several relatively recent findings in the psychological literature on probabilistic judgment. In general, the phenomena of over-confidence (judged probabilities are too extreme) and conjunction violations (conjunctions of two events are judged more likely to occur than one of the events alone) are largely eliminated when subjects respond in the "frequency in a reference class" format of Question B (Fiedler 1988; Gigerenzer 1994; Gigerenzer, Hoffrage, and Kleinbölting 1991). Moreover, failures of Bayesian reasoning are also greatly reduced by this response format (Cosmides and Tooby 1996; Gigerenzer and Hoffrage 1995). To properly deploy this format, the participant must make judgments about nonsingleton reference classes: in plainer language, the participant cannot be asked to make judgments about the probability of a unique event (I am employed on this particular day), but rather about the frequency of outcomes in a sufficiently large reference class. Question B "depersonalizes" a respondent's judgment, but that is not the purpose of this question format. Rather, it eliminates judgment about unique events, replacing it with a frequency judgment about a class, and avoids an explicitly counterfactual phrasing.

A reference class must be defined for this format, and Proposal B treats this as a feature rather than a bug. By tailoring reference classes to resemble each participant, the survey can provide "conditional participant evaluations" to match the planned subgroup impact estimates of the formal evaluator or econometrician.

We think of Proposals A and B as two ends of a continuum. Proposal A is simpler to implement and may work reasonably well, but it still has some potential problems based on our understanding of the psychological literature. Proposal B arguably remedies those potential problems. However, the Question B format is more difficult to implement for several reasons. First, the survey question must be tailored to the respondent because a reference class based on the respondent's subgroup must be described. Second, it requires still more planning and foresight on the part of a research team. In essence, Question B asks respondent i to give an estimate of $E[Y(0)|X_j = X_S]$, where S is a subgroup identical to the reference class defined in the respondent's question. If the research team intends to test the covariance proposition in Expression (7.1), the reference classes in the survey question must properly anticipate the subgroups that the analyst will use to estimate subgroup impacts.

Some Issues

In thinking about our proposals, a number of common issues arise. We consider four issues in turn: 1) the use of numerical probabilities, 2) validity issues more generally, 3) reliability, and 4) what to do about treatment group members who drop out of a program in an experimental evaluation or about participants who start but do not complete a program more generally.

First, how well do respondents handle requests for numerical probability (chances or frequencies) estimates? Depending on which authors you read, this glass appears either half empty or half full. Tourangeau, Rips, and Rasinski (2000) praise attempts by economists to measure numerical probabilities (rather than using vague scales such as "likely," "very likely," and so on). At the same time, they note evidence from the psychology literature showing that respondents have trouble with probabilities near zero and one and that they can fall victim to problems such as the conjunction fallacy. More generally, the literature on "heuristics and biases" in probability judgment is now an old one: large and influential surveys are by now nearly 40 years old (Kahneman, Slovic, and Tversky 1982).

At the same time, other findings in Dominitz and Manski (1997a), Hurd and McGarry (1995), and Manski (2004) provide a more optimistic view. As well, Dominitz and Manski (1997b) find that respondents do a good job of estimating the probability of loss of employment or health insurance in the coming year (though they do less well with the probability of being burglarized). Hurd and McGarry (1995) find that respondents in the Health and Retirement Study, a longitudinal survey of older Americans, do a remarkably good job of estimating their probability of death at particular ages. We think it makes good sense to try probability or frequency elicitations like those in Questions A and B, for three reasons. First, there is value in having numerical probability estimates in order to calculate the expected value of employment in the counterfactual state. Second, in the context of evaluating active labor market programs, this probability likely lies well away from zero or one for most respondents. And third, there is reasonably positive evidence available in the literature regarding predictions of job loss. Moreover, as discussed earlier, the Question B format puts some recent findings in the psychological literature to work to arguably minimize some common biases.

We also worry about the problem of the "bunching" of responses at 50 percent, particularly under Question A. De Bruin has studied this phenomenon in a series of papers—see, for example, De Bruin and Carman (2012) and the citations therein, as well as the discussion and proposed remedy in Manski and Molinari (2010). De Bruin finds empirically important bunching, as well as evidence that respondents, particularly low-education respondents, use 50 percent as a "don't know" response. Without pretesting, we can only speculate regarding the importance of this phenomenon for our questions, though the literature clearly suggests the value of following up on responses of 50 percent with a question probing the respondent's level of uncertainty about the response.

Turning now to our second issue, how valid are responses to Questions A or B likely to be? Three comments suffice for this discussion. One, we can hardly do much worse than the existing measures if the results in Chapters 4, 5, and 6 hold more broadly. Two, because our questions embody a measurable dependent variable, namely employment, and include numerical probability estimates, we can easily examine their validity by looking at employment outcomes in the counterfactual state, as represented either by the control group in an experimental evaluation or by an econometrically adjusted comparison group in a nonexperimental evaluation. Such an analysis would mirror existing analyses in the literature just mentioned that look at the validity of forecasts of employment or health insurance loss as well as mortality. Indeed, the fact that Dominitz and Manski (1997a) find a reasonable level of validity for a similar question involving forecasts of own employment (as opposed to own employment in a counterfactual world) makes us cautiously optimistic regarding the likely performance of our measure.

Three, there are two recent papers in the development economics literature that have fielded versions of one or both of our Questions A and B. In work developed independently from our own, McKenzie (2018) asks versions of our Question A of both treatment and control group members in his evaluation of a "large-scale business plan competition" in which some semifinalists were randomly assigned to receive large business grants, thereby enabling an experimental analysis. He finds rather disappointing results, as both treatment and control group members systematically overestimate the implicit treatment effect.

Brudevold-Newman et al. (2017), directly inspired by our own work, implement versions of our Questions A and B in the context of their evaluation of two interventions designed to relax credit constraints among the poor in urban Kenya. They ask their two treatment groups two versions of Question B, one about the treated outcome for a reference group and one about the untreated outcome for a reference group. They then construct implicit participant evaluation impact estimates by subtracting one from the other. This differs from our approach, suggested above, of comparing elicited beliefs about the counterfactual for a reference group with realized outcomes for the treatment group. Their approach does quite well at replicating their experimental impact estimate for the outcomes they examine. Indeed, it does better than our approach would because they find that respondents provide biased estimates of both the treated and untreated outcome levels for the reference group, but that the biases largely cancel each other out in constructing the impact estimate. Their implementation of Question A does poorly when compared to actual control-group outcomes in their data, but their respondents tend to underestimate the treatment effect in this case, rather than overestimating it like the respondents in McKenzie (2018).

Our third issue concerns the reliability of Questions A and B. Reliability here means that the same person will answer the same question in the same way, given repeated queries (and conditional on the relevant circumstances not having changed). Other than the ACSI measures, we do not know of research on the reliability of the participant evaluation questions considered in the preceding section. In (possibly) related research, Krueger and Schkade (2007) find a two-week test-retest reliability of 0.6 for a standard life-satisfaction question. Not surprisingly, we also do not know the reliability of the measure we propose here, for the simple reason that no one has examined it yet. It is something we would like to examine in the right context.

Our fourth issue centers on how Questions A and B should be modified, if at all, in cases where individuals drop out of a program.[11] This can occur in the case of experiments when, for example, individuals in the treatment group do not in fact participate in the program because of the placement of random assignment prior to enrollment. As noted in Heckman et al. (2000), the existence of dropouts constitutes the norm in the literature on active labor market programs, with a large fraction of the experimental treatment group not receiving treatment in many experimental evaluations. In nonexperimental evaluations, the treatment group typically only includes individuals who participate in the program at least somewhat, but even in this context, some individuals will start but not complete a program.

In experimental cases with treatment group respondents who did not participate, two solutions come to mind. One solution simply assumes that the treatment-group outcome equals the control-group outcome for such individuals, so that their person-specific impact equals zero. This assumption underlies the common procedure (a simple instrumental-variables estimator) of dividing the experimental impact estimate by the fraction of the treatment group that does not drop out; see, e.g., Bloom (1984) or Heckman, Smith, and Taber (1998) for discussion. The alternative solution would ask individuals about their employment chances had they been randomly assigned to the control group. This latter formulation presumes that the respondent recalls random assignment and, conditional on that, recalls assignment to the treatment group.

The case of partial participation does not require any modification, as the counterfactual of interest consists of what would have happened had the respondent not participated, whether or not he or she completed the program.

Variants

We have also considered a number of variations of the participant evaluation question described above. The first variation would just replace employment with earnings. In this case, two routes are possible. The first is that we could ask respondents to estimate mean earnings in the counterfactual state—that is, $E[Y_i(0)|Z_i]$. This is simple and quick, and sufficient to test the covariance proposition in Expression (7.1). In many laboratory experiments, such estimates (especially of the behavior of others) can be quite good (e.g., Croson 2000; Gächter and Renner 2010).

The second route comes into play because researchers sometimes want more information about respondents' subjective distributions. One could then rely on the formulation used in Dominitz and Manski (1997b) and collect responses to construct a subjective cumulative distribution function (CDF) of earnings. This method asks a sequence of questions about the probability that earnings will not exceed an increasing sequence of earnings levels (we speak here in terms of Proposal A, but a similar modification of Proposal B is straightforward). The necessity of repeating the question for several earnings values, in order to obtain a reasonable approximation to the distribution, means a much larger impact on survey duration than simply asking respondents to report a mean. Also, we expect that (implicitly) predicting various points on the CDF of earnings implies a larger cognitive burden on the respondent than simply making a binary prediction about employment at a given point in time, or merely asking the respondent to report mean earnings. Despite these concerns, Dominitz (1998) finds that earnings questions of this sort do reasonably well in the context of respondents' predicting their own earnings in the next year (rather than counterfactual earnings in the same year).

The second variation would bolster questions with additional information, meant to prompt respondents to consider what they might have done had they not participated in the program. For instance, a modified Question A could read as follows:

> *"Suppose that the program shut down right before you were scheduled to participate. Think about things you might have done instead, such as looking for work, looking for another program, or leaving the labor force. Given your most likely choice of other activities, what do you think is the percent chance (what are the chances out of 100) that you would be employed today?"*

A "debiasing" literature in experimental psychology suggests that consideration of alternative outcomes or events can reduce biases in probability judgment (e.g., Fischhoff 1982). Of course, if a list of alternatives can alter how the respondent thinks about the question and his or her response, researchers may want to try out multiple lists. Thirty years ago, psychologists recommended that respondents first be asked to produce their own list of alternatives before stating a probability, but it is now known that this can backfire and produce greater bias than with no intervention, so we do not recommend it (Sanna, Schwarz, and Stocker 2002). Instead, supplying a short list of perhaps two or three considerations makes sense in light of the available research.

A third variant would put the question about counterfactual earnings in the baseline interview—that is, prior to participation—rather than at the time of the follow-up interview, after participation.[12] In this case, we would suggest a pair of questions, one about earnings or employment conditional on participation, as with NJCS Question E24 in Box 7.7, and one about earnings or employment in the non-participation state. These questions could be asked of both treatment and control group members prior to random assignment. Comparing the prospective responses regarding the participation state with the realizations might allow a calibration of any general forecast bias due to, say, excessive optimism, as found in Dominitz (1998). Having an estimate of this bias would allow adjustment of the prospective measure for the counterfactual state as well.

Last, a fourth variant would involve putting our suggested question ahead of a standard question, to see if getting respondents thinking about the counterfactual world of nonparticipation would change their responses to the usual questions. The survey literature provides many examples where making a particular idea, event, or line of reasoning salient through asking a preceding question can affect responses; see, for example, the experiment on sequencing of political and economic judgments in surveys reported by Wilcox and Wlezien (1993) or the discussion of context effects in Chapter 7 of Tourangeau, Rips, and Rasinski (2000). Undertaking this variant would provide some information about whether a rewording of the standard question that incorporated an explicit cue to the respondent to think about what would have happened in the absence of participation might perform better than the usual questions appear to do at present.

Finally, we think it would be highly desirable to begin learning something concrete about the reliability of these continuous-response formats, whether these are stated as probabilities of outcomes or as mean outcomes. To that end, we would like to see a survey design that repeats one or more of these kinds of questions—once relatively early in the survey, and then again later (after at least a few minutes in which the respondent has answered other items). This knowledge would help put statistical limits on the usefulness and uses of these survey responses. Without independent knowledge of reliability, it is nearly impossible to know what a poor model fit means (when these responses are dependent variables) or how to correct for measurement error (when these responses are regressors).

SUMMARY AND CONCLUSIONS

This chapter has described and critiqued existing participant evaluation measures collected by surveys used in evaluating active labor market programs. Our own opinion is that these existing measures hold little promise as substitutes for experimental or econometric program evaluation: we do not believe any of them would "work better" than the three measures we examined in detail in earlier chapters. But we also think that the potential promise of participant evaluation cannot really be tested with the existing questions. We developed "desiderata" for questions that might permit such a test, and none of the existing questions truly fit the bill. Given that view, we also made the case for some alternative measures that better reflect our existing state of knowledge and our desiderata for questions that would allow for a more definitive test of participant evaluation.

Notes

1. We have reformatted the questions to correct errors and inconsistencies and to match standard Upjohn practice, while leaving the substance alone.
2. A large literature makes use of the experimental (and related nonexperimental) data from the National JTPA Study (NJS). See Orr et al. (1996) and Bloom et al. (1993) for official summaries of the results. The NJS data are available from Abt Associates and the Upjohn Institute: http://www.upjohn.org/node/952 (accessed October 21, 2018).

3. See Hollister, Kemper, and Maynard (1984) for more about the program and the evaluation results. The NSW data are available from the Inter-university Consortium for Political and Social Research (ICPSR): http://www.icpsr.umich.edu/icpsrweb/ICPSR/studies/7865.

4. The final evaluation report is Bloom et al. (2000); the data and related documentation are available from MDRC at https://www.mdrc.org/available-public-use-files.

5. The final evaluation report is Decker et al. (2000). The data and related documentation are available from the Upjohn Institute: http://www.upjohn.org/node/944.

6. The final evaluation report is Quint, Bos, and Polit (1997). The data and related documentation are available from MDRC; see the information at https://www.mdrc.org/available-public-use-files.

7. The final evaluation report is Bloom et al. (2002). The data and related documentation are available from MDRC; see the information at https://www.mdrc.org/available-public-use-files.

8. The final evaluation report using administrative data for longer follow-up is Schochet, McConnell, and Burghardt (2003). Many additional evaluation reports are available at the Mathematica Policy Research website: www.mathematica-mpr.com. To inquire about accessing the experimental data, email info@mathematica-mpr.com.

9. See, e.g., https://wdr.doleta.gov/directives/corr_doc.cfm?DOCN=1263.

10. See www.theacsi.org and www.cfigroup.com.

11. As discussed in Barnow and Smith (2016), parts of the literature make a useful distinction between "no shows" who never receive any program services and dropouts who start but do not complete a program. For our purposes here, we have in mind mainly individuals assigned to the treatment group who receive no (or only very minimal) services. More extensive partial service receipt raises distinct but related questions.

12. Bell and Orr (2002) investigate ex ante questions regarding outcomes and impacts asked of caseworkers in an active labor market program. They find that caseworkers do reasonably well at predicting untreated outcomes but have no idea which participants will benefit most from treatment.

8
Conclusion

In this book, we have studied survey measures that ask participants in social programs to evaluate the programs in which they have participated. To our knowledge, our work represents the first attempt to rigorously examine the information content of such measures despite, as documented in Chapter 7, their widespread use in program evaluation practice. In a broad sense, we make six contributions: 1) we develop a set of theoretical frameworks within which to think about participant evaluations, 2) we describe an econometric framework for studying them using data from program evaluations that contain participant evaluation responses, 3) we empirically examine the correlation between participant evaluations and compelling estimates of program impacts, 4) we investigate the determinants of positive participant evaluations more generally within the context of our theoretical frameworks, 5) we document the range of participant evaluation measures available in the literature that evaluates active labor market programs, and 6) we propose alternative measures that build on our findings as well as on the broader literature.

While we frame our discussion in terms of active labor market programs and we draw our case studies from that literature (because that is where we can find experimental data that include participant evaluation measures), we think, with a caveat or two, that our work has implications well beyond that narrow context. First, even within the labor market program context, our three case studies all relate to programs that serve a disadvantaged population in one particular developed country, namely the United States. We see no reason to think our findings would not generalize to similar populations in other developed countries. In contrast, generalizing to disadvantaged populations in the developing world would typically mean a substantial reduction in the literacy and numeracy levels of the respondents, which could impact response patterns. In the other direction, we would expect less disadvantaged populations in the developed world to have (on average) greater cognitive capacity, which could improve the performance of survey measures like those we study. Generalizing across contexts rather than populations, we see parallels to our findings in the literature on placebos in medicine, where the evidence suggests that individuals rely on lay theories related to, for example, branding (Branthwaite and Cooper 1981) and pill colors (Blackwell, Bloomfield, and Buncher 1972) when evaluating the effectiveness of the pills they consume.

More broadly, individuals' ability to learn from experience, and then to use that knowledge to accurately represent outcomes associated with available alternatives, lies at the heart of rational models of human behavior. Participants who think they can determine whether they have benefited from an intervention but actually cannot may make faulty future choices based on the mistaken knowledge they think they have gained. From this perspective, the lay science interpretation of our findings may appear to challenge the notion that people accurately represent alternatives and their future consequences when making decisions. Yet the heart of Nisbett and Wilson's (1977) and Ross's (1989) surveys is a dissociation between experimentally measured causes of subject behavior and subjects' own verbal reports on those causes. Nisbett and Wilson remind us that though subjects sometimes tell more than they can know, they also clearly know more than they can tell (Polanyi 1964). There is no paradox here: skilled performance, which can depend crucially on neural processes hidden from consciousness, does not imply a capacity for accurate verbal description of the processes underlying such performance. A neoclassical economist gives no important ground by embracing a lay science interpretation of participants' inability to accurately *report* program impacts. The capacity for verbal report and the capacity for decision making are simply two different things.

FINDINGS

We have two main empirical findings from the analyses in Chapters 4, 5, and 6. The first is that participant evaluations from the three experimental evaluations we examine have little or no relationship with econometric impact estimates based on two different identification strategies. Interpreted in the light of the theoretical frameworks presented in Chapter 2, this evidence argues against the second of the two decision theory viewpoints captured in Equation (2.7). We also find some empirical evidence against the first decision theory viewpoint, which implies the bounds in Expression (2.5), despite the width of those bounds and the consequent weakness of our test. Given our critique of the extant participant evaluation survey measures in Chapter 7, we tend to blame not decision theory but rather poor question design for these empirical failures.

The one partial exception to this broad negative finding comes from the Jobs First evaluation in Chapter 6. We attribute the somewhat (and it is only somewhat) better performance of the participant evaluation measure in that study to the underlying survey question, which focuses on a specific outcome under the control of the respondent and also pushes the respondent to think about the counterfactual world in which she did not participate in the program. We document in Chapter 7 that the participant evaluation measure in the Jobs First data represents something of an anomaly in having these useful features. As a result, we do not view the Jobs First evidence as a counter to our first general conclusion: *Existing, widely used participant evaluation measures do not constitute reasonable or evidence-based substitutes for serious experimental or econometric evaluation, and they should not be interpreted as such in presenting evaluation results.*

Our second finding is that the participant evaluation measures we study do have consistent relationships with crude proxies for impacts, such as measures of service type (a proxy for resources expended on the participant), labor market outcome levels (which measure impacts only if the counterfactual state consists of no employment or earnings, which it does not for the vast majority of our samples), and before-after comparisons. These findings provide strong support for the view that respondents avoid the cognitive burden associated with trying to construct (implicitly or explicitly) the counterfactual outcome they would have experienced in the control group. Instead, they appear to act as lay scientists, using readily available proxies and simple heuristics to conclude, for example, that if they are employed at the time of the survey or if their earnings have risen relative to the period prior to random assignment, the program probably helped them find a job or get a better job. At the same time, our evidence does not rule out the view that respondents consider factors in their answers not captured in our experimental and econometric impact estimates, such as expected impacts in later periods or subjective and direct costs and benefits associated with the services they received. For example, we find it difficult to explain the positive participant evaluations for respondents with zero earnings in the postprogram period we observe in the JTPA data in Chapter 4 other than through the subjective rationality view. More generally, the proxy variables motivated by the lay scientist framework leave much variation in the participant evaluation measure to be explained by other factors.

We borrow our "lay science" interpretation of our results from a large literature in social psychology on the fallibility of self reports. The "study skills" experiment of Conway and Ross (1984) is the most parallel study we know of. Conway and Ross recruited subjects from one large introductory psychology course who expressed interest in taking a three-week study skills class, and then randomly assigned them to either the class (treatment) or a waiting list (control). Both groups gave self reports on their own study-skill proficiency both before and after the three-week class. After the three-week class, both groups were also asked to recall what their self-report of their study skills from three weeks earlier had been (before assignment to treatment or control). Finally, both groups also directly reported changes in their study skills over the three-week period of the class. Since subjects came from one course, and the experiment took place between the midterm and final in that course, comparable performance measures (in the form of grades on the midterm and final in the same class) were available to Conway and Ross, as were overall semester grades collected from registrar records.

The objective measures confirmed what professional evaluators of such classes, e.g., Gibbs (1981), have found: the class had no statistically significant effect on outcome measures (grades in the course or on the final, or for the semester overall). Yet treatment subjects reported significantly greater change in their study skills, and expected significantly better grades, than did control subjects. Curiously, the former effect seems mainly traceable to a biased recall of their preclass study-skill level. Although treatment and control subjects did not actually differ in their before-after self-reports of their study skills, treatment subjects' recall of their "before" study skills—at the time of the "after" survey—were statistically lower than they had actually reported in "before" surveys, while control subjects showed no such bias.

Conway and Ross (1984) interpret these results as showing that their subjects act as lay theorists. In other words, the subjects have a theory that a study skills class will improve study skills. Treatment and control subjects' "after" evaluations of their study skills differ little; put differently, there is no evidence that treatment subjects are exaggerating their "after" skill. If their memory of their "before" study-skill level is hazy, the treatment-group subjects may instead opt to theoretically infer positive change from the class and then postdict their preclass study-skill level on the basis of that theoretical prediction. This kind of process wholly explains Conway and Ross's findings.

The literature on using surveys to measure expectations, as discussed in Manski (2004), provides some hope that more sophisticated survey questions might do a better job of measuring the underlying objects of interest. Depending on whether human minds normally construct expectations and evaluations, and just how they do so, recall processes could be a crucial part of such expectations and evaluations. It is worth mentioning that some forms of biased recall of "before" judgments (similar but not identical to the kind studied by Conway and Ross [1984]) are known to be mitigated if the subject's actual "before" judgment is known and the subject is given a real incentive to correctly recall it, as in Aderman and Brehm (1976). Put differently, the experimental economist's normal emphasis on incentive-compatible mechanisms for truthful reports might be helpful here, and such methods are increasingly incorporated into various surveys.

Overall, we conclude that ex post survey-based participant evaluations of the type analyzed here are very poor substitutes for rigorous experimental or nonexperimental estimates of program impact. Although our work is (to our knowledge) the first to seriously study what these questions actually measure using data from social experiments, the discussion above shows that our findings, and our interpretations of them, are far from unique: very similar results can be found in many laboratory experiments conducted by social psychologists—and, indeed, we have drawn our "lay science" interpretation from this literature. We can think of no better summary warning than the one Ross (1989, p. 354) gave in his musings on the implications of Conway and Ross (1984):

> The biased retrospections evidenced by participants in improvement programs may cause them to remain in worthless programs and not to search for more effective treatments. Indeed, when self-reports are a primary indicant of improvement, a conspiracy of ignorance may emerge in which both the helper and the helped erroneously believe in the achievement of their common goal.

References

Abadie, Alberto, Joshua Angrist, and Guido Imbens. 2002. "Instrumental Variables Estimates of the Effect of Subsidized Training on the Quantiles of Trainee Earnings." *Econometrica* 70(1): 97–117.

Aderman, David, and Sharon S. Brehm. 1976. "On the Recall of Initial Attitudes Following Counterattitudinal Advocacy: An Experimental Reexamination." *Personality and Social Psychology Bulletin* 2(1): 59–62.

Ashton, Robert H. 1990. "Pressure and Performance in Accounting Decision Settings: Paradoxical Effects of Incentives, Feedback, and Justification." *Journal of Accounting Research* 28(Supplement): 148–180.

Barnow, Burt, and Jeffrey A. Smith. 2004. "Performance Management of U.S. Job Training Programs: Lessons from the Job Training Partnership Act." *Public Finance and Management* 4(3): 247–287.

———. 2016. "Employment and Training Programs." In *Means Tested Transfer Programs in the United States, Vol. 2*, Robert Moffitt, ed. Chicago: University of Chicago Press, 127–234.

Bell, Stephen H., and Larry L. Orr. 2002. "Screening (and Creaming?) Applicants to Job Training Programs: The AFDC Homemaker–Home Health Aide Demonstrations." *Labour Economics* 9(2): 279–301.

Bitler, Marianne P., Jonah B. Gelbach, and Hilary W. Hoynes. 2005. "Distributional Impacts of the Self-Sufficiency Project." NBER Working Paper No. 11626. Cambridge, MA: National Bureau of Economic Research.

———. 2006. "What Mean Impacts Miss: Distributional Effects of Welfare Reform Experiments." *American Economic Review* 96(4): 988–1012.

———. 2017. "Can Variation in Subgroups' Average Treatment Effects Explain Treatment Effect Heterogeneity? Evidence from a Social Experiment." *Review of Economics and Statistics* 99(4): 683–697.

Blackwell, Barry, Saul S. Bloomfield, and C. Ralph Buncher. 1972. "Demonstration to Medical Students of Placebo Responses and Non-Drug Factors." *Lancet* 299(7763): 1279–1282. https://doi.org/10.1016/s0140-6736(72)90996-8 (accessed October 15, 2020).

Bloom, Dan, James J. Kemple, Pamela Morris, Susan Scrivener, Nandita Verma, and Richard Hendra, with Diana Adams-Ciardullo, David Seith, and Johanna Walter. 2000. *The Family Transition Program: Final Report on Florida's Initial Time-Limited Welfare Program*. New York: Manpower Demonstration Research Corporation (MDRC).

Bloom, Dan, Susan Scrivener, Charles Michalopoulos, Pamela Morris, Richard Hendra, Diana Adams-Ciardullo, and Johanna Walter, with Wanda Vargas. 2002. *Jobs First: Final Report on Connecticut's Welfare Reform*

Initiative. New York: Manpower Demonstration Research Corporation (MDRC).

Bloom, Howard. 1984. "Accounting for No-Shows in Experimental Evaluation Designs." *Evaluation Review* 8(2): 225–246.

Bloom, Howard, Larry Orr, George Cave, Stephen Bell, and Fred Doolittle. 1993. *The National JTPA Study: Title II-A Impacts on Earnings and Employment at 18 Months*. Bethesda, MD: Abt Associates.

Bohm, Peter. 1984. "Are There Practicable Demand-Revealing Mechanisms?" In *Public Finance and the Quest for Efficiency*, Horst Hanusch, ed. Detroit, MI: Wayne State University Press, pp. 127–139.

Branthwaite, A., and P. Cooper. 1981. "Analgesic Effects of Branding in Treatment of Headaches." *British Medical Journal* 282(6276): 1576–1578. https://doi.org/10.1136/bmj.282.6276.1576 (accessed October 15, 2020).

Brudevold-Newman, Andrew, Maddalena Honorati, Pamela Jakiela, and Owen Ozier. 2017. "A Firm of One's Own: Experimental Evidence on Credit Constraints and Occupational Choice." World Bank Policy Research Working Paper No. 7977. Washington, DC: World Bank.

Calónico, Sebastian, and Jeffrey A. Smith. 2017. "The Women of the National Supported Work Demonstration." *Journal of Labor Economics* 35(S1): S65–S97.

Card, David, and Daniel Sullivan. 1988. "Measuring the Effect of Subsidized Training Programs on Movements In and Out of Employment." *Econometrica* 56(3): 497–530.

Carrell, Scott E., and James E. West. 2010. "Does Professor Quality Matter? Evidence from Random Assignment of Students to Professors." *Journal of Political Economy* 118(3): 409–432.

Conway, Michael, and Michael Ross. 1984. "Getting What You Want by Revising What You Had." *Journal of Personality and Social Psychology* 47(4): 738–748.

Cosmides, Leda, and John Tooby. 1996. "Are Humans Good Intuitive Statisticians After All? Rethinking Some Conclusions from the Literature on Judgment under Uncertainty." *Cognition* 58(1): 1–73.

Couch, Kenneth. 1992. "New Evidence on the Long-Term Effects of Employment Training Programs." *Journal of Labor Economics* 10(4): 380–388.

Croson, Rachel. 2000. "Thinking Like a Game Theorist: Factors Affecting the Frequency of Equilibrium Play." *Journal of Economic Behavior and Organization* 41(3): 299–314.

De Bruin, Wändi Bruine, and Katherine G. Carman. 2012. "Measuring Risk Perceptions: What Does the Excessive Use of 50% Mean?" *Medical Decision Making* 32(2): 232–236.

Decker, Paul, Robert Olsen, Lance Freeman, and Daniel Klepinger. 2000.

Assisting Unemployment Insurance Claimants: The Long-Term Impacts of the Job Search Assistance Demonstration. Washington, DC: Mathematica Policy Research.

Dehejia, Rajeev H., and Sadek Wahba. 1999. "Causal Effects in Nonexperimental Studies: Reevaluating the Evaluation of Training Programs." *Journal of the American Statistical Association* 94(448): 1053–1062.

———. 2002. "Propensity Score-Matching Methods for Nonexperimental Causal Studies." *Review of Economics and Statistics* 84(1): 151–161.

Devine, Theresa, and James Heckman. 1996. "The Structure and Consequences of Eligibility Rules for a Social Program." In *Research in Labor Economics, Vol. 15*, Solomon Polachek, ed. Greenwich, CT: JAI Press, pp. 111–170.

Djebbari, Habiba, and Jeffrey A. Smith. 2008. "Heterogeneous Program Impacts: Experimental Evidence from the PROGRESA Program." *Journal of Econometrics* 145(1–2): 64–80.

Dolton, Peter, and Jeffrey A. Smith. 2011. "The Econometric Evaluation of the New Deal for Lone Parents." IZA Discussion Paper No. 5491. Bonn, Germany: Institute of Labor.

Dominitz, Jeff. 1998. "Earnings Expectations, Revisions, and Realizations." *Review of Economics and Statistics* 80(3): 374–388.

Dominitz, Jeff, and Charles Manski. 1996. "Eliciting Student Expectations of the Returns to Schooling." *Journal of Human Resources* 31(1): 1–26.

———. 1997a. "Perceptions of Economic Insecurity: Evidence from the Survey of Economic Expectations." *Public Opinion Quarterly* 61(2): 261–287.

———. 1997b. "Using Expectations Data to Study Subjective Income Expectations." *Journal of the American Statistical Association* 92(439): 855–867.

Doolittle, Fred, and Linda Traeger. 1990. *Implementing the National JTPA Study*. New York: Manpower Demonstration Research Corporation (MDRC).

Dunnett, Charles W., and Ajit C. Tamhane. 1992. "A Step-Up Multiple Test Procedure." *Journal of the American Statistical Association* 87(417): 162–170.

Edwards, Ward. 1968. "Conservatism in Human Information Processing." In *Formal Representations of Human Judgment*, Benjamin Kleinmuntz, ed. New York: Wiley, pp. 17–52.

Eyal, Yonatan. 2010. "Examination of the Empirical Research Environment of Program Evaluation: Methodology and Application." *Evaluation Review* 34(6): 455–486.

Fiedler, Klaus. 1988. "The Dependence of the Conjunction Fallacy on Subtle Linguistic Factors." *Psychological Research* 50(2): 123–129. https://doi.org/10.1007/BF00309212 (accessed October 15, 2020).

Fischhoff, Baruch. 1975. "Hindsight Is Not Equal to Foresight: The Effect of

Outcome Knowledge on Judgment under Uncertainty." *Journal of Experimental Psychology: Human Perception and Performance* 1(3): 288–299. https://doi.org/10.1037/0096-1523.1.3.288 (accessed October 15, 2020).

———. 1982. "For Those Condemned to Study the Past: Heuristics and Biases in Hindsight." In *Judgment under Uncertainty: Heuristics and Biases*, Daniel Kahneman, Paul Slovic, and Amos Tversky, eds. Cambridge: Cambridge University Press, pp. 335–352.

Gächter, Simon, and Elke Renner. 2010. "The Effects of (Incentivized) Belief Elicitation in Public Goods Experiments." *Experimental Economics* 13(3): 364–377.

Gibbs, Graham. 1981. *Teaching Students to Learn: A Student-Centred Approach*. Milton Keynes: Open University Press.

Gigerenzer, Gerd. 1994. 'Why the Distinction between Single-Event Probabilities and Frequencies Is Important for Psychology (and Vice Versa)." In *Subjective Probability*, George Wright and Peter Ayton, eds. Chichester, UK: John Wiley and Sons, pp. 129–161.

Gigerenzer, Gerd, and Ulrich Hoffrage. 1995. "How to Improve Bayesian Reasoning without Instruction: Frequency Formats." *Psychological Review* 102(4): 684–704.

Gigerenzer, Gerd, Ulrich Hoffrage, and Heinz Kleinbölting. 1991. "Probabilistic Mental Models: A Brunswikian Theory of Confidence." *Psychological Review* 98(4): 506–528.

Grether, David M. 1980. "Bayes Rule as a Descriptive Model: The Representativeness Heuristic." *Quarterly Journal of Economics* 95(3): 537–557.

Grogger, Jeffrey, and Lynn A. Karoly. 2005. *Welfare Reform: Effects of a Decade of Change*. Cambridge, MA: Harvard University Press.

Harrison, Glenn. 1992. "Theory and Misbehavior of First-Price Auctions: Reply." *American Economic Review* 82(5): 1426–1443.

———. 2013. "Field Experiments and Methodological Intolerance." *Journal of Economic Methodology* 20(2): 103–117.

Heckman, James J. 1997. "Randomization as an Instrumental Variable." *Review of Economics and Statistics* 78(2): 336–341.

Heckman, James J., Carolyn J. Heinrich, Pascal Courty, Gerald Marschke, and Jeffrey A. Smith, eds. 2011. *The Performance of Performance Standards*. Kalamazoo, MI: W.E. Upjohn Institute for Employment Research.

Heckman, James J., Carolyn J. Heinrich, and Jeffrey A. Smith. 2002. "The Performance of Performance Standards." *Journal of Human Resources* 37(4): 778–811.

———. 2011. "Do Short-Run Performance Measures Predict Long-Run Impacts?" In *The Performance of Performance Standards*, James J. Heckman, Pascal Courty, Carolyn J. Heinrich, Gerald Marschke, and

Jeffrey A. Smith, eds. Kalamazoo, MI: W.E. Upjohn Institute for Employment Research, pp. 273–303.

Heckman, James J., Neil Hohmann, and Jeffrey A. Smith, with Michael Khoo. 2000. "Substitution and Dropout Bias in Social Experiments: A Study of an Influential Social Experiment." *Quarterly Journal of Economics* 115(2): 651–694.

Heckman, James J., Robert J. LaLonde, and Jeffrey A. Smith. 1999. "The Economics and Econometrics of Active Labor Market Programs." In *Handbook of Labor Economics, Vol. 3A*, Orley C. Ashenfelter and David Card, eds. Handbooks in Economics 5. Amsterdam: North-Holland, pp. 1865–2097.

Heckman, James J., and Jeffrey A. Smith. 1995. "Assessing the Case for Social Experiments." *Journal of Economic Perspectives* 9(2): 85–110.

———. 1998. "Evaluating the Welfare State." In *Econometrics and Economic Theory in the 20th Century: The Ragnar Frisch Centennial Symposium*, Steinar Strøm, ed. Econometric Society Monograph Series. Cambridge: Cambridge University Press, pp. 241–318.

———. 1999. "The Pre-Programme Earnings Dip and the Determinants of Participation in a Social Programme: Implications for Simple Programme Evaluation Strategies." *Economic Journal* 109(457): 313–348.

———. 2000. "The Sensitivity of Experimental Impact Estimates: Evidence from the National JTPA Study." In *Youth Employment and Joblessness in Advanced Countries*, David Blanchflower and Richard Freeman, eds. Chicago: University of Chicago Press for NBER, pp. 331–356.

———. 2004. "The Determinants of Participation in a Social Program: Evidence from a Prototypical Job Training Program." *Journal of Labor Economics* 22(2): 243–298.

Heckman, James J., and Jeffrey A. Smith, with Nancy Clements. 1997. "Making the Most out of Programme Evaluations and Social Experiments: Accounting for Heterogeneity in Programme Impacts." *Review of Economic Studies* 64(4): 487–535.

Heckman, James J., Jeffrey A. Smith, and Christopher Taber. 1998. "Accounting for Dropouts in Evaluations of Social Programs." *Review of Economics and Statistics* 80(1): 1–14.

Heinrich, Carolyn J., Gerald Marschke, and Annie Zhang. 1998. *Using Administrative Data to Estimate the Cost-Effectiveness of Social Program Services*. Technical report. Chicago: University of Chicago.

Hirshleifer, Sarojini, David McKenzie, Rita Almeida, and Cristobal Ridao-Cano. 2014. "The Impact of Vocational Training for the Unemployed: Experimental Evidence from Turkey." IZA Discussion Paper No. 8059. Bonn, Germany: Institute for the Study of Labor.

Hoffmann, Florian, and Philip Oreopoulos. 2009. "Professor Qualities and Student Achievement." *Review of Economics and Statistics* 91(1): 83–92.

Hollister, Robinson. 1984. "The Design and Implementation of the Supported Work Evaluation." In *The National Supported Work Demonstration*, Robinson Hollister, Peter Kemper, and Rebecca A. Maynard, eds. Madison: University of Wisconsin Press, pp. 12–49.

Hollister, Robinson, Peter Kemper, and Rebecca A. Maynard. 1984. *The National Supported Work Demonstration*. Madison: University of Wisconsin Press.

Holt, Charles, and Susan Laury. 2002. "Risk Aversion and Incentive Effects." *American Economic Review* 92(5): 1644–1655.

Human Resources and Skills Development Canada. 2009. *Summative Evaluation of Employment Benefits and Support Measures in the Ontario Region, October 2009.* Canadian government document SP-AH-933-01-10E. Ottawa: Human Resources and Skills Development Canada.

Hurd, Michael D., and Kathleen McGarry. 1995. "Evaluation of the Subjective Probabilities of Survival in the Health and Retirement Study." *Journal of Human Resources* 30(Special Issue): S268–S292.

Jacob, Brian, and Lars Lefgren. 2008. "Principals as Agents: Subjective Performance Measurement in Education." *Journal of Labor Economics* 26(1): 101–136.

Juster, F. Thomas. 1964. *Anticipations and Purchases: An Analysis of Consumer Behavior*. Princeton, NJ: Princeton University Press for the National Bureau of Economic Research.

———. 1966. "Consumer Buying Intentions and Purchase Probability: An Experiment in Survey Design." *Journal of the American Statistical Association* 61(315): 658–696.

Kahneman, Daniel, Paul Slovic, and Amos Tversky, eds. 1982. *Judgment under Uncertainty: Heuristics and Biases*. Cambridge: Cambridge University Press.

Kelley, Harold H., and Anthony J. Stahelski. 1970. "Social Interaction Basis of Cooperators' and Competitors' Beliefs about Others." *Journal of Personality and Social Psychology* 16(1): 66–91. https://doi.org/10.1037/h0029849 (accessed October 15, 2020).

Kelly, George A. 1955. *The Psychology of Personal Constructs, Vol. 1: A Theory of Personality*. New York: Norton.

Kemple, James, Fred Doolittle, and John W. Wallace. 1993. *The National JTPA Study: Site Characteristics and Participation Patterns*. New York: Manpower Demonstration Research Corporation (MDRC).

Kline, Patrick, and Christopher R. Walters. 2016. "Evaluating Public Programs with Close Substitutes: The Case of Head Start." *Quarterly Journal of Economics* 131(4): 1795–1848.

Koenker, Roger, and Gilbert Bassett Jr. 1978. "Regression Quantiles." *Econometrica* 46(1): 33–50.

Kornfeld, Robert, and Howard S. Bloom. 1999. "Measuring Program Impacts on Earnings and Employment: Do Unemployment Insurance Wage Reports from Employers Agree with Surveys of Individuals?" *Journal of Labor Economics* 17(1): 168–197.

Kristensen, Nicolai. 2014. "What Do We Learn from Self-Evaluations of Training? A Comparison of Subjective and Objective Evaluations." Unpublished manuscript, University of Aarhus, Denmark.

Krueger, Alan B., and David A. Schkade. 2007. "The Reliability of Subjective Well-Being Measures." NBER Working Paper No. 13027. Cambridge, MA: National Bureau of Economic Research.

Kuhlman, D. Michael, and David L. Wimberley. 1976. "Expectations of Choice Behavior Held by Cooperators, Competitors, and Individualists across Four Classes of Experimental Games." *Journal of Personality and Social Psychology* 34(1): 69–81. https://doi.org/10.1037/0022-3514.34.1.69 (accessed October 15, 2020).

LaLonde, Robert J. 1986. "Evaluating the Econometric Evaluations of Training Programs with Experimental Data." *American Economic Review* 76(4): 604–620.

Lichtenstein, Sarah, Baruch Fischhoff, and Lawrence D. Phillips. 1982. "Calibration of Probabilities: The State of the Art to 1980." In *Judgment under Uncertainty: Heuristics and Biases*, Daniel Kahneman, Paul Slovic, and Amos Tversky, eds. Cambridge: Cambridge University Press, pp. 306–334.

Liu, Wei. 1997. "Stepwise Tests When the Test Statistics Are Independent." *Australian Journal of Statistics* 39(2): 169–177.

Manski, Charles F. 1990. "The Use of Intentions Data to Predict Behavior: A Best-Case Analysis." *Journal of the American Statistical Association* 85(412): 934–940.

———. 1999. "Analysis of Choice Expectations in Incomplete Scenarios." *Journal of Risk and Uncertainty* 19(1–3): 49–65.

———. 2004. "Measuring Expectations." *Econometrica* 72(5): 1329–1376.

Manski, Charles F., and Francesca Molinari. 2010. "Rounding Probabilistic Expectations in Surveys." *Journal of Business and Economic Statistics* 28(2): 219–231.

Markman, Keith D., and Matthew N. McMullen. 2003. "A Reflection and Evaluation Model of Comparative Thinking." *Personality and Social Psychology Review* 7(3): 244–267.

Masters, Stanley, and Rebecca Maynard. 1981. *The Impact of Supported Work on Long-Term Recipients of AFDC Benefits.* New York: Manpower Demonstration Research Corporation (MDRC).

McKelvey, Richard D., and Talbot Page. 1990. "Public and Private Information: An Experimental Study of Information Pooling." *Econometrica* 58(6):

1321–1339. http://www.jstor.org/stable/2938318 (accessed October 15, 2020).

McKenzie, David. 2018. "Can Business Owners Form Accurate Counterfactuals? Eliciting Treatment and Control Beliefs about Their Outcomes in the Alternative Treatment Status." *Journal of Business and Economic Statistics* 36(4): 714–722. https://www.tandfonline.com/doi/full/10.1080/07350015 .2017.1305276 (accessed May 25, 2021).

Merz, Russ. 2007. "The American Customer Satisfaction Index (ACSI) Technology: A Methodological Primer." CFI Group white paper. Ann Arbor, MI: CFI Group.

Mosteller, Frederick, and Cleo Youtz. 1990. "Quantifying Probabilistic Expressions." *Statistical Science* 5(1): 2–12. https://projecteuclid.org/download/ pdf_1/euclid.ss/1177012242 (accessed October 15, 2020).

Nisbett, Richard E., and Lee Ross. 1980. *Human Inference: Strategies and Shortcomings of Social Judgment*. Englewood Cliffs, NJ: Prentice-Hall.

Nisbett, Richard E., and Timothy D. Wilson. 1977. "Telling More than We Can Know: Verbal Reports on Mental Processes." *Psychological Review* 84(3): 231–259.

Offerman, Theo, Joep Sonnemans, and Arthur Schram. 1996. "Value Orientations, Expectations, and Voluntary Contributions in Public Goods." *Economic Journal* 106(437): 817–845.

Orr, Larry, Howard Bloom, Stephen Bell, Fred Doolittle, Winston Lin, and George Cave. 1996. *Does Training Work for the Disadvantaged? Evidence from the National JTPA Study*. Washington, DC: Urban Institute Press.

Philipson, Tomas, and Larry V. Hedges. 1998. "Subject Evaluation in Social Experiments." *Econometrica* 66(2): 381–408.

Polanyi, Michael. 1964. *Personal Knowledge: Towards a Post-Critical Philosophy*. New York: Harper and Row.

Quint, Janet, Johannes Bos, and Denise Polit.1997. *New Chance: Final Report on a Comprehensive Program for Young Mothers in Poverty and Their Children*. New York: Manpower Demonstration Research Corporation (MDRC).

Ross, Michael. 1989. "Relation of Implicit Theories to the Construction of Personal Histories." *Psychological Review* 96(2): 341–357.

Roy, A. D. 1951. "Some Thoughts on the Distribution of Earnings." *Oxford Economic Papers* 3(2): 135–146.

Sanna, Lawrence J., Norbert Schwarz, and Shevaun L. Stocker. 2002. "When Debiasing Backfires: Accessible Content and Accessibility Experiences in Debiasing Hindsight." *Journal of Experimental Psychology Learning Memory and Cognition* 28(3): 497–502. https://doi.org/10.1037//0278 -7393.28.3.497 (accessed October 15, 2020).

Schochet, Peter Z., John Burghardt, and Sheena McConnell. 2008. "Does Job Corps Work? Impact Findings from the National Job Corps Study." *American Economic Review* 98(5): 1864–1886.

Schochet, Peter Z., Sheena McConnell, and John Burghardt. 2003. *National Job Corps Study: Findings Using Administrative Earnings Records*. Princeton, NJ: Mathematica Policy Research.

Simon, Herbert A. 1957. "A Comparison of Game Theory and Learning Theory." *Psychometrika* 21(3): 267–272.

Smith, Jeffrey A. 1997. "Measuring Earnings Levels among the Poor: Evidence from Two Samples of JTPA Eligibles." Unpublished manuscript. University of Western Ontario, London.

Smith, Jeffrey A., and Petra E. Todd. 2005a. "Does Matching Overcome LaLonde's Critique of Nonexperimental Estimators?" *Journal of Econometrics* 125(1–2): 305–353.

———. 2005b. "Rejoinder." *Journal of Econometrics* 125(1–2): 365–375.

Smith, Jeffrey A., and Alexander Whalley. 2020. "How Well Do We Measure Public Job Training?" Unpublished manuscript. University of Michigan, Ann Arbor.

Tourangeau, Roger, Lance J. Rips, and Kenneth Rasinski. 2000. *The Psychology of Survey Response*. New York: Cambridge University Press.

U.S. Department of Education. 2005. *Evaluation of the Teaching American History Program*. Washington, DC: U.S. Department of Education, Office of Planning, Evaluation, and Policy Development.

U.S. Department of Labor (USDOL). 1976. "Insured Unemployment under State Programs." Table E.1. *Employment and Earnings* 22(7): 132.

U.S. General Accounting Office (USGAO). 1996. *Job Training Partnership Act: Long-Term Earnings and Employment Outcomes*. Report HEHS-96-40. Washington, DC: U.S. General Accounting Office.

Vavra, Terry G. 1997. *Improving Your Measurement of Customer Satisfaction: A Guide to Creating, Conducting, Analyzing, and Reporting Customer Satisfaction Measurement Programs*. Milwaukee, WI: ASQ Quality Press.

Wallsten, Thomas S., David V. Budescu, and Rami Zwick. 1993. "Comparing the Calibration and Coherence of Numerical and Verbal Probability Judgments." *Management Science* 39(2): 176–190. https://doi.org/10.1287/mnsc.39.2.176 (accessed October 15, 2020).

Wilcox, Nathaniel T. 1993. "Lottery Choice: Incentives, Complexity, and Decision Time." *Economic Journal* 103(421): 1397–1417.

Wilcox, Nathaniel, and Christopher Wlezien. 1993. "The Contamination of Responses to Survey Items: Economic Perceptions and Political Judgments." *Political Analysis* 5(1): 181–213.

Wilson, Timothy D. 2004. *Strangers to Ourselves: Discovering the Adaptive Unconscious*. Cambridge, MA: Belknap Press.

Wood, Michelle. 1995. "National JTPA Study—SDA Unit Costs." Abt Associates Memo to Jerry Marsky [*sic*] and Larry Orr." Rockville, MD: Abt Associates.

Wright, William F., and Mohamed E. Aboul-Ezz. 1988. "Effects of Extrinsic Incentives on the Quality of Frequency Assessments." *Organizational Behavior and Human Decision Processes* 41(2): 143–152.

Wright, William F., and Urton Anderson. 1989. "Effects of Situation Familiarity and Financial Incentives on Use of the Anchoring and Adjustment Heuristic for Probability Assessment." *Organizational Behavior and Human Decision Processes* 44(1): 68–82.

Authors

Tanya Byker is an associate professor of economics at Middlebury College. She teaches courses in regression and the economics of gender. Professor Byker graduated from Swarthmore College and earned her PhD from the University of Michigan. She has published for the National Bureau of Economic Research, the Center for Economic Policy Research, and in the *American Economic Review*. Her research falls under the categories of labor and development economics and focuses on the interrelated choices individuals make about education, work, and parenthood. She has studied how birth-related career interruptions in the United States vary by mother's education, and the ways that parental leave laws impact those labor-supply decisions. In a developing-country context, she has studied how access to family planning impacts fertility and longer-term outcomes such as schooling and employment in Peru and South Africa.

Sebastian Calónico is an assistant professor in the Department of Health Policy and Management at Columbia University. His research focuses on program evaluation and causal inference, applying innovative quantitative methods to the study of relevant empirical problems in an interdisciplinary context, including economics as well as other social, medical, and statistical sciences. His work has been published in *Econometrica*, the *Journal of the American Statistical Association*, and the *Review of Economics and Statistics*. Sebastian was born in Argentina, where he completed a BA in economics at Universidad de Buenos Aires and an MA in economics at Universidad Torcuato Di Tella. He received a PhD in economics from the University of Michigan, where he also obtained an MA in statistics. Prior to joining Columbia University in 2019, he was a faculty member in the Department of Economics at the University of Miami.

Jeffrey Smith is the Paul T. Heyne Distinguished Professor in Economics and the Richard A. Meese Professor in Applied Econometrics at the University of Wisconsin–Madison, where he also serves as associate director of research and training for the Institute for Research on Poverty. He holds a master's and a PhD in economics from the University of Chicago and bachelor's degrees in computer science and economics from the University of Washington. He is a coauthor of *The Performance of Performance Standards*, published in 2011 by the Upjohn Institute, and has published in the *American Economic Review*, *Journal of Labor Economics*, and the *Journal of Economic Perspectives*, among other journals. His research centers on experimental and nonexperimental methods for the evaluation of interventions, with particular application to social and educational programs. He has also written papers examining the effects of university quality on educational and labor market outcomes, and the use of statistical treatment rules to assign persons to government programs.

Alexander Whalley is an associate professor of economics in the Haskayne School of Business at the University of Calgary. He also serves as a Lab Economist at the Creative Destruction Lab—Rockies and a research fellow with the Westman Centre for Real Estate Studies. He holds a PhD in economics from the University of Maryland–College Park, an MA from the University of British Columbia, a BA from the University of Western Ontario, and was a visiting scholar at Stanford University and the University of California, Berkeley. His publications include the *Journal of Political Economy*, the *Review of Economics and Statistics*, and the *Journal of Public Economics*. He researches the economics of innovation, urban economics, labor economics, and economic history. In these fields, he looks at the determinants of productivity, how university technology affects regional growth, and the effects of accountability on government performance.

Nathaniel Wilcox is a professor of economics at Appalachian State University. He earned a PhD in economics from the University of Chicago, was a visiting graduate student at the universities of Arizona and Michigan, and received a BA in economics from Binghamton University. He has published in such academic publications as the *American Economic Review*, *Econometrica*, the *Journal of Risk and Uncertainty*, and the *American Journal of Physical Anthropology*. He served as Georgia State University's program director for econometrics at its Center for the Economic Analysis of Risk, and he serves on the editorial boards of the academic publications *Experimental Economics* and the *Journal of the Economic Science Association*. His research interests include the economics and psychology of decisions, learning, and beliefs; applied statistics and econometrics; and experimental methods.

Index

Note: The italic letters *b, f, n,* or *t* following a page number indicate a box, figure, note, or table on that page. Double letters mean more than one such consecutive item on a single page.

Family Transition Program (FTP)
  evaluations contractor for, 201–202
  survey questions for, 205*b*, 220
Florida
  FTP in, 201–202, 205*b*, 220
  JSA in, 202, 206*b*–208*b*, 232*n*5
Folk theories, lay scientist views and, 20,
    21, 72
FTP (Family Transition Program), 201–
    202, 205*b*, 220

GED (General Equivalency Diploma)
    receipt
  high-school dropouts without, and
    NSW eligibility, 103
  as Job Corps outcome, 11–12
  JTPA program and, 11–12, 73
Georgia, NSW site in, 137*b*

Health and Retirement Study, human
    judgment and probability from,
    225–226
Human capital, increases in, 145
Human judgment, 234, 237
  probability and, 225–226, 229–230
Human Resources and Skills
    Development Canada, 3

ICPSR (Inter-university Consortium for
    Political and Social Research),
    231*n*3
Illinois, NSW site in, 137*b*
Impact estimation
  econometrics and, 22, 25–26
  participant evaluations and, 32–35
  proxy variants and, 72–73, 82
  quantile differences and, 29–32
  subgroups and, 26–29, 101
Impact proxies
  as determinants of positive participant
    evaluations, 86, 88
  estimation with proxy variants, 72–
    73, 82
  lay scientist views and, 22, 23*n*2, 36,
    91

participant evaluation relationships
    with, 235–236
Inter-university Consortium for Political
    and Social Research (ICPSR),
    NSW data available from, 231*n*3

Job Corps Study
  evaluation of, 202, 213*b*, 215, 217,
    220, 232*n*8
  outcome impacts of participation in,
    11–12, 14
Job search assistance (JSA)
  evaluation of, demonstrations, 202,
    206*b*–208*b*, 215, 220
  federally provided, in JTPA program,
    41, 73, 78
  low-intensity, in Jobs First, 41, 150
Job Training Partnership Act (JTPA,
    1982) program, 40–41
  authors' empirical case study of, 4–5,
    39, 91*n*1
  (*see also* National Job Study
    [NJS])
  eligibility rules for, 40, 46*t*–47*t*, 91*n*2
  NSW demonstration and, participants,
    40, 101–103
  rank preservation and, 31
  services and costs of, 41, 73, 91*n*3
  survey questions in participant
    evaluation of, 44–45, 45*b*
Jobs First program, 145–195, 178
  as authors' empirical case study, 4, 5
  compared to other survey-based
    participant evaluation studies, 103,
    145, 147–148, 150, 178
  components of, 40, 146–147
  data and sample design of, 148–149,
    179*nn*1–3, 181*t*, 211*b*–212*b*
  empirical descriptive statistics,
    outcomes and impacts in,
    153–158, 154*t*–155*t*, 156*t*, 179*n*5,
    183*b*–184*b*, 184*t*–185*t*
  (*see also under* Bivariate
    correlations, Jobs First)
  evaluations contractor for, 103–104

About the Institute

The W.E. Upjohn Institute for Employment Research is a nonprofit research organization devoted to finding and promoting solutions to employment-related problems at the national, state, and local levels. It is an activity of the W.E. Upjohn Unemployment Trustee Corporation, which was established in 1932 to administer a fund set aside by Dr. W.E. Upjohn, founder of The Upjohn Company, to seek ways to counteract the loss of employment income during economic downturns.

The Institute is funded largely by income from the W.E. Upjohn Unemployment Trust, supplemented by outside grants, contracts, and sales of publications. Activities of the Institute comprise the following elements: 1) a research program conducted by a resident staff of professional social scientists; 2) the Early Career Research Award program, which provides funding for emerging scholars to complete policy-relevant research on labor-market issues; 3) a publications program and online research repository, which provide vehicles for disseminating the research of staff and outside scholars; 4) a regional team that conducts analyses for local economic and workforce development; and 5) the Employment Management Services Division, which administers publicly funded employment and training services as Michigan Works! Southwest in the Institute's local four-county area.

The broad objectives of the Institute's activities are to 1) promote scholarship and evidence-based practices on issues of employment and unemployment policy, and 2) make knowledge and scholarship relevant and useful to policymakers in their pursuit of solutions related to employment and unemployment.

Current areas of concentration for these programs include the causes, consequences, and measures to alleviate unemployment; social insurance and income maintenance programs; compensation and benefits; workforce skills; nonstandard work arrangements; and place-based policy initiatives for strengthening regional economic development and local labor markets.